COMMUNICATION
AND
CONFLICT
MANAGEMENT

——————➤》》》 《《《←——————

IN CHURCHES
AND CHRISTIAN
ORGANIZATIONS

COMMUNICATION
AND
CONFLICT
MANAGEMENT

➤➤➤➤ ◄◄◄◄

IN CHURCHES
AND CHRISTIAN
ORGANIZATIONS

KENNETH O. GANGEL
and
SAMUEL L. CANINE

BROADMAN PRESS
NASHVILLE, TENNESSEE

4230-09
ISBN: 0-8054-3009-1

Dewey Decimal Classification: 254
Subject Heading: CHURCH ADMINISTRATION //
CONFLICT MANAGEMENT // COMMUNICATION
Library of Congress Catalog Card Number: 91-9967
Printed in the United States of America

Unless otherwise indicated, Scripture quotations are from the Holy Bible, *New International Version*, copyright © 1973, 1978, 1984 by International Bible Society. Used by permission. References marked NASB are from the *New American Standard Bible*. © The Lockman Foundation, 1960, 1962, 1963, 1968, 1971, 1972, 1973, 1975, 1977. Used by permission. References marked NEB are from *The New English Bible*. Copyright © The Delegates of the Oxford University Press and the Syndics of the Cambridge University Press, 1961, 1970. Reprinted by permission. References marked KJV are from the *King James Version*.

Library of Congress Cataloging-in-Publication Data
Gangel, Kenneth O.
    Communication and conflict management in churches and Christian
organizations / by Kenneth O. Gangel, Samuel Canine.
        p. cm.
    ISBN 0-8054-3009-1
    1. Church controversies.   2. Communication—Religious aspects—
Christianity.   3. Conflict management—Religious aspects—Christianity.
4. Communication in organizations.   I. Canine, Samuel, 1941– .   II. Title.
BV652.9.G35   1992
254—dc20   91-9967
                                                               CIP

PREFACE

A few years ago I took a group of doctoral students to the American Airlines training center just south of the Dallas/Fort Worth International Airport. Upon taking my turn in the cockpit simulator, I asked the pilot hosting our visit what he considered to be the most important function carried out in flight among the members of the cockpit team. Without any hesitation he replied, "Crew coordination." The pilot, copilot, and navigator must have a constant working relationship—a harmony of duties—or trouble can break out at any time.

This book is about "crew coordination"—not in an airplane cockpit, but in churches and Christian organizations. In the insightful article cited at the beginning of our first chapter, Robert W. Kirkland suggests, "The church lives in the midst of a world in conflict. The world is searching for solutions. The church's ability to handle its own conflicts properly will influence its own vitality and its impact on the world. Properly managed conflict is one of church's greatest assets."

My colleague Dr. Samuel Canine is an expert in communication and my own expertise rests in administrative process and organizational supervision. Together we have designed a book that emphasizes the integration of communication and conflict management. We have placed strong emphasis on interpersonal relationships and tried to develop not only theoretical foundations (as important as those are), but also show how solid theology and communication theory can be put into practice in environments in which Christians work together.

It is our viewpoint that the major problem facing sincere Christians in this decade has little to do with theology, the occult, secularism, or humanism. These genuine threats have been with us since the inception of the New Testament gospel. Far more insidious, however, is our inability to work together, to function harmoniously and creatively, and to constructively manage conflict when it does erupt. In short, we have not been very effective at "crew coordination."

The following chapters draw from the disciplines of administration, education, sociology, psychology, and theology to explain and interpret how communication works and how it serves conflict management. We treat such basic topics as "learning to listen." We demonstrate conflict management examples from Scripture and church life, and we show how all of this impacts such practical and constant leadership functions as recruitment, training, and supervision. It is our wish and prayer that the book will serve the broad body of Christ and its many functions in the world at the end of the twentieth century.

Kenneth O. Gangel

CONTENTS

COMMUNICATION
AND
CONFLICT
MANAGEMENT
—————————➤➤➤ ◀◀◀—————————
IN CHURCHES
AND CHRISTIAN
ORGANIZATIONS

WHY COMMUNICATION
IS IMPORTANT

Writing in the summer 1990 issue of *Search*, Robert Kirkland recorded what he called "a shocking discovery—the literature related to conflict management in the church is in its infancy." He cited only three works of merit on the subject and proposed a suggestion as to why more helpful material has not been produced.

> Perhaps the church has tried to keep its conflicts hidden in the church closet. I propose that image in my efforts to help the contemporary church regarding the managing of conflict. Recent writers have brought the fact of the church's struggle with conflict out of the church closet. Now everyone knows that Christians experience conflict![1]

Not only can we document almost 2,000 years of conflict in the church, but the history of management science might well be told as a study of role conflict between individuals and institutions, between persons and organizations. Down through the years, experts have employed different terminologies to describe this phenomenon and the leadership style related to it. Perhaps most common are the terms *nomothetic* (institution oriented) and *idiographic* (individual oriented).

In this case, one emphasis in conflict with the other emphasis only adds up to one confusing question: How can we keep a ministry producing and achieving while at the same time keeping its workers satisfied and self-actualized? Enter the role of interpersonal relations (IPR) and interpersonal communication (IPC). Somehow leaders must coordinate roles and responsibilities of people in a work group, their relationships with each other, and their individual and collective relationships to the organization. Just when the leader expects people to be consistent, logical, and perfect, they turn out to be inconsistent, illogical, and imperfect.

In the church, the problem can be alleviated or compounded. The oil of the Holy Spirit provides a supernatural lubricant not available to secular organizations. When properly lubricated, the organization will work very well toward achieving both individual goals and the total objectives of the congregation. To this extent the church is organism *before* it is organization. Our problems come when we try to think *only* in terms of organism (the supernatural and invisible union of the body), forgetting that the church must also be viewed as organization, or when we think *only* of organization, forgetting organism.

If a Christian ministry (particularly the church) operates in accordance with Scripture, it will be the most exquisite demonstration of interpersonal relations principles the world has ever seen. A spirit of *koinonia* and unity can permeate the body and radiate from it to all its surrounding environment.

Review of Foundational Sociology

Studies of both interpersonal relations and communication are part of the broader perspective of the social sciences and, more specifically, sociology. When studied as a part of management science, these subfields bring together a social psychology. Within the church and other Christian organizations, we deal with the integration of faith and learning, making it necessary for us to review aspects of sociology within the light of Scripture. Even more elementary, we must return to the field itself.

Nature of the Discipline

Sociology offers a scientific study of the processes and products of human interaction. In interpersonal relations all human conduct involves a plurality of actors. Sociology asserts that human beings develop their human abilities in social interaction. All that is human must be embodied in language in some way. The word *culture* describes the way of life of people (or of *a* people), essentially made up of prominent social institutions like family, religion, government, recreation, economy, education, and welfare. Within these categories communication goes on continuously among friends, groups, clubs, churches, and other forms of people-gatherings.

Human beings live in constant group relationship. Social interaction follows given patterns; therefore, our study of interpersonal communication must presuppose collectivity, as is illustrated in the following hypothetical story of a 35-year-old Christian man named Brian.

Sample Application

Brian's day begins in a small collectivity called a household or family. When he leaves that group, his path leads to another small group at work (meanwhile his children are at school and his wife at the club or at Bible study). Yet even on his way between these primary groups, Brian joins other small groups, such as his car pool or people he may meet for coffee just before work begins.   When the work day ends, Brian may stop at a fitness center interacting with a com-pletely different group. (Meanwhile his children are at basketball and cheerleading practice, and his wife is shopping.) Shortly after he regathers with the family group. They all head out to some school activity such as a musical program or an athletic event. *In an ordinary day most individuals move in and out of at least five or six other small-group settings*.

Although this may be a bit early in our study to narrow our thinking on dialogue, the interpersonal episode between two people provides the foundation of all communication. Interpersonal dialogues produce social activity and create culture, but *only when people believe and act upon a shared concept does it become significant to the interpersonal relationship*.

Practical Implications

One general exception to all of this is what sociologists call "audience behavior." Think about that exception in relationship to large classrooms, church services, political rallies, and even television viewing. We know that audience behavior does not easily create behavioral change in people. We also know that large organizations consist of many small groups. Several practical implications seem to emerge immediately:

1. A study of interpersonal relations and communications must focus on dialogue and small groups—not organizations and institutions.
2. Interpersonal communication is essential for interpersonal relations.
3. Interpersonal communication and interpersonal relations provide the context for social maturity and spiritual growth.
4. Our "audience behavior" society does not generally lend itself to the advancement of strong interpersonal communication/interpersonal relations.

Understanding Human Groups

While we are reviewing sociological theory it might be useful to begin with groups. One classic work on the subject (*The Human Group* by George Homans) develops a conceptual scheme focusing on three elements of human behavior that determine group outcomes: activity, interaction, and sentiment. Homans places a good deal of importance on interaction but also emphasizes a number of other elements that must be taken into account in the study of human behavior. One of the major hypotheses of the book states that "If the interactions between the members of a group are frequent in the external system, sentiments of liking will grow between them, and these sentiments will lead in turn to further interactions."[2]

Let us purge ourselves immediately of the view that communication always implies media and hardware. That is a form of communication but not the dimension we will be studying. You will want also to distinguish carefully between *communication theory* and *information theory*. The latter deals with terms like sender, receiver, message, encoding, decoding, and feedback. It forms the basis from which media communication has developed. Our concern in this book centers in interpersonal communication which deals exclusively with people and primarily with words. But let us get back to our three code words.

Mutuality, Presentality, Simultaneity

When we think about group members interacting and communicating, three words surface, again from the writings of

sociologists, particularly symbolic interactionists: *mutuality,*
presentality, and *simultaneity.*

Mutuality deals with what happens in communication when
all the parties recognize their responsibility for *message* and
meaning. To put it another way, IPC and IPR are always
mutual, never singular, always dialogue, never monologue.

Presentality tells us communication must be explained in
terms of the here and now. Two weeks ago Brian may have felt
very warm about his job, very confident and secure in his
future. Then the company announced layoffs, cutbacks, and a
possible relocation to another state. Details will still be forth-
coming; but as Brian goes to work after such an announcement, immediate policy, not how the company may have
related to him in the past, is the issue.

The idea of *simultaneity* argues that we cannot think of
communication as a table tennis game in which messages are
batted back and forth. Unlike the philosophical psychology of
behaviorism, communication cannot be viewed as stimulus—
response. Both (all) figures act simultaneously. Look again at
the story of Brian.

Something went wrong at the basketball game, and on the
way home Brian finds himself in an argument with his junior-
high son Terry, age 13. In the heat of the discussion, Brian
may be tempted to use an expression common to our culture:
"You make me mad." However, that would be inaccurate, a
denial of mutuality. An exact rendering of what happened 🖈
between father and son during the forty-minute drive home
would have to emphasize that Brian and Terry did it together.
Both were involved in Brian's being upset.

Generalized Others and Significant Others

Like almost any professional field, sociology has its own
jargon. People at work or church with whom we must speak on
occasion or even quite regularly are called "generalized others." When our generalized others are "with us" in the communication flow, both meaning and message seem positive.
Theoretically, if we could all be constantly in a state of openness, vulnerability, and transparency rejecting our hiding
mechanisms, insecurities, and defensiveness, we would face very

few communication problems. When they did arise, we would feel comfortable in asking one another for explanations.

Parallel to the generalized other is the "significant other." We develop and share ideas in the presence of people significant to us. We anticipate and act upon ideas in ways we believe these significant others see us. We then build this relationship by repetition and habit. This helps explain why sons or daughters often act the same way in the presence of a mother or father as they did ten, twenty, or thirty years ago or why deacon-pastor conflicts tend to be so difficult to solve, even over long periods of time.

Most husbands and wives think they know each other well, and that may be largely true. They might be amazed in some cases, however, to really know how the other thinks and acts in unusual situations. Social theorists argue that persons can change in any direction at any time if they can change significant others, generalized others, and their handling of language.

Our emphasis in this book has nothing to do with changing significant others or generalized others; in fact, we reject that notion (from such a view comes divorce, running away from home, stamping out of church meetings, etc.). But changing language? Understanding the process of IPR and IPC? Now we are talking about possibility! We will come back to these as the study proceeds.

The Nature of Communication

Communication does not occur in isolation, and it does not have to be verbal. The process of socialization within groups takes place primarily through interpersonal communication even when it results in hostility rather than agreement. Effective leaders learn to participate in the communication process in such a positive way that their involvement bolsters the unity of the group and enhances the quality of interpersonal relationships.

Definition of Communication

Perhaps a simple definition might be helpful here: *communication is meaning exchange, not word exchange*. As someone once remarked, "I'm sure you believe you understand what you think I said, but I am not sure you realize that what you heard was not what I really meant." Such is the problem we tackle in this book.

Keep in mind the context of our study—group leadership in Christian organizations. We have to focus first on Interpersonal Communication as a dialogue between two people. In the broader sense, however, the communication process has to reach out to the organization: church, mission, parachurch ministry, publishing house, and whatever other setting you envision. Ernest Bormann and associates speak primarily from an information-processing point of view, but they pick up the difficulty of transferring the communication process into the wider context.

> Communication problems are intensified by the fact that persons in an organization are in a continual state of flux. Staff additions and replacements may be hired. New policies and procedures are continually modifying the hierarchical structures.
>
> All other things being equal, people will communicate most frequently with the people geographically closest to them.
>
> All other things being equal, people will communicate most frequently with people closest to their own status within the organization.
>
> All other things being equal, people will communicate most frequently with people in their own unit.[3]

Context of Communication

We have not said much about the social situation in which messages are produced. Context deals with the general surroundings of any given communication transaction, and the personal elements people bring to the context are far more important than the physical environment. For example, *sensitivity*, one's skill and ability to perceive and interpret with empathy, is crucial to the process. *Self-disclosure* deals with revealing the truth about oneself including desires, needs, or goals, and doing so honestly and candidly. *Trust* makes self-disclosure possible. It gives us "permission" to disclose ourselves to others. *Risk* (the willingness to accept adverse outcomes that may result from trusting other people in the

relationship/communication milieu) is also a factor within the
context of communication. Gerald Wilson explains these four
aspects:

> Thus feedback, sensitivity, self-disclosure, trust, and risk
> are interrelated. The ability to interact in a game-free
> exchange—one in which the participants are open to each
> other; one in which they grow—depends on these interper-
> sonal events.[4]

One non-technical way of thinking about context is to substitute the word *climate*. One thinks immediately about tem-
perature, sunshine or rain, and other aspects of the physical
environment. We also talk commonly about *climate* with respect to interpersonal communication. An angry husband and
wife, staring sullenly at one another across the table in frozen
silence, have created a certain climate for that moment. Obviously they have rejected self-disclosure and trust and therefore have designed a very poor climate for communication.

Communication and Organizational Theory

Three Eras of Theory

If we were to review the history of organizational structure,
we might agree with Amitai Etzioni that the twentieth century has contained essentially three eras: (1) classical theory
of scientific management, (2) the human relations era, and (3)
the structuralist approach that, more or less, synthesized the
first two. One senses that we are in a change mode now,
moving from structuralism toward a cybernetic-systems approach appropriate for the knowledge explosion at the end of
this century.

Early years of research ushered in the human relations
era (about 1925-1950), moving management away from its
obsession with formal organizations, rational behavior, and
maximal production, toward the view that the most satisfying or rewarding organization would be most efficient. However, the pendulum swung too far, failing to deal with the
balance.

Goal Achievement and Communication

We are now in the latter days of the synthetic period of structuralism in which goal achievement and the meeting of human needs have been recognized as constant, ever-present competing forces in every organization. Most organizations, including churches and seminaries, still err in the direction of goal achievement rather than interpersonal communication and need-meeting.

Years ago Amitai Etzioni wrote:

> The ultimate source of the organizational dilemmas reviewed up to this point is the incomplete matching of the personalities of the participants with their organizational roles. If personalities could be shaped to fit specific organizational roles, or organizational roles could fit specific personalities, many of the pressures to displace goals, much of the need to control performance, and a good part of the alienation would disappear.[5]

When I first read that, my eyes began to sparkle, and my mind moved forward in anticipation, only to find this noted authority suggesting that such personality shaping and role matching is virtually impossible. A great deal of research has been done since the publication of that work more than thirty years ago, but the problems have not changed. If they had, it would hardly be necessary to prepare this book on communication and conflict management, which many church leaders believe may be the most dominant problem Christian organizations face at the end of the twentieth century.

Cyclical Organizational Patterns

Part of this problem may simply arise from the cyclical pattern of an organization. Dissatisfaction with existing structures tends to produce an incipient organization, which then gives way to formal organization through the rise of visionary leadership. The organization then moves toward maximal efficiency during which rational organizational structure (bureaucracy) replaces the initial charismatic leadership. First generation leaders die off, and administration comes to be viewed as a means and not an end.

Then the program of the institution becomes all-important, and what was *communication process* becomes *information process*. Now workers in the organization no longer doubt they exist to serve it, whether or not it serves them at all. Ultimately overinstitutionalization ensues, and death comes in one form or another. Death may not be extinction but merely spiritual, moral, or social stagnation. Apply that formula to any organization you know—a church, a Christian college or seminary, a mission board, or even a family—and you will discern, to a greater or lesser extent, how each of the various phases fit.

Philosophy of Ministry and Leadership

Eugene Habecker said one of the reasons for leadership "is that the primary makeup of the organization is people." Using the Bible to explain, he went on to say:

> Scripture well illustrates the point that people change and leaders change. The Israelites were a different people under the leadership of Moses or Joshua than they were under subsequent leaders. The apostles performed differently after Jesus rose from the dead and returned to heaven than they did while He was still on earth. In the context of our families, our priorities as parents are different when the children are all under age ten than when all of them are in their teens. People change, leaders change, and organizations change. Leaders must be sensitive to these kinds of changes and respond accordingly.[6]

Review of the Literature

A great deal of literature was written during the 1980s on the subject of leadership. Perhaps the general social vacuum created such a need that some felt constrained to attack the problem directly. David Klopfenstein has provided a masterful review of that literature, with special focus on the models used to illustrate what he called "some Christian concerns of leading." Like many before him, Klopfenstein ended up with an emphasis on Bennis and Nanus and their book, *Leaders: The Strategies for Taking Charge*:

These new leaders are identified by four strategies: vision, communication, trust, and empowerment. While these strategies may be qualities of Christian ministry and leadership, the authors were in fact describing business executives. To the Christian leader, these social science data are most helpful in shaping our questions of inquiry, refining our methods of research and teaching, building our models of ministry, and contributing to the field of leadership.[7]

Principles of an Effective Management Philosophy

What kind of philosophy of ministry creates a climate in which IPC and IPR can flourish, not only as a means but also as a biblical end? In our opinion, which has been developed in greater detail in a recent book entitled *Feeding and Leading*[8], it will be a decentralized ministry that rejects autocratic leadership except in the most unique and demanding situations. The ministry will be one in which the body functions together as a team, providing a wide variety of need-meeting instructive experiences.

We obtained these principles of ministry by generalizing the way the disciples understood the teaching of Jesus and applied that teaching in the Book of Acts and in the preparation of the New Testament Epistles. Teaching and preaching may be essential, but they are carried out within a climate of caring and nurture that not only makes possible IPC and IPR but elevates them to a major goal within the organization. In short, a people-centered ministry provides congregations with the privilege and responsibility to think and strategize about ministry without having everything so absolutized and programmed that people merely serve the bureaucracy.

Conclusion

We close this first chapter by referring to the words of Peter Drucker, widely viewed as the father of modern management. At Claremont Graduate School where Drucker teaches, the curriculum of the Peter F. Drucker Graduate Management Center centers in the belief that management cannot be viewed merely as a set of quantitative skills, but it should be seen as a profoundly human activity. The classes do not emphasize specialization but integration. Drucker himself acknowledged, "Management always lives, works, and practices in and for an institution. An institution is a human community held together by a bond that, next to the tie of family, is the most powerful human bond—the work bond."[9]

If leaders want to win and develop people, they must know their followers—their spiritual conditions, their personal abilities and limitations, their weaknesses and strengths, and their needs. That knowledge presupposes a highly developed, indeed, a spiritually sophisticated network of interpersonal relations and interpersonal communication—a goal toward which this book is dedicated.

Notes

1. Robert W. Kirkland, "Conflict Management in the Church," *Search* (Summer 1990): 13.

2. George C. Homans, *The Human Group* (New York: Harcourt Brace Jovanovich, 1950).

3. Ernest G. Bormann, et al., *Interpersonal Communication in the Modern Organization* (Englewood Cliffs, N.J.: Prentice-Hall, 1969), 47-48.

4. Gerald L. Wilson, et al, *Interpersonal Growth Through Communication* (Dubuque, Iowa: William C. Brown Publishers, 1985), 16.

5. Amitai Etzioni, *Modern Organizations* (Englewood Cliffs, N.J.: Prentice-Hall, 1964), 75.

6. Eugene B. Habecker, *The Other Side of Leadership* (Wheaton: Victor Books, 1987), 29-30.

7. David E. Klopfenstein, "Research in Leadership," *Christian Education Journal* (Winter 1989):52.

8. Kenneth O. Gangel, *Feeding and Leading* (Wheaton: Victor Books, 1989).

9. Peter Drucker, *Chronicle of Higher Education*, February 10, 1988, 83.

2

————→>>> <<<←————

COMMUNICATION MODELS

Introduction

Many believe that changes in the fast-moving world of communication have left the church behind. Could it be that congregational fights, church splits, and the generally short tenure of ministerial staffs stem from something as basic as communication deficiencies? Not only *could* it be, it probably *is* in many of those unfortunate cases.

Over fifty-five years ago Elton Mayo wrote a book entitled *The Human Problems of an Industrial Civilization*. The industrial civilization has given way to the information society, but the human problems persist. One must understand, Mayo was a product of his time, basically chronicling the transfer in management studies from the scientific management era of Frederick Taylor to the human relations era that followed the Hawthorne studies.

Much of Mayo's emphasis on human factors is still highly relevant today. For example, he argued that "the chief difficulty of our time is the breakdown of the social codes that formerly disciplined us to effective working together," and "we have too few administrators alert to the fact that it is a human-social and not an economic problem which they face."[1] These ideas, still applicable in the 1990s, bring us back again to the emphasis on interpersonal communication as *the transmission of ideas between persons in a language common to both*.

No two people can meet without transmitting and reacting to signals of some kind. Communication of one depends on the response of the other and vice versa. Positive communication promotes appropriate attitudes and actions. For Christians, those attitudes and actions must line up with biblical standards for communicating persons and the roles they hold.

Of course, language does not merely consist of words: it includes any means by which we convey facts, ideas, attitudes, and feelings to other people. Sometimes language can be a barrier to communication because abstract words and evaluative terms become ambiguous. Even concrete terms achieve their true significance only in the mind of the person using them. In so far as the users are able to transmit their meanings to others, they have achieved genuine communication.

Over the past fifty years communication models have been developed in industry to enhance communication in the organizational setting. For example, the *rational-logical model,* based on Aristotelian logic and organizational structure, used as its foundation the work of Korzybski and others. The *persuasion-emotional need model* deals with motivations, emotions, and territories and again links to Korzybski, or perhaps even more to Roethlisberger. The *social/nonrational model,* emphasizing group and self-space, consists of emphases on sentiments, social structure, status, group roles, and syndromes. The latter takes its cue from the work of Pareto and Henderson.

Primarily because of their complexity and the necessity of having some background in social psychology to really draw any value from such models, we only mention them for some advanced students who will want to look further. In this chapter, however, we want to draw upon five more-basic models that provide a balance between information theory and communication theory.

Field of Experience Model

This has been a favorite communication model for a quarter century. Developed by Dr. Donald Ely at Syracuse University, the model is both complete and simple. Dr. Ely wrote about his concept:

> The communication process is dynamic, ongoing, ever changing, and continuous. There is no beginning, no ending, not even a fixed sequence. The components within a process

interact, each element affecting another. When the process
is diagrammed, as in the drawing, we arrest its dynamism
and analyze it as a static representation. But it is not at rest.
It is always moving.[2]

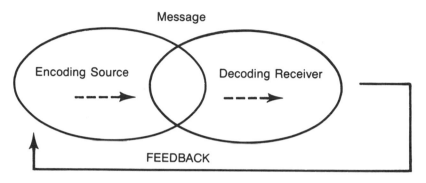

Reprinted, by permission, from Donald P. Ely, "Are We Getting Through to Each Other?"
International Journal of Religious Education (May 1962).

The title of the model emphasizes that broad climate or
milieu in which all communication takes place. We discussed
this in chapter one. Leaders can ensure better reception of
their message if they take into consideration the "field of
experience" with which followers must deal. Included in such
a field are attitudes, intellectual levels, cultural backgrounds,
emotional readiness, and numerous other elements.

The *source* of an idea in person-to-person communication is
the mind of the communicator. When a message has been
decided on, it must be verbalized or symbolized in some way so
it can be communicated to other people. Information theorists
refer to this as *encoding*. Encoding is futile unless accompanied by an adequate process of *decoding*, and two things are
significant here. First, if the originator of the message wishes
the receiver to decode properly, he or she must take pains to
encode the message clearly in a form that will be understand-
able to the *receiver*. Furthermore, the sender must be somewhat confident that the receiver has the wherewithal to carry
on the decoding process.

The term *receiver* represents the person for whom the
message is intended: work group, wife or husband, children,
students, or a friend. Feedback helps the source interpret

whether or not the receiver has understood and internalized the message.

The central poignant idea of the Ely model shows that *no message gets through until decoding overlaps encoding.* Ely would add that two people engaged in a relationship must possess some level of overlapping experience if they hope to achieve successful communication. Each must understand what the other thinks in terms of his or her own world.

Interpersonal Episode Model

Only slightly more complex than the Ely model is the Interpersonal Episode Model (IEM) that definitely focuses on human-interaction rather than the information-processing slant of communication.

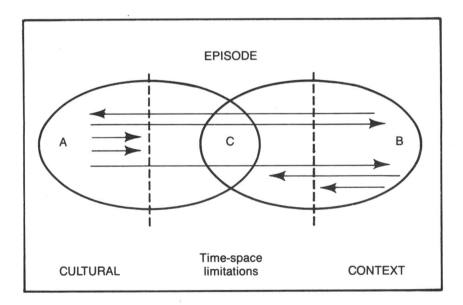

In the model, C equals concepts, categories, and constructs that are shared. The episode takes place within time-space limitations in a cultural context. Each person (A and B) brings his or her concepts to the episode, and the overlap represents the commonality of persons in interaction. Remember, this all happens simultaneously.

Some of A's statements to B (or B's to A) proceed through the commonality (note the arrows), but others do not because of the many impeding elements that hinder communication, such as the time-space limitation. The cultural context dilutes interpersonal meanings. Concepts and categories are not all held in commonality. A and B talk *to* each other, sometimes talk *by* each other, and hopefully talk *with* each other.

Transactional Model

Although management science research deals with changing either individuals or institutions, many experts have decided on the transactional approach connecting the nomothetic and idiographic dimensions. In reality, these dimensions exist in constant relationship to and interaction with one another, rather than in separate spheres. Individuals' values will determine their behavior unless they compromise their values for some item of secondary importance, such as salary or position. Therefore, organizational values must somehow be integrated with those of individuals.

The model below, developed by Getzels and Guba, clarifies the kind of difficulties that arise in the institution-individual balance game.[3] The top line indicates institutional plans and

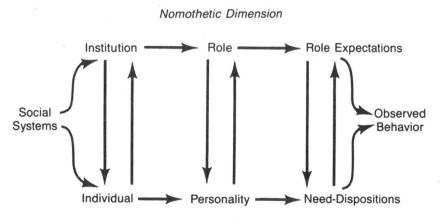

Reprinted from *Competent to Lead* by permission of the author: Kenneth O. Gangel, p. 135. Copyright 1974 by Moody Press.

roles. The bottom line focuses on the individual. The vertical arrows show the necessity of bringing the conflict into creative tension to achieve harmony in the organization.

Certainly both the organization and the individual can change, but an emphasis on changing either one to the sacrifice of the other will lead to confusion and turmoil.

The Scripture figuratively speaks of the church as a building and of its members as various blocks of stone in the framework of that building. Just as the architects of a physical building take into account the qualities of the materials with which they work, so must the organizational architects of the church (or other Christian organizations) consider the characteristics of the personnel who make up the structure of their institutions.

The tasks of the human architect are considerably more complex. We know so little about the qualities of human materials, and they are notoriously changeable. Some people reject the organization because they feel they have given but not received. Others pose the opposite problem of taking but wanting to give nothing in return. That results in a sterile organization, which if Christian, becomes a liability rather than an asset to the ongoing ministry of God's work in the world.

If IPR and IPC are to thrive in the contemporary church, we must move to flexibility rather than rigidity in coping with institutional tension. Spontaneity and openness provide the new materials out of which creative energy can come to recharge the communication batteries of Christian organizations in these days of opportunity.

We seek not to baptize secular research and stuff it, still damp, into the organizational potholes on the road the church must travel. Rather, we apply biblical principles to communication, better understood because we have taken the time to grapple with the secular research.

Management Process Model

R. Alec MacKenzie is a name as common to students of administrative process as Peter Drucker or Douglas MacGregor. As a consultant, MacKenzie has attempted to pull together in one single (and quite overwhelming) diagram all the various components of the management process.[4] Represented here are only four concentric rings of a nine-ring oval. Since the inclusion of components expands toward the outward boundaries of the oval, we also have here the most simple and foundational segment of the diagram.

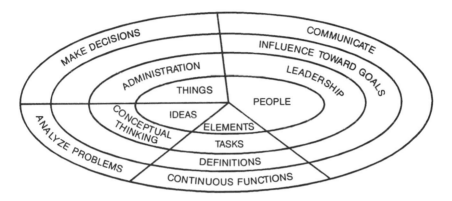

Reprinted by permission of *Harvard Business Review*. An exhibit from "The Management Process in 3-D" by R. Alec MacKenzie, November/December 1969. Copyright © 1969 by the President and Fellows of Harvard College; all rights reserved.

Notice that *communication,* along with *analyzing problems* and *making decisions,* appears as a continuous function because it occurs throughout the management process rather than in any particular sequence. Communication must be ongoing for many (perhaps all) functions and activities to be effective. In reality, of course, the whole process merges and if not kept dynamic and active, tends to collapse on itself and implode.

Who is responsible for sustaining the continuous functions, notably communication? One could correctly answer, "Everyone in the organization"; however, as always, the buck stops at the desk of the leader. The senior pastor is responsible for the communication of the church staff and other leadership.

Harold Westing observed a parallel between divorce and church staff disintegration: "Counselors suggest that 86% of American divorces are brought about by poor communication.

We're convinced that the percentage would be similar in the breakdown of staff relationships."[5] Westing suggested that no committee or board in a church should meet without the rest of the staff seeing the agenda and minutes of those meetings. There should be no surprises among team members, no hidden agenda, no politicking to advance oneself at the expense of other members of the team.

Westing included a chart showing that the amount of communication heard and understood by persons in business firms may diminish by 70 percent over five levels of the organization chart (president at 90 percent, nonmanaging member at 20 percent). He concluded: "Lest this happen in church, everyone, but especially the senior pastor, must keep working on communication skills constantly. He has to be thinking all the time about seeing that everyone is informed, not only on the team, but in the congregation."[6]

Hard and Soft Organizational Model

Closely related to Getzels and Guba is this Hurst model that first appeared in *Harvard Business Review* (May-June 1984). It focuses on the contrasts between a hard, rational approach to communication and one that is soft and intuitive. We can identify a major premise here: the key to a functioning harmonious group is for members to understand that they

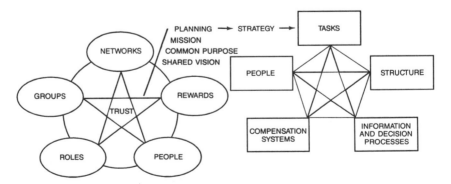

Reprinted by permission of *Harvard Business Review*. An exhibit from "Of Boxes, Bubbles, and Effective Management" by David K. Hurst, May/June 1984. Copyright © 1984 by the President and Fellows of Harvard College; all rights reserved.

might disagree with each other because they are in two different contexts.[7]

The model, though complex, speaks for itself when studied carefully. Hard, rational leadership types tend to focus on tasks, structure, information processes, compensation systems, and a view of people characterized by the five words that appear on the chart. Soft, intuitive leadership types, on the other hand, like to talk about roles, groups, networks, or rewards and think about people in a social atmosphere creating, imagining, inspiring, and even playing.

Boxes (hard, rational types) are closed; they have walls and lids. Bubbles (soft, intuitive types) are flexible and transparent; they can easily expand and join with other bubbles. One needs only a modicum of imagination to see the Pharisees of Jesus' day functioning like boxes. For them, ethical and biblical behavior had severe and easy explainable boundaries. Today we might call it "black and white" interpretation.

In contrast we can see the disciples during their formative years learning to be "bubbles." They acted like boxes at times, but the Lord repeatedly rebuked them for such behavior and developed their flexibility and cooperation. Today we might say that ethical and biblical behavior in leadership roles suffer when we function in closed, stringent, and dogmatic ways. We become hard box leaders banging against other boxes rather than blending our ministries with theirs to bring about mutual achievement. Hurst used the interesting analogy of judo in which a person does not resist an attacker but "goes with the flow," thereby adding his strength to the attacker's momentum. Hurst further developed the box/bubble analogy by referring to "father and mother roles" and said, "The family is the original team, formed to handle the most complex management task ever faced. Of late, we seem to have fired too many of its members—a mistake we can learn from."[8]

Hurst's metaphor is limited of course, as are all the models of this chapter. Our purpose is certainly not to memorize models nor pit the values of one against another. The idea is to understand communication so that we may practice it more effectively. For that to happen, we must understand the various component parts and how they all come together to form a communication system or network. Communication between husband and wife seems very different than communcation between boss and employee. However, when analyzed in accordance with accepted models, those differences quickly shrink leaving us with very dependable patterns and principles which relate to virtually every communication situation.

Let us close our chapter on that *family* note. In my files I found a "Communication Covenant" (source unknown) prepared by a congregation for husbands and wives. Here are a few of the points:

1. We will express irritations and annoyances we have with one another in a loving, specific, and positive way rather than holding them in or being negative in general.
2. We will not exaggerate or attack the other person during the course of a disagreement.
3. We will attempt to control the emotional level and intensity of arguments.
4. We will never let the sun go down on our anger or never run away from each other during an argument.
5. We will both try hard not to interrupt the other person when he or she is talking.
6. We will carefully listen to the other person rather than spending time thinking up a defense.
7. We will not toss in past failures of the other person in the course of an argument.
8. When something is important enough for one person to discuss, it is that important for the other person.

Good advice for families—and for Christian organizations.

Notes

1. Elton Mayo, *The Human Problems of an Industrial Civilization* (New York: The Viking Press, 1960), 180.

2. Donald P. Ely, "Are We Getting Through to Each Other?" *International Journal of Religious Education* 38, no. 9 (May 1962):4-5.

3. J. W. Getzels and E. G. Guba, "Social Behavior and the Administrative Process," *The School Review* 65 (Winter 1957):423-41; and Jacob W. Getzels, "Administration as a Social Process" in *Administrative Theory in Education,* ed. Andrew W. Halpin (Chicago: University of Chicago, 1958), 156.

4. R. Alec MacKenzie, "The Management Process in 3-D," *Harvard Business Review* (November-December 1969):80.

5. Harold Westing, *Multiple Church Staff Handbook* (Grand Rapids, Mich.: Kregel, 1985).

6. Ibid., 35-36.

7. David K. Hurst, "Of Boxes, Bubbles, and Effective Management" *Harvard Business Review* 3 (May-June 1984):83.

8. Ibid., 87.

3

COMMUNICATION MESSAGES

LAURA: Will you stay home tonight? I think I have the flu.

FRED: I'm already committed to see Joe from my office.

LAURA: (*If he won't do this small favor for me, how can I count on him when I have a major problem?*) You never want to stay home. I very rarely ask you to do anything.

FRED: (*If she insists on keeping me home for such a small thing, what will happen when something big happens—like when we have kids?*) I'm sorry, but I really have to go.

LAURA: (*I should get out of the relationship while I can and find somebody I can depend on.*) Go ahead if you want to. I'll find somebody else to stay with me.

The above conversation, adapted from *Love Is Never Enough* (New York: Harper and Row, 1989) clearly demonstrates both the existence and the abuse of various messages of communication. Beck directs the Center for Cognitive Therapy at the University of Pennsylvania. He and other cognitive therapists have concluded that much of what goes wrong in communication, particularly in discussions between couples, has to do with what happens in the parenthetic thoughts of the communicants.

Once they lose initial trust, people begin hesitating to say what they really mean. They misread each other's messages, impute improper motives, and overgeneralize their complaints. Hostility arises, and communication seems all but dead. Understanding how communication processes work, how we receive and deliver messages, may revive both our trust and our communication.

Psychologists who work in this area talk about personal "scripts" that people carry with them. Perhaps the young wife's script has her coming in second best, because that is precisely where her parents placed her during childhood. Or, the husband reads from a script that insists he understands, even if he has no clue to his wife's feelings. Other scripts emphasize saying the right things, or saying what a spouse or boss or friend might want to hear, rather than what one really means.

It is probably too early to pass judgment on the successes of the cognitive therapy approach, but early reports seem encouraging. Marriage is worth saving, and therapists should work diligently at clarifying communication messages.

Other relationships face the same issues, including those in churches and parachurch organizations. Deacons can distort messages around a conference table as easily as husband and wife across the dinner table. Elders and pastor might very well lose each other while "reading scripts" in the very same family room in which noncommunicative script-relationships took place between husband and wife just hours before. Both family and church need to understand communication processes.

Understanding Communication Processes

The word *messages* in the title of this chapter carries a technical meaning among communication specialists. *Messages* are those selectively perceived behaviors to which each person in an interpersonal transaction adapts his or her own behavior. Smith and Williamson noted that "in interpersonal communication transactions, messages have three levels of meaning: the denotative level, the interpretive level, and the relational level."[1] The key word here is *meaning*, since perception and interpretation vary widely. Once we "take in" communication signals, we must determine what they mean and how we will respond. To grasp this aspect of communication processes, we must understand these three levels of meaning and how they work.

Denotative Level: Definitions from Dictionaries

Denotation refers to literal meanings, those we find in dictionaries and other authoritative sources. For example, a dictionary will tell us that the word *compromise* means "a settlement of differences by arbitration or by consent reached by mutual concessions." The dictionary also reminds us that *compromise* might be "a concession to something derogatory or prejudicial." One could use *compromise* in either sense and in doing so might deliver a different message than the one intended. How the message is received is influenced by the context and culture of the audience (one person or many) who may bring a completely different interpretation than the speaker delivered.

Interpretive Level: Definitions from Culture and Context

Messages represent the various languages and behaviors of other people to which we as listeners and observers assign meaning. The meaning of any given message depends on the context in which it occurs and, in a broader sense, the culture in which it must be interpreted.

Let us get back to our word *compromise*. I once used that word in a thoroughly positive sense with an undergraduate class. I intended to convey the healthy results that come when people subordinate their own personal rigidity and dogmatism to achieve a blended result mutually beneficial to all of them. One student took immediate exception. In his home, *compromise* offered no promise of benefit. On the contrary, it meant giving in to another's viewpoint and thus losing one's own. Reluctance to accept my definition of compromise stemmed from both his context and culture. Our differences in those areas blocked meaningful communication.

The interpretive level is quite complex, instigated by a set of cues which tell the other people in the transaction how the message should be understood. Was there an upward inflection? Did he laugh when he said it? Did she have fire in her eyes? What cultural and contextual meaning separated listener and speaker?

Relationship Level: Definitions from Personal Contacts

Several things tend to happen in the communication process. Since people change over a period of time, we lose detail and tend to distort the words we actually heard. Nonsense ideas seem to fade while certain central concepts hang on.

Uniquely emotional moments such as a mode of language ("I love you" or "I never want to see you again") stay with us. Touching behavior, so essential to adequate communication in our culture, lingers, and the words spoken in those moments last longer in our minds.

Picture a pastor and board chairman. During a meeting, they exchange words. After the meeting, they ask for forgiveness and promise to pray for one another. That moment will remain long after the business items of the evening have faded. The restored relationship, not the harsh words, has defined the meeting.

Three levels of communication process—each important, each often misunderstood, and each closely related to the others. Smith and Williamson condense that relationship in a cogent paragraph.

> The denotative level of meaning is *content* oriented. It conveys the meanings associated with specific objects, behaviors, or experiences. The interpretive and relational levels of meaning are about the nature of the message itself. They tell us how to interpret the content; they tell us how to modify our roles in relation to each other in order to understand the content.[2]

Whether engaged in individual communication, small groups, or large assemblies, we must remember that prejudice tends to attach to fact. What may appear to us to be simple to understand at the denotative level, can become clouded as we interpret and reinterpret, constantly adding baggage to what we thought we once knew. The real terror comes when the communication process continues without awareness that the baggage has been attached. In supervising the work of others, administrative communication becomes particularly crucial. It, too, is subject to all the levels we have already discussed and, according to many experts, provides the "glue" that holds the whole administrative process together.

Understanding Administrative Communication

Organizations (including churches and parachurch organizations) are held together by communication, not structure.

For some reason, we have difficulty getting seminary students to grasp the difference between church polity and leadership style. They somehow feel that certain leadership styles are forced upon them by certain forms of church polity. We maintain to the contrary that both polity and leadership styles interact in ministry, but they should remain two distinct items. A well-formed leadership style can normally operate in virtually any kind of polity, assuming it does not run counter to the leader's theology.

In the administrative process, communication is not merely one of the functions; it permeates *all* functions and links them together. Organizing, planning, staffing, delegating, co-ordinating, and motivating—which of these or any other administrative function can be carried out without effective communication? Engstrom and Dayton warn, "Communicate or else."

> An effective organization needs clear and *communicable goals, adequate resources, motivated people,* and *good communication.* If the objectives of the group are understood and accepted by all its members, and if they have the corporate resources to attain their objectives, *then* what each member of the group needs is information on what to do, how to do it, when to do it, and where to do it. In order to maintain his commitment to the task, he also needs to know what progress he and the rest of the organization are making toward reaching their goals.[3]

Since organizational communications pose such an ongoing task, we want to observe several very important guidelines:

1. *Communicate objectives repeatedly and clearly.* Experienced leaders have come to understand, sometimes in the most difficult way, that one cannot overcommunicate something as central as ministry goals.

2. *Protect the emotional tone of the communication.* Keep in mind interpretive and relational dimensions as well as denotative. Do not assume all members of a listening group receive a communication in the same way. Carefully consider how every recipient feels about what you said.

3. *Identify clear channels for communication.* People need to know whom to talk to, whom to ask, and who has the

authority to direct their activities. These things should not arise by way of a solution to a problem, but they should be established and reenforced by simple administrative maintenance.

4. *Recognize different levels of communication.* One could talk here about volume level, but importance levels are also crucial. Constant intensity in communication creates tension for the communicants, whether lovers or leaders. Good administrators find ways to lower intensity levels repeatedly.

5. *Teach people to communicate.* You model it in your own leadership style; but you also need to offer seminars, provide demonstrations, and develop methodology.

6. *Evaluate yourself as a communicator.* Do not assume all is well. Assume that many of the problems you experience relationally in your organization (or your marriage) stem from inadequate communication.

Understanding Feedback

Since communication is exchange of meaning, we should expect constant complication in clarifying our meanings within the communication process. Obviously *misinformation* and *disagreement* pose barriers for communication, but they appear as nothing when compared to *misunderstanding.* How many times have fathers pleaded with their teenagers, "I know you don't *agree* with what I said, but do you *understand* it?"

All leaders would like to avoid misinformation and achieve agreement. However, those ends, noble as they may be, are not always attainable. Furthermore, we may never attain them if we do not deal with the real problem of misunderstanding, ignorance, or refusal to solicit and utilize feedback.

We apply the word *feedback* in a much broader sense than its common use in a strictly information-processing communication model. Rather than merely viewing it as information a receiver gives back to a sender about a message, we want to think of feedback as *describing* a relationship between transactional partners in the communication system.

Keep in mind that in any communication situation (particularly one in which you are the sender), you can allow your orientation to fix on at least three different dimensions of the process—the *sender,* the *message,* or the *receiver. Immature communicators* are primarily source oriented. They fix an egocentric attachment to their own words, motives, or objectives and then ask later, "Why didn't they understand me?"

Improving communicators focus primarily on the message. They want to be sure they choose the right words, that the terminology and sequencing fits the setting, and that they have spoken precisely what they intended to say. That is much better than being source oriented, but it still will not get the job done.

Feedback becomes the target for *impressive communicators,* since they constantly want to know what their message has conveyed to others. Motive arises here, as in all aspects of Christian leadership. Our desire for feedback must be intended to help the recipient, not to gain favor for ourselves. Serious communication does not seek church foyer levels; it looks beyond the "that was a beautiful sermon" mentality of feedback. Persons to whom we speak need to understand our meanings; they need to understand something of the spirit in which we offer our communication; and they need to understand what we would like them to do with what we have said. Consider these specific guidelines for feedback:

1. *Feedback should be specific not general.* If the other person(s) in the relational episode misunderstands, needs further clarification, or disagrees, he or she must point as precisely as possible to that part of the verbiage that creates the problem.

2. *Feedback depends on mutual trust between/among the communicators.* Trust helps me tell you what I thought of your ideas without fear of reprisal. Trust tells me you will really do something about my pleas for clarification or my disenchantment with the direction the organization is taking.

3. *Solicited feedback will usually be better received than that which is unsolicited.* Some people do not mean it when they ask, "Do you agree with me?" They really mean, "You had better agree with me." The responsibility here is mutual, like everything else in the communication process. Both parties should solicit, genuinely want, and freely provide feedback.

4. *Feedback should be descriptive of how the receiver responds and the effects of those words or deeds,* not threatening

and judgmental about his or her person. All parties need to separate words and ideas from those who have offered them, as difficult as that is to do. When we respond, we should respond to what has been *said*, not what we think a person might *feel*.

5. *Feedback needs to be checked and rechecked to ensure its validity.* Sometimes that checking needs merely another question to ensure that meanings stay on the same wave length. Other times it might mean contacts with other staff members to verify the general tone of the feedback.

Ernest Bormann and associates offer a terse paragraph directing our attention to the only adequate and mature focus for communicating leaders. Interestingly, they refer to effective communicators as "consciously competent individuals."

> Consciously competent individuals are primarily receiver-oriented when they attempt to achieve an objective through speech-communication. If one is interested in the results of the message beyond whatever ego-gratification comes from expressing feelings, then he must help his receivers achieve understanding of his meanings. The source and the message are important only as they contribute to gaining the desired action from the receiver(s). Hence, the favored attitude for a person interested in communicating to accomplish specific objectives is to be receiver-oriented.[4]

Understanding the Rules of Communication

Twenty-five years ago the American Management Association released a memo entitled "Ten Commandments of Good Communication. I do not have access to the detailed documentation, but I have retained a copy in my files. The overview seems so helpful I reproduce it here with brief annotated paragraphs that represent our understanding of the way Christian leaders can implement these ideas in ministry.

1. *Seek to clarify your ideas before communicating.* Even the best communication can often be misunderstood. When ideas and goals seem fuzzy in our own minds, we put our people at risk by thrusting them into a position of required understanding when the ideas may still be indecipherable.

2. *Examine the true purpose of each communication.* In

education and in administration, goals are nearly everything. Language, tone, approach, timing, and sequence—all serve the objectives of the communication. Do not misunderstand here: the objective of the communication may have nothing to do with task achievement or organizational advancement. Christian leaders often speak to heal wounds or encourage people, but those are very precise and important goals and require very specific kinds of communication.

3. *Consider the total physical and human setting whenever you communicate.* This places us back again in earlier chapters on the communication climate, simultaneity, presentability, mutuality, and episodic relationships. Considering immediate context, social climate, physical setting, and timing, do not forget the less obvious but equally important organizational and emotional mind-set of the recipient.

4. *Consult with others, where appropriate, in planning communication.* Where should we meet? When should we meet? Do we agree to any limits on what we will say on this occasion? Who will speak first? Can we agree to feedback honestly on the basis of how we feel?

5. *Be mindful, while you communicate, of the overtones as well as the basic content of your message.* To review, denotative, interpretive, and relational dimensions must all be kept in balance with a primary focus on the third of that triplet. Volume, tone, and a host of nonverbal cues dramatically affect the message and the response.

6. *Take the opportunity, when it arises, to convey something of help or value to the receiver.* The happiness and improvement of the people with whom we serve must be every leader's deep concern. Those colleagues quickly understand whether our attempts at communication exist for our own benefit, for the benefit of the organization, or whether their own welfare receives appropriate attention.

7. *Follow up your communication.* We have discussed this at some length earlier in the chapter under the general heading of "Understanding Feedback."

8. *Communicate for tomorrow as well as today.* Every communication episode provides another link in the transactional chain. Other links have preceded it, and others will follow. It cannot be divorced from those on which it now builds, nor

should it be expected to stand alone apart from what will follow. To put it another way, every opportunity at communication ought to increase, perhaps even multiply, other opportunities for communication.

9. *Be sure your actions support your communication.* How did Jesus put it? "These people honor me with their lips, / but their hearts are far from me" (Matt. 15:8). Leaders often talk a lot but frequently may be perceived as having little heart for the kind of follow through that makes the talk worthwhile.

10. *Seek not only to be understood but also to understand —be a good listener.* This tenth law introduces our next chapter. Listening is one of the most crucial, difficult, and abused aspects of the communication process. As someone has said, "If we are to understand the inner man [or woman], we must listen with the inner ear."

In this chapter we have explained why the complications of the communication process often distort those messages, how we can clarify those messages through effective organizational communication, how a proper use of feedback can assist all communicators, and how following some simple rules will help us become more effective in communication.

Remember Fred and Laura? How might their conversation have been different if they had observed a few of the simple lessons of this chapter? Have a look.

LAURA: "Will you stay home tonight? I think I have the flu."

FRED: "I'm already committed to see Joe from my office."

LAURA: (I know this is really an important business contact for him, yet I do feel very ill.) "I'm sorry to ask, but this is one time I really need your help. Would it be at all possible to reschedule your meeting with Joe? If not, I'll understand and make other arrangements."

FRED: (She really does look sick, but Joe and I have to rearrange that contact within the next 48 hours. Laura rarely asks for something this earnestly, maybe I should stay home with her.) "I'll do my best; let me call Joe and see if he'll be available for an early breakfast."

LAURA: (He really cares how I feel and really wants to help me. Whatever he decides, I'm at least thankful that he's considerate enough to try to rearrange his schedule.) "Thanks darling. It would be great if you could be here; but, if Joe can't make it in the morning, please go ahead to your meeting tonight, and I'll find somebody else to stay with me."

Notes

1. Dennis R. Smith and L. Keith Williamson, *Interpersonal Communication* (Dubuque, Iowa: William C. Brown, 1977), 76.

2. Smith and Williamson, 84.

3. Ted Engstrom and Ed Dayton, "Communicate or Else..." *Christian Leadership Letter,* February 1973, 1.

4. Ernest G. Bormann, et al., *Interpersonal Communication in the Modern Organization* (Englewood Cliffs, N.J.: Prentice-Hall, 1969), 148.

4

LEARNING TO LISTEN

In June of 1815 the Battle of Waterloo raged to a conclusion on the northern coast of France. The outcome was immediately communicated across the English Channel by means of semaphore, the signaling of flags. The three-word message announced, "Wellington defeated Napoleon." Fog filled the channel after the second word, and messengers rushed back to London with the news, "Wellington defeated." Rothschild's messenger, however, "listened" for the full message, brought back the accurate report, and as a result, Rothschild cleaned up in a crashed market the next morning. Sometimes it pays to listen to the entire message before taking action.

Most of us are poor listeners. As a skill, listening seems considerably easier to develop than speaking. Furthermore, it may be in much greater demand. Everyone craves a good listener, one who can affect the flow of conversation by attentive responses and reactions. Good listeners turn opposition to support, increase knowledge, enhance appreciation, and make peace in organizations.

Good listeners function as a sounding board. They give their energy and concentration to sense, attend to, understand, and remember what they hear as others talk. In *sensing* they receive stimuli through the senses. In *attending* they select one or more of the stimuli and allow it (them) to register in their brains. In *understanding* they interpret and evaluate what they have sensed. In *remembering* they recall the understood message and, if necessary, act upon it.

Everyone of us wants precisely that kind of behavior in other people—employees, spouses, children, and even strangers we meet for the first time. The least we can do, therefore, is develop those qualities in ourselves.

Improving Listening Skills

One of the best and briefest treatments regarding the improvement of listening skills appeared many years ago in *The Nation's Business*. The article was entitled "Listening Is a 10-part Skill," and much of this first section is adapted and revised from that article by Ralph Nichols.[1]

1. *Find areas of interest.* Bad listeners decide after a few minutes that a speaker or subject is dull and irrelevant to their needs. Good listeners ask constantly, "What's being said here that I can use?" Picture yourself in a congregation listening to a sermon from a preacher less educated and skilled than yourself. You are tempted to let the time slip by with an occasional nod or smile to encourage the speaker. This first guideline, however, suggests that you attack the text, work at being involved intellectually and spiritually, and allow God to apply the truth of His Word to your heart.

2. *Judge content, not delivery.* That is tough to do for those who are trained in thespian and homiletical techniques. A good listener quickly gets by the distractions of inadequate delivery to concentrate on what the speaker has to say and, therefore, to apply guideline number 1.

3. *Hold your fire.* Overstimulated listeners get too excited too soon, either positively or negatively. Reaction is important every time we hear someone speak, but it should be deferred. Good listeners understand what speakers say from the speaker's perspective, not just their own. In nonformal interpersonal communication, feedback questions can help us get a better empathetic understanding and dampen those fires of early reaction.

4. *Listen for ideas.* Good listeners grasp the flow of what others say. They look for characteristic language, structure, repetition, transitions, and other signposts of communication. Remember, these things work not only with formal speeches and sermons, but in conversation as well.

5. *Be flexible.* Remember people communicate in many different ways so we have to listen in many different ways. Some speak with highly organized minds and move right through a series of items in order. Others ramble, testing our listening patience, looking for the right nonverbal feedback,

wondering whether empathy will greet the ideas they struggle to express. Wise leaders (good listeners) make the necessary mental adjustments to accommodate the differences in speakers. This flexibility factor applies to everything from taking notes in a different way to maintaining control over body language and nonverbal feedback.

6. *Work at listening.* Faking attention heads the list of the most common problems of poor listeners, yet it is the one most easily corrected. Listening is hard work and calls for dedication and even sacrifice. It requires eye contact, appropriate posture, and the kind of body language that helps communicators express themselves more freely and more clearly.

7. *Resist distractions.* You can spot poor listeners in any congregation. Every noise at the back causes heads to turn; every fussy baby creates frowns in that direction; every handy piece of paper serves as an outlet for excess mental energy. Good listeners fight distraction. They mute or turn off the television, refuse to turn their necks toward extraneous noise, and fix their concentration on the speaker.

8. *Exercise your mind.* Bad listeners lack experience. They have not struggled through difficult material, stretching ideas and content from fields with which they are not familiar. Like children, they only show interest in comfortable, relatively easy concepts that do not require them to exercise their minds. Good listeners do not "turn off" what they do not want to hear and "turn up" what they do like to hear. In the spirit of guideline number 1, they stretch for whatever new and helpful concepts they might find in a conversation or an address.

9. *Keep your mind open.* We all have biases that may or may not be the right way of viewing ideas and situations. The first step in open-mindedness brings our biases to the foreground, recognizing and admitting them. Then, as we listen to another speak, we ask ourselves five basic questions clearly spelled out by Gerald Wilson:

What is the topic of conversation? (Topic)
What is the speaker's position on the topic? (Position)
Do I agree or disagree with his position? (Agreement)
How strongly do I agree or disagree? (Strength)
Do I consider this an important issue? (Importance)[2]

10. *Capitalize on thought speed.* The thinking-speaking ratio stands at approximately four to one. Most people speak at a speed of about 125 words a minute, and most listeners can listen or think at the rate of about 500 words per minute. Even with slight adjustment either way we notice that most of us have between 300 and 400 words of excess thinking time during every minute a person talks to us. It is quite easy to let our minds wander and center on things more interesting to us but totally unrelated to the immediate conversation. Listening experts suggest, however, that we anticipate where the speaker is going, mentally summarize what he or she has already said, evaluate and reach some preliminary judgments on response, and always interpret in the light of the overall context (particularly the speaker's point of view). In short, we "listen between the lines" much in the same way we read between the lines in an article or book.

Listening to Superiors

Most management literature deals with listening to subordinates, as well it might for leaders unable to listen will be unable to lead. However, every leader is also a follower. Presidents and pastors must answer to boards, deans and assistant pastors must answer to presidents and pastors, middle management to top management, and so it goes.

Assurance of Meaning

Crucial to listening from a subordinate point of view is an assurance of a supervisor's meaning. When the boss speaks, whether giving instructions or just providing general information, the employee must understand what the boss says and means. Here rephrasing feedback provides a useful tool.

Be careful not to exaggerate what sounds good. As followers, we want to be sure our leaders can help us meet needs we identify in ourselves, not just fulfill the objectives of the organization. Nevertheless, we want to avoid getting so excited or pleased about some positive statement that we miss the big picture of what the boss really said.

Concentration

Concentration counts too. Sometimes business meetings go on interminably, and other people present ask questions whose answers we have known for some time. Nevertheless, it is useful to listen to the chairperson's response to see whether we have understood the chair's position accurately, or for that matter, whether that position remains the same now as when we discussed that matter two weeks ago.

Unfamiliar Messages

Listen, too, for unfamiliar "messages." Is there something new here? Have I misunderstood the boss previously? Does the arrangement of data I hear today conflict with what I thought I heard last week? Remember communication is a mine field; the more carefully we walk, the more safely we will get through.

Bosses may get by from time to time with a passive listening style, but subordinates need to be actively involved in listening at all times.

Listening to Subordinates

An old story once made the rounds in organizational communications circles. Two derelicts were sunning themselves on a park bench. "The reason I'm here," said one, "is that I refused to listen to anyone." "That's funny," said the other. "The reason I'm here is because I listened to everyone."

Balanced Response

Listening to subordinates may be extremely important, but balanced response provides the key to effective leadership listening. We like to know that our boss's door (and mind) stands open to our ideas and suggestions. So do the people who serve under our leadership. The way bosses respond to subordinates' attempts to communicate with them has a great deal to do with the morale of those who serve in that office.

The rules for listening to subordinates do not differ greatly from things we have looked at already in this chapter. Rephrase and restate what seems useful; pay attention; avoid preconceived ideas; discipline your reaction so that you show no anger or surprise; consider the source continuously by trying to understand the cultural, social, and emotional milieu out of which this employee speaks; and finally, don't interrupt even if you are the boss.

Follow-Through

When you respond, you have now assumed the feedback role, reacting to ideas initiated by the other person. To achieve effective follow-through, remember three things:
1. The subordinate needs to understand your response.
2. The subordinate needs to be willing to accept your response.
3. The subordinate needs to be able to do something about your response if he or she so chooses.

Sufficient Access

Remember, prior to all of this you have created access for those subordinates to speak with you in the first place. If you are not available with respect to time or place, or have not built a reputation for listening to other people, listening guidelines are irrelevant—you will never need them.

Underlying Assumptions

Edward Dayton and Ted Engstrom suggested several assumptions that underlie a boss's willingness to encourage and even solicit ideas and suggestions from subordinates.

People have good ideas.
People closest to the work are more likely to know what's going on than people who are supervising the work.
People enjoy participating and making the work and the work place better.
People need a channel to be heard.
People need to *believe* they have been heard.
People should be rewarded and/or affirmed in some way for good ideas.[3]

Listening as a Means of Solving Interpersonal Problems

Why do human relations problems often seem more severe in a Christian organization than in a secular organization?

Does not such a complaint indict us in view of everything we have learned about love, peace, and brotherhood among the saints? Can Evangelical theology and management science be brought together to explain this nagging phenomenon?

The following paragraphs do not exhaust the subject, nor do they offer any final answer. Perhaps they do at least suggest how we might attack the problem. It is our opinion that human relations problems often plague Christian organizations:

1. *Because of unrealistic expectations.* People in Christian organizations, especially those coming in from secular organizations, expect utopia. However, Christians do not check their old natures at the door when signing contracts or securing employment in a Christian organization. Failure to listen to the realities of the job may have clouded preparation to function in that situation. This happens commonly with seminary graduates moving out to first-time ministry positions. Their unrealistic expectations seem to close their ears to warnings and guidelines offered by friends, professors, and sometimes even those who serve in the Christian organization or church where they seek work. Unrealistic expectations of millennial conditions throw people off their guard, and the old nature has a chance to manifest itself in much greater proportion than if those same persons were operating in the pagan surroundings of a secular organization. There they would be constantly checking themselves to see whether the differential of godliness shined through.

2. *Because of Satan's overtime activity.* Why should the evil one bother a secular organization already furthering his goals in the world—materialism, consumer exploitation, perhaps even the manufacture of damaging materials, such as tobacco, alcohol, etc.? Having no concern there, he can work overtime by concentrating his demonic troops on organizations seeking to teach Christlike values, to train for Christian service ministries, to carry out the Great Commission, or to offer a place of witness, fellowship, and worship in an otherwise satanic surrounding.

3. *Because of the ignorance of managerial processes.* The application of "human relations" techniques in the administration of organizations is a complex and professional skill. It

does not just happen because employees are "good people," or because they happen to be Christians. Good people, especially those who serve in leadership roles, dare not be ignorant in managerial process and the crucial role that listening skills play in that process. By listening effectively (both to subordinates and superiors) good people become effective people and spiritual people become competent people. Peter Drucker said, "There are no good people, there are only people good for certain things." Of course, such a statement issues out of a theological vacuum and legitimately expresses the truism that everyone must find his or her proper niche in the organization to function effectively and happily. However, the theological truth is that there *are* good people, at least in their standing before God, and those good people ought to become better people each day in the process of sanctification.

4. *Because the demands are greater on both sides of the person-in-organization conflict.* An organization that hires Christians usually demands more of them in terms of ethics, output, loyalty, and role fulfillment than one that operates on the basis that all employees will cheat the company if they can. Many Christian organizations almost have a Theory Y pattern built into their philosophies. Management says, "Our people are Christians; they will automatically be better workers and higher achievers."

At the same time, "labor" focuses on the idiographic dimension and says, "The administration is composed of Christians; therefore, we will receive sympathetic treatment, better employee practices, and a constant sensitivity to our needs and individual personalities." When these things do not emerge, friction sets in, and each side blames the other for not "being Christian"!

What then is the solution? Perhaps we need a realistic understanding that God is not finished with any one of us yet, and that the old nature will come out every time it gets a chance. Certainly the potential for positive human relations seems infinitely greater in the Christian organization, or our Evangelical pneumatology needs adjusting. What does all this have to do with listening? In every team situation, and especially in times of great demand, communication may very well be the difference between success and failure. Listening amounts to more than just applying the skills we have discussed earlier in this chapter. It is an attitude, a willingness to value what others says to us and, when necessary, act upon what we hear. Human relations problems will never go away, but they can be significantly alleviated by people who know how to listen and respond. We commonly say, "Think before you speak." We might also add, "Listen before you speak."

If it really is possible for a believer to possess and display the fruit of the Spirit (Gal. 5:22) and a loving, caring, burden-bearing attitude toward others (Phil. 2:1-4), then the capacity for constant *koinonia* must be present. Yet we lack the knowledge of how to make it work on a realistic, carefully designed pattern in the trenches.

Our obsession with Christian perfection in other brothers and sisters also needs to be reexamined. If we can exchange that critical spirit for a Christlike willingness to work at the task, any Christian organization can be a management model of human relations even though it consists of imperfect people from top to bottom.

Quite obviously, improvement of listening skills must start at the top, and they must start with calculated instruction regarding the nature of human relations. In brief, the leader explains what we can be because of God's grace and because we can learn to integrate scriptural truth with managerial process.

At the same time the leader warns what we will become if we allow the god of this world to infest the organization. Such a process does not divorce theology from managerial effectiveness, but rather marries spirituality and competence to form the basis for a happy family. In business and industry, human relations only offers a means to an end. In the Christian organization, it is both means and ends.

The New Testament speaks to these issues. Christian leaders in Christian or secular organizations need to constantly study and teach the truth of Scripture regarding how believers must relate to each other. The following passages represent a fair listing of the key New Testament texts:

Matthew 5:3-20,38-48; 7:1-5; 18:15-17,21-35
Luke 6:20-45; 14:25-35; 22:24-27

John 13:1-17,34-35; 14:9-17; 17:20-26
1 Corinthians 3:1-3; 10:23-24; 13:1-7
Galatians 5:13-26
Ephesians 4:1-3,29-32
Philippians 2:1-4
Colossians 3:12-17; 4:6
1 Thessalonians 2:7-8; 3:11-13; 4:9-12; 5:12-13
2 Timothy 2:23-26
Titus 3:1-2
Hebrews 12:14-15
James 1:19-26; 3:1-4; 4:11; 5:9
1 Peter 3:8-12; 5:6-10
1 John 2:9-11; 3:13-18; 4:7-13,18-21

One more warning: just as institutional morale is probably suspect when people in any given organization constantly talk about it, so the organization that claims it has no human relations problems is probably greatly self-deceived or deliberately hiding its dirty laundry. *We can best find the source of human relations problems by looking in a mirror, not across the counseling desk.*

Until those of us who hold managerial positions willingly understand our own abrasiveness to people, our own failures in communication, our own selfishness; until we understand how each subordinate views himself or herself and grasp the social context out of which he or she comes; until we institute clearly defined training programs that focus on listening skills as well as on long-range planning, delegation techniques, and the rest of the managerial process—until these changes take place we can continue to anticipate that the Christian organization will have a poor track record in harmonizing the idiographic and nomothetic dimensions to produce a positive human relations climate.

Listening to Nonverbal Messages

Definition of Nonverbal Communication

We have talked a good bit about nonverbal feedback but primarily in the context of using our own body language to encourage and affirm people speaking to us. Let us conclude this study by looking briefly at reading nonverbal communication. Technically, nonverbal communication "refers to communicative messages which are nonlinguistic, analogic, and processed primarily by the brain's right hemisphere."[4] We are talking here about gestures, facial expressions, physical appearance, touching behavior, and other forms of language. Sign language does not qualify since it is definitively linguistic.

Influence of Nonverbal Communication

Janis Andersen cited some amazing statistics regarding the influence of nonverbal communication on human interaction. For example, she quoted studies by Albert Mehrabian that claimed 93 percent of the meaning in human interaction comes from nonverbal messages and only 7 percent from verbal messages! Those figures may be high, but most studies acclaim nonverbal communication as more important than verbal. We will talk more about nonverbal communication in chapter 7; our main focus here deals with how to read (listen to) these important messages.

Nonverbal Symbols

Important here is a recognition of whether these nonverbal cues have been sent intentionally or unintentionally. The way a person dresses, for example, might very well indicate something about the message the person is trying to send you. Consider the massive literature on "dressing for success" and the way all of us want to dress appropriately when going for a job interview.

Communication experts talk about "gross body movements" and "gestures." In the first category they include "emblems," which are deliberate movements translatable into words (pointing); "illustrators" used to reinforce a verbal message (smiling); "regulators," movements facilitating interaction (holding up a hand signaling "stop"); "affect displays," which demonstrate intensity of feelings (crying); and "adaptors," any gesture used as a means to alleviate tension (closing one's eyes). Considerably less subtle are the readings we must make of posture, facial and eye symbols, touching or nontouching behavior, and personal distancing.

In summary we quote from Gerald Wilson:

The point of all of this discussion was that the human communication systems we use, especially in interpersonal communication events, is comprised of a complex system of interacting cues and variables other than words, which accompany the language we speak. To become more sensitive to the subtlety and complexity of this system is to become a better communicator. And especially when trouble exists in our relationships it is useful to be able to identify what is being communicated nonverbally and to talk about our interpretations. By doing this, and only by doing this, can we assure ourselves that our guesses really are shared meaning.[5]

Reading about listening skills will probably not improve them very much. Now that we know some of the issues involved we can come to a very good starting place—self-assessment. Try the following for starters:

- I usually respond quickly to the first statement.
- I often control the conversation in order to lead it off in directions I want it to go.
- I frequently convert conversations to personal stories or illustrations called to mind by something the other person has said.
- I do most of the talking during conversations or even in group meetings.
- I usually find out what is going on in my organization indirectly and often after the fact.
- I have rarely, if ever, been concerned about body language, either giving or reading it.
- I have paid a lot of attention to communicating to my subordinates but very little to listening to them.
- I frequently let my mind wander when someone is telling me something I am not really interested in.
- I usually lose patience with people who cannot communicate well, assuming the responsibility for failure is theirs.

If you have to answer yes to most or many of the above statements, you are a prime candidate to get serious about learning to listen.

Notes

1. Ralph Nichols, "Listening is a 10-part Skill," *Nation's Business* 45 (July 1957):56.

2. Gerald Wilson, et al., *Interpersonal Communication in the Modern Organization* (Englewood Cliffs, N.J.: Prentice-Hall, 1969), 111.

3. Edward R. Dayton and Ted W. Engstrom, "Suggestions," *Christian Leadership Letter,* June 1986, 1.

4. Janis Andersen, "Instructor NonVerbal Communications: Listening to Our Silent Messages," *Communicating in College Classrooms: New Directions for Teaching and Learning* 26 (June 1986):43.

5. Wilson, *Interpersonal Communication,* 224.

5

SELF-CONCEPT
AND COMMUNICATION

Perhaps the words "Know thyself" first appeared on the temple wall at Delphi. Leaders need to understand their own abilities, gifts, strengths, limitations, and aspirations. Few things in the natural domain help one through life and fit one for leadership roles like a knowledge of who one really is or what one can do. Perhaps one of the saddest symptoms associated with a lack of individuality is the sensation of this loss of identity. Impressionable people suffer distress when they have no clear conception of who they are, why they are, and where they are going.

Psychologists refer to this as "self-concept," a term that describes a combination of the characteristics one believes about oneself and the images one presents to others.

> Imagine that all your personal information is contained in a little box that you carry around. When you meet others, you select identifying items from the box to present to them. There is some information that you want most people to see, so you select those bits most frequently. There are other things about yourself that you want only select individuals to see, and so you reserve these bits for special situations. There are still other parts of you that you keep entirely to yourself. These are things known only to you. And finally, there is information tucked in the corners of the box that you don't even know exists.[1]

In actuality this concept is far more ancient than the oracle at Delphi and comes from a much more reputable source. In Proverbs 23:7 we read, "For as he thinketh in his heart, so is he" (KJV). Some have argued that people are what they eat, and surely that idea contains some truth. However, one thing seems clear not only from the Proverbs passage but from the teaching of Jesus as well: *we are what we think.*

Self-Concept as a Communication Model

Johari Window Model

The Johari Window was developed by psychologists Joseph Luft and Harrington Ingham. Using the familiar four-quadrant model they described information known to others or not known to others and known to self or not known to self.[2]

	Known to self	Not known to self
Known to others	*OPEN*	*BLIND*
Not known to others	*HIDDEN*	*UNKNOWN*

From *Group Processes: An Introduction to Group Dynamics* by Joseph Luft, by permission of Mayfield Publishing Company. Copyright © 1984, 1970, and 1963 by Joseph Luft.

Reading clockwise around the quadrants beginning with the upper left we find the words *open, blind, unknown,* and *hidden.* The diagram reflects behaviors known to others but not known to self (blind) and behaviors not known to others and not known to self (unknown). Some of us can deal with the left side of the diagram, admitting both open and hidden characteristics. Secular psychologists would argue that the key objective in self-concept awareness is *appropriateness,* presenting a correct image for each relationship and context. We disagree. The biblical response, and a biblical value for studying self-concept psychology, centers in insight (know thyself), truth (vulnerability), and transparency to other people.

In *A Passion for Excellence* Tom Peters reminded us that "The only magic is brute consistency, persistence and attention to detail. Leaders act in ways consistent with their beliefs, they are persistent in pursuit of their visions, and they are always vigilant about the little things that make a big difference."[3]

Insight and Truth

Growth in self-concept must be growth toward insight and truth. Every leader needs to bring his or her self-concept in line with reality, thereby perceiving *actual*, not *mythical* strengths and weaknesses. Each individual consists of several selves: dad, doctor, democrat, duck hunter, and deacon. This concept of the multiple self causes great conflict and demonstrates the necessity for discipline and integrated behavior.

Generally, mature people resist change, yet growth in the self-concept requires it. Furthermore, harmony in the organization demands not only a coherence of the multiple selves to each individual involved but also a cementing of relationships among all the individuals, particularly at the leadership level. Here communication comes in. Though they do not speak theologically, Smith and Williamson described the paradox of human communication:

> The self is created and maintained through interpersonal communication transactions. The infant does not come into the world as a fully formed person, only with the potential for learning the significance and use of message systems. The interpersonal transactions within the context of the family, community, and society are then responsible for shaping the self, the perception of self, and the perception of others. On the other hand, we must now observe that the individual is not completely determined. There is evidence to indicate that the individual decides what perspectives he or she will adopt in interacting with others. To say that the self is molded by forces that form the environment of the self, and at the same time assert that the self has the freedom to adopt a view of life and the universe that transcends the social environment, is to confront a basic paradox in the nature of interpersonal communication.[4]

Self-Growth and Spiritual Formation

Christians, of course, add numerous other spiritual dimensions here and talk not only about a growing self-concept but also about spiritual formation. The innate power of God's Word, the control of the Holy Spirit, the dynamic of prayer, the influence of godly friends—these and many more internal and environmental factors help form the self that God wants us to be and also give us clarity and understanding about that self.

On the one hand, we remind ourselves of God's grace, how much He loves us, and the significance of self-esteem. After all, one cannot love one's spouse or neighbor as oneself if one finds only disgust and repulsiveness in the self. The other extreme, however, takes us to Romans 12:3 where Paul wrote, "For by the grace given me I say to every one of you: Do not think of yourself more highly than you ought, but rather think of yourself with sober judgment, in accordance with the measure of faith God has given you." Attitudinal inflation looms at least as dangerous as feelings of inferiority. God calls us to a happy balance.

Self-Concept and Latent Roles

Lessons From the Hawthorne Studies

In the literature of management science the concept of latent roles comes to us primarily from those famous and historic Hawthorne experiments. The Massachusetts Institute of Technology conducted a series of studies at the Western Electric Company's Hawthorne Works in Chicago (actually Cicero) lasting from 1924 until 1932 and testing the response of workers under varying work conditions. The oversimplified description of "Hawthorne effect" describes the influence of responses from causes other than the ones the researcher is measuring. At the Western Electric plant, no matter what they did with the workers, production went up. Years later Roethlisberger and Dickson referred to the Hawthorne experiments as "the systematic exploitation of the simple and the obvious," namely, that people will work better when management pays attention to them.

From the Hawthorne studies we learn that the requirements of the individual and the institution must somehow be kept in balance. Years of research and reams of literature were produced over the next fifty years precisely to emphasize that strategic point.

Centrality of Interaction

Counselors who followed up the Hawthorne experiments learned that *interaction* was the important element in their contact with employees. At the point of interaction the greatest insights come, and the findings can be best understood. What surfaced came to be known as "latent roles."

Most individuals find themselves involved in a variety of interpersonal relationships, the work group being only one of them. People play many roles as they fit into numerous activities, hence a variety of selves enter the complex concept. *At issue here is the fact that all roles other than the one being played at a given time become latent.* The counselors discovered that latent role characteristics lend themselves to improving human problems when handled properly by a trained counselor, but results only come at the point of interaction.

When a latent role emerges in interaction, a nonthreatening atmosphere is created. Each party takes a comfortable role and freedom settles into the relationship.

Latent Roles and Closure

The idea of closure is foreign to the latent role because when closure occurs, learning stops and stereotyped patterns begin. Careful here. The change does not come about only because the persons are "trying to please" but because they really *accept* a new role without vacillation or equivocation.

People want to be clear on self-concept. Especially those in whom the Spirit of God dwells and who take seriously the Bible's call for openness and vulnerability. They want to be individuals with values of their own not submerged in church or organizational regulations.

Let us remember that great difference between latent roles and deviant roles. Deviants are against everything except doing it precisely their way. The latent role player struggles only against the binding structure of environmental norms, usually the stubbornness of the organization.

Leaders must be aware that the self is created, developed, and maintained through communication and interaction with others. Think about the personality of an infant. At the age of two or three months there is hardly any difference among normal healthy infants though we often talk about one "having more personality" than another. At the age of one year or eighteen months, very distinct patterns emerge. Those patterns reflect precisely what parents or other omnipresent adults have been saying and the way they have been behaving around that child during those crucial impressionable months.

The same kind of thing happens with neophytes in the Christian organization. The Christian self fully blossoms through a process of maturing. The way spiritual "adults" around new Christians respond to their needs and handle both primary and latent roles will, to a large extent, determine what they become in the years ahead. Once again, the major challenge aims at leaders actively and consciously involved in the process of training other leaders.

Self-Concept and Threat

Students with keen insight into the field of psychology will immediately note that the ideas of this chapter have been informed primarily by the work of Arthur Combs and Donald Snygg. Their research and a great deal of supporting documentation from professional colleagues down through the years emphasizes how threat restricts the perceptive field. If their basic assumption holds up, namely, that intelligence is a function of the richness and breadth of the phenomenal field, the effect of threat on that field represents a dangerous imposition.[5]

Negative Results of Threat

Threat concentrates attention on the perceived rather than the real or possible. Threat, researchers remind us, is the perfect device of the manipulator and the autocratic leader. It provides the means by which people can be prevented from exploring widely within their own experience and self-concept while at the same time being held rigidly and unquestionably to the beliefs and values the manipulator wants them to treasure.

Threat and Tunnel Vision

We find one common and popular result of threat in what we have come to call *tunnel vision*. Tunnel vision dramatically limits our perceptions. Illness in the family, personal trauma, and imminent danger—these and lesser environmental hazards cause the self-concept to shrink, narrowing its focus on a singular role even to the point of fixation.

A second effective threat on the self-concept is the *defense reaction* induced in people when they feel threatened. A good example here would be the way people react when first told of some dramatic change in a church program. If leadership does not handle that announcement properly, fields of vision narrow, wide perceptions are rendered impossible, and the opportunity for perceptual revision is dramatically reduced. In short, under threat, behavior becomes rigid.

Threat and Challenge

Another dramatic difference is that between threat and challenge. A threat carries feelings of jeopardy and inadequacy to deal with what one faces. In challenge, people experience a degree of adequacy to meet the challenge (assuming it has been presented as challenge and not threat). Maybe the difference has to do with a self-concept of competence or incompetence in dealing with the task.

Perhaps what Toynbee once said about societies can also be said about churches. The more intelligent face a crisis and learn to cope while those without crisis, or in which crisis overwhelms intelligence and resources, produce very little positive response and perhaps even collapse entirely. Donald Snygg and Arthur Combs put it this way:

> A free society requires independent, thinking people of wisdom and perspective; it requires unthreatened citizens, people who are challenged but not threatened. A complex, interdependent society like ours requires people who are flexible, not rigid; who can perceive broadly rather than narrowly; who are not so bound to the necessity of self defense as to have little time or energy to devote to the

problems of their fellow human beings. In our kind of society not all possibilities can be readily foreseen, and it is necessary for us to be able to rely not on the brains of a few, but on the interacting creative efforts of millions. Rigidity, narrowness and preoccupation with self defense are the very antithesis of what a fluid, open, dynamic modern society requires. Fear and threat have no place in such a society.[6]

If we substitute the word *church* for the word *society* in the above paragraph, we get some glimpse of the practicality of this research.

Self-Concept and Significant Others

This subject may be viewed from two radically different but equally important dimensions. First of all, our self-concepts are shaped by what we have called in an earlier chapter "significant others"—family members, friends, religious leaders, teachers, and other important personalities. This says a great deal about the kind of people we spend time with and call our friends. It also reemphasizes the tragedy of the breakdown of family and church in modern society. Quite obviously, the health of the self-concepts of those who serve as our significant others holds a determinative effect on the health and growth of our own self-concept.

Interplay of Self-Concepts

The other dimension has to do with recognizing our influence on those who consider us "significant others." A senior pastor with a staff of three certainly represents a significant other to those associates. Their self-esteem and feelings of self-worth largely depend upon the way he responds to them week after week. Evaluation and even criticism of persons may at times be necessary but never without recognizing that their sense of importance, the health and growth of their self-concepts, depend on his leadership. Wise leaders take time to observe what people have done well and tell them about it. Making subordinates feel needed is a major task of leadership and a major influence in the development of their self-concepts.

Remember too that we are not born with the ability to lead others. Leadership is learned behavior, often developed through trial and error. Even visionary leaders, able to inspire and motivate others, often make poor supervisors simply because they have not learned various aspects of communication and interaction essential to the maintenance of self-concept in relationships.

Handling Anger in Significant Others

As one of the most common strong emotions, anger can destroy families, friendships, and leader-follower relationships. Angry people lose control and become precisely the kind of threat that narrows perceptions and weakens the self-concepts of others. Angry people tend to do things instinctively, and they repeatedly return to their anger because it seems natural and even momentarily satisfying.

Good leaders cannot afford that moment. They have committed themselves to maturity and discipline. Their awareness of the destructive effects of anger on their own self-concepts and those of others requires that they allow God's Holy Spirit to identify the kind of angry behavior that can only be called sin. Not all anger is sin. However, Christian leaders out of control and reeking havoc on the self-concepts of those around them must be viewed as engaging in sin.

Ego and the Love Ethic

We and those who serve with us need to approach ministry with a proper attitude. Serious commitment to the love ethic of 1 Corinthians 13 and its practical outworking in the lives of others is central in the development of the self-concept. Christian leaders must not be self-seeking nor egotistical. Like an effective quarterback, they hand off the ball while fans cheer the running back who gets the twenty-yard gain.

In the functioning of biblical responsibility in the church, workers must know their tasks and believe them to be important, understand and support the objectives of ministry, and be conscious of their relationship to others in the program. They achieve that in healthy and growing self-concepts when they can be free from an atmosphere of intimidation and have a significant role in congregational ministry.

Notes

1. Gerald L. Wilson, et al., *Interpersonal Growth Through Communication* (Dubuque, Iowa: William C. Brown Publishers, 1985), 36.

2. Joseph Luft, *Group Processes: An Introduction to Group Dynamics*, 2d ed. (Palo Alto, Calif.: National Press Books, 1970), 11.

3. Tom Peters and Nancy Austin, *A Passion for Excellence* (New York: Random House, 1985), 324.

4. Dennis R. Smith and L. Keith Williamson, *Interpersonal Communication* (Dubuque, Iowa: William C. Brown, 1977), 307.

5. Arthur W. Combs and Donald Snygg, *Individual Behavior* (New York: Harper and Row, 1959), 180-88.

6. Ibid., 189.

6

LANGUAGE AND INTERPERSONAL RELATIONS

Ancient Babylonian inhabitants of the plain of Shinar built that primitive ziggurat to reach to heaven and establish the unity of the nations. The record in Genesis 11 tells us that their greatest fear came to pass when God scattered them all over the earth with different languages. There was no longer a mark for the fugitive, no ray of hope, no token of grace.

Language as a Reflection of Ourselves

Out of the confusion God chose one nation with one language to carry forth His Word and be His people on the earth. Of course they too failed, and they too were scattered, until today Jews speak almost every language on the face of the civilized earth. In the future God will do it again, as He pulls together a unification of nations in the millennial kingdom where everyone will speak one pure language and worship in God's holy mountain (Zeph. 3:9-11). The miracle of languages at Pentecost may well have been a first-century demonstration of this yet future event.

Language Reflects Values

Meanwhile, language continues to be the major factor in human relationships. In the twentieth century we have seen that nations with identical or similar languages ban together in times of world war; nations with diverse languages draw swords against one another. Civil war represents an exception to that, but the general principle has prevailed throughout history.

So it is in families, churches, and businesses. The way we

talk provides the best barometer of our lives and values. We talk about things we care about. Think about your friends and yourself. Everyone has a three- or four-point personal agenda that keeps coming up like the reruns on summer television. Golf, sports, job, children, cars, and the list goes on. Given an opportunity to dominate the conversation, we rarely turn the spotlight on other people, preferring to bask in our own interests.

Language Reflects Attitudes

Furthermore, we reflect negative or positive attitudes by the way we talk. Some folks use language offensive to Christians while the language of others is simply depressing. The words come from attitudes that work for or against us as negative thinking and pessimism become a self-fulfilling prophecy. However, we have the power to choose our own attitudes and certainly the power to choose our own words. That is what this chapter is all about. Paul wrote to the church at Colossae, "Let your conversation be always full of grace, seasoned with salt, so that you may know how to answer everyone" (4:6). Let us accept that marvelous reminder as we consider the topic before us.

Language—Scientific or Magical?

Communication specialists have done a good bit of work on the nature of language and semantics. For example, they hold essentially two basic views of language, the *scientific view* and the *magical view*. The former holds that language is essentially *representational* in that its various levels of abstraction from reality form the basis of the process of inference. The connection between a word and the object it represents, therefore, becomes somewhat arbitrary, and consequently problems arise from the abstraction and arbitrariness of language. Korzybski said it well: "The map is not the territory."

The *magical view* of language suggests that words are *constitutive* rather than representational. Here is the way Smith and his colleagues explain that:

> When a word is used, it is a reality. Words carry with them inherent meanings which have been transmitted from gen-

eration to generation by a language throughout the history of the culture. Language not only embodies the evocation of experience with objects and events; it also carries with it the unconscious meanings attached to words throughout history. The magical view of language is prominent in our legal and political systems today as well as in our everyday use of language. Persuasion, healing and religion would not be possible without the constitutive nature of language.[1]

Which view is correct? Surely both contain truth and values. We will do well to understand and remember both the scientific and magical views as we work to improve our use of language in interpersonal relations.

Language and General Semantics

Two Meanings of Every Word

To scientific theorists of language (general semanticists, among others) words only represent reality in the same sense that a map represents the state it depicts. How foolish it would be to stand on a map of Indiana, for example, and argue that one is in the state, if indeed this discussion were taking place in California. Words, therefore, as symbols consist of the *referent* (the reality to which the word points) and the *reference* (the internalized interpretations of the user).

Consider the late twentieth-century understanding of the word *fundamentalist*. To the secular news media, *fundamentalism* represents everyone from the demented ravings of an ayatollah to committed biblical inerrantists on the faculty of an Evangelical seminary. However, a fundamentalist could also be a conservative school teacher who believes in getting back to phonics and other basics in elementary reading programs. *Two meanings may occur every time a word is used in conversation—the meaning of the user and the meaning of the hearer.*

Wilson's Triangle of Meaning

Gerald Wilson's triangle of meaning depicts the concept of referent and reference in a simple diagram.[2]

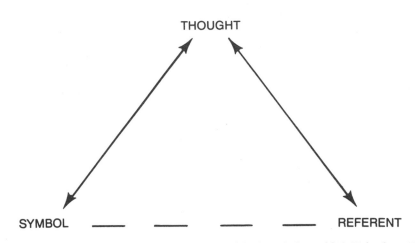

Adapted from *The Meaning of Meaning*, 8th ed. by C. K. Ogden and I. A. Richards, p. 11.
Printed in 1946 by Harcourt, Brace & World.

The word *referent* describes what the communication is about. *Thought* represents the speaker's perception and interpretation of the referent. *Symbol* stands for something else, in this context, a word or a set of words. Notice that the solid lines represent a clear connection between thought and symbol or thought and referent. The dotted line suggests that there may or may not be any connection between the two elements—the map is not the territory; the symbol is not the referent. According to Wilson:

> You can see that language provides a set of symbols that you use to transmit your thoughts to others. Experiences of people, events, and objects are reconstructed in symbolic form, which becomes talk about those experiences. In using language, you choose words (symbols) that represent the idea you intended to communicate....
>
> The words you use vary in terms of abstraction level. The more abstract your language, the further you are from direct experience, the more territory your language covers, and the less specific detail about the characteristics of the experience are included in your message.... If such a process of abstracting is going on inside you, it is also going on inside the other person with whom you're talking.[3]

Language and Perception

Improper use of language gets us into trouble when we incorrectly perceive what people say to us. For example, we often consider ourselves targets and say things like "he always gets mad at me" or "she just likes to pick on me." With those statements we imply that we know other people's motivation which is not commonly true. We have no idea what irritation (other than ourselves) has created a situation which seems to make us the targets of other people's anger.

Part of our problem here comes from thinking of ourselves as objects rather than subjects. In using language we must recognize that we do not become mere objects of another's antagonism but actually enter into the mutuality, presentality, and simultaneity of interpersonal relationships. That does not mean we are to blame for everyone else's bitterness; it does mean we can never divorce ourselves from all aspects of the communication episode.

Symbolic interactionists like to argue that rejection is always mutual. For example, if a husband holds unconditional love for his wife, she can only reject him at surface levels; in his heart and being he fends off the rejection of the moment in order to retain and sustain the ongoing contact. Although difficult to do over a long period of time, that is the essence of solid communication.

Several slogans can help us understand the self-referential nature of symbolic interaction.

1. *"You are not the target."* To say "you are mad at me" is probably incorrect most of the time. Surely some other irritation causes A to attack B. As a matter of fact, one may really like or even love B (consider a quarrel between husband and wife), but because of certain known or unknown irritants one appears to be "mad" at the other at some given point in time.

2. *"You are a subject."* The contrast, of course, is the word *object*. In using language we must recognize that we are not merely objects of another's antagonism but rather a part of the mutuality, presentality, and simultaneity in interpersonal relationships.

3. *"Rejection is always mutual."* This one is a bit more difficult to grasp unless we really have a handle on the mutu-

ality and simultaneity of interpersonal relationships. For example, if a husband holds unconditional love for his wife, she can only reject him at surface levels; in his heart and being, he fends off the rejection of the moment in order to retain and sustain the ongoing contact.

Korzybski's Non-identity and Non-allness

Korzybski's use of dashes characterizes his concern that single words fail to communicate as scientific language. In addition to the principle of *non-identity* (the map is not the territory) he advanced the principle of *non-allness*, arguing that a word does not represent all the object since what is abstracted at one level does not represent what may be abstracted at other levels. The abstracting process (perception), he would say, is self-reflexive. We use language to talk about language and make statements about statements. We are constantly making abstracts of abstracts, binding ourselves more deeply into the struggles of perception.

Perception as the Product of Experience

Donald Snygg and Arthur Combs offer two very helpful statements about the relationship of language and perception. They are almost self-explanatory:

1. *What we perceive does not exist, but what we believe exists.* Notice how the self-concept framework fits this understanding of perception. Courts constantly face this problem in evaluating the credibility of witnesses. What did they really see? Experience may be essential to perceiving, but what one perceives is determined by his or her perceptual field, which certainly includes more than direct experience.

2. *We perceived what we have learned to perceive as a result of our past opportunities or experiences.* Consider children raised in extreme isolation and then placed in a new and socius environment. What do they make of a bath tub, for example? How would you explain television to a nine-year-old who had never seen nor heard of it before? Indeed, how do you explain God the Father to children whose drunken earthly fathers beat and curse them every night of their lives?[4]

No, perception is largely a learned call. The ancient proverb "seeing is believing" does not work. Indeed, Jesus tried to turn that notion around for His friends, arguing that believing is seeing (John 11:40).

Language and Meaning

Meanings in People

Communication researchers repeatedly remind us not to search for meaning in statements alone. According to Berlo, *"Meanings are in people,* [they] are covert responses contained within the human organism. Meanings are learned. They are personal, our own property.... To the extent that people have similar meanings they can communicate. If they have no similarities in meaning between them, they cannot communicate."[5]

Denotation and Connotation

Remember these two words from an earlier chapter? They fit here as well. *Denotation* refers to a simple dictionary definition apart from relationships, environment, and context. Denotation is extremely important in preparing business reports, preaching sermons, offering testimony on a witness stand, and any other time one wants to be precise.

Connotative meaning refers to a word in environment and context, influenced by what is said, by who said it, by the topic of conversation, and by all of those mutual, simultaneous happenings that color the communication process. Several times I have seen television shows do a take-off on this particular issue. They will show a three- or four-minute clip of an event as seen from the perspective of one character, then rerun precisely the same event as seen from the perspective of another character. Obviously, what we view seems like two totally different happenings. That is connotation.

We can be pleased to work both with connotation and denotation. We must remember that both exist, that both are useful, and we must be alert to both at all times in the communication process.

Language and Relationships

Since language is the most dominate aspect of culture, students of communication must grasp how we pull together the use of language, perceptions, and meanings to assist in the ultimate goal of strengthened interpersonal relations. Culture, of course, forms the general frame of reference for the language we use, giving identity to the people who form a society.

Relationships Ascribe Meaning

The language we use in talking to and about people in our various relationships reveals a great deal about ourselves and how we view others.

We are concerned in this text with the practical application of the connection between language and relationship. Remember this connection is a two-way street: language influences relationships (creates, sustains, and destroys them), but relationships also influence language.

The roles we take in a relationship control and moderate our pool of symbols. (One does not use the language of a lover when speaking to one's sister-in-law or grandmother.) As we have already noted, different kinds of meaning can be assigned across relationships, and language reflects the view we assign to a relationship, as illustrated in the following case study:

> Ben's job requires a good bit of travel, and he often calls Leanne, especially if he has to be on the road several days. On one such occasion, however, he was extremely busy in meetings throughout two days and had forgotten to call. Meanwhile, at home, Leanne had struggled through a tough day with the kids. She needed to talk, unload, be encouraged and affirmed in how she had handled the crisis.
>
> Thus she called Ben who picked up the receiver while surrounded by piles of documents, plans, and reports. He was glad to hear from Leanne, but his mind was elsewhere; and in the twenty-minute conversation he failed to convey any emotion about Leanne's problem. He inadequately expressed his love, and he unconsciously gave the impression he was too busy to seriously consider any issues at home.
>
> Leanne hung up disappointed, frustrated, and angry. How could he let her down like that? Why would he be so insensitive? Well, she would show him. No more calls. If he wanted

to talk to her on business trips, from now on the move was his! Furthermore, when Ben came home, she would use the silent treatment—no interest in events of his trip until he apologized for that terrible behavior on the phone.

Communication as Punishment

However faulty Ben's handling of the call, Leanne has chosen to violate a cardinal axiom of communication: *never use a vehicle or channel of love to threaten, punish, or manipulate the loved one.* In this case the vehicle was a telephone. Other examples might be letters, conversation, and, ultimately, the biblical mandate dealing with marital sex (1 Cor. 7:3-5).

The one way Ben and Leanne can share their love while he travels is the telephone. When she chooses to hold that means hostage until he behaves the way she wants him to, she is being manipulative. Furthermore, if Ben needs her loving voice in those lonely hotels, it may also be giving punishment. Ben also needs to realize his part in the problem. He must see that Leanne also has struggles at home each time he is away.

Please note that Ben and Leanne have no reason to punish each other; they really love each other and want to be supportive. *It is the nature of communication that we use its processes against its purposes* and then wonder why we create problems in interpersonal relations.

Repairing Communication Breakdown

What should Leanne have done? Several good options existed, depending on how long Ben was to be gone.

1. Leanne could have said on the phone, "Ben, are you hearing me? Do you understand what I mean? I need your love and support. I'm really coming unglued down here."

2. She could have waited until Ben returned (assuming it was only a day or two) and placed a discussion of the telephone problems high on the immediate discussion agenda.

3. She could have called back either the same day or the next day (instant maintenance), attempting to clarify and solve the problem.

4. When he returned, she and Ben could have set some rules for telephone conversations, especially if he tends to be less able to share openly through a "cool" medium like the telephone.

Whatever her choice, the basic principle remains: Do not punish a loved one by threatening to cut off a necessary channel of love or by using language (or withholding language) as the necessary symbol to convey that love. Quite obviously, perceptions and meanings ran amok in those twenty minutes. Consider what Ben's response might have been: "What's her problem? I'm out here working hard to support her and the kids. How can I solve her problems from a thousand miles away? Well, if that's the way she wants it, that's the way it will be. No calls from her—no calls from me."

There you have it. Communication cutoff between two people who really love each other, caused by immature action followed by immature reaction. You can count on it; it is all down hill from there until one of them denies self, willingly becomes vulnerable, answers manipulation with love, and uses language in the proper way to get communication going again.

The case study shows a very practical implementation of the use of language and interpersonal relations. There are others as well. The writing of business letters, such a mundane aspect of administration, requires sincerity, optimism, and an imaginative treatment of the subject matter.

Expressing appreciation to fellow workers requires the right words and the right environment accompanied by the right inflection and the right nonverbal signals. Common courtesy (or should I say uncommon courtesy) is a matter of language.

Teach secretaries and receptionists to answer a phone as though they are pleased to receive the call and happy to help strangers who enter the office. Genuine courtesy springs from a concern for other people's feelings. Like leadership, it is learned behavior. The use of language is learned behavior that is absolutely crucial to interpersonal communication and interpersonal relations.

Notes

1. Dennis R. Smith and L. Keith Williamson, *Interpersonal Communication,* (Dubuque, Iowa: William C. Brown Publishers, 1977), 185.

2. Gerald L. Wilson, et al., *Interpersonal Growth Through Communication* (Dubuque, Iowa: William C. Brown Publishers, 1985), 161.

3. Ibid., 165-66.

4. Arthur W. Combs and Donald Snygg, *Individual Behavior* (New York: Harper and Row, 1959), 84-89.

5. David K. Berlo, *The Process of Communication* (New York: Holt, Rinehart and Winston, 1960), 175.

CONFLICT AND
NONVERBAL COMMUNICATION

In the mid-1800s a supposedly valid story circulated about a most amazing horse living in Germany. His name was Clever Hans. Someone discovered that this horse could calculate mathematical problems. If someone asked Clever Hans to add two plus two, he would strike his hoof on the ground four times and stop. Psychologists studied the animal and put him through rigorous tests to make him miss a calculation, but he never missed any simple math question. If asked for ten minus two, he would strike his hoof eight times. He performed addition, subtraction, multiplication, and division with equal skill. The leading thinkers of the day were baffled. How could a horse respond so accurately to math problems?

The answer came one day quite by accident. A little girl asked Clever Hans a math problem, but she did not know the answer. He missed. As they repeated the experiment over and over, they discovered that the horse was supersensitive to the slightest nonverbal cues. An eyebrow or a slight change in facial expression would cause him to stop hoofing the answer. When the interrogator observed Clever Hans had reached the accurate answer, he or she would send out a nonverbal message, and immediately the horse would stop. The world of nonverbal communication is an important and fascinating world in which we communicate far more often than we realize.

In this nonverbal world we focus on a language that communicates beyond our use of verbal symbols. This is no easy task to accomplish. Edward Sapir defined nonverbal as "an elaborate code that is written nowhere, known by none, and understood by all."[1] Nonverbal messages prove to be difficult to analyze but powerful in establishing and maintaining relationships.

Why Nonverbal Communication Is Important

"At least 65% of all social meaning in interpersonal communication is conveyed through nonverbal stimuli."[2] When we limit communication to the emotional area, nonverbal communication accounts for 93 percent of all our relationship messages.[3] Conflict usually falls more into the emotional domain than the cognitive arena. This frequency factor argues for the importance of understanding the dynamics of nonverbal messages.

Nonverbal communication demonstrates the accuracy of the statement, "You cannot not communicate."[4] The concept of a continual flow of information between people is supportable only when we consider nonverbal messages. The face, the eyes, the posture send out messages demanding to be processed. The issue is not *whether you will* communicate, but *how you are* communicating. The conflicting party in the heat of the battle may think he or she is not communicating when the debate appears stalemated, but even in the silence we send and receive profound messages. Therefore nonverbal communication becomes more than important; it becomes essential in order to make sense of our circumstances.

Nonverbal communication levels tend to be more accurate than verbal. Somehow our mouths find it easier to send out false messages than our bodies.

Nonverbal communication also reveals more emotional elements than does verbal. We understand a sad or happy face before a person utters a word. Every day we recognize the rapid pace or a sluggish walk in those we meet. We may misread the nonverbal message, but we will read it first before we process any verbal message. Therefore, we must study nonverbal communication if we are to understand communication and conflict as we should.

What Nonverbal Communication Does

Replaces Verbal Communication

Nonverbal communication can *replace* verbal communication. Picture yourself sitting across the table from an adversary in a conflict setting. As you seek to make your point in the discussion, you notice your antagonist starting to move his head from side to side signaling he does not agree with what you are saying. You may be able to continue unless he adds a smirk on his face, rolls his eyes at certain points you make, or looks away in dismay that anyone could be so stupid as to believe what you have just said.

Up to now your adversary has not uttered a word. However, he has sent volumes of information nonverbally, and everyone present has processed these messages to some degree. In a less controversial way, a nonverbal message frequently replaces the verbal message. For example, when a seventeen-year-old boy says hello to a sixteen-year-old girl and she replies with a smile, the meaning is infinitely more valuable to him than any polite verbal response she might have used.

We use nonverbal communication routinely as we wave good-bye or hello, use a thumb's-up or thumb's-down signal, and hold up the palms of our hands to motion to an individual to stop. In each of these instances, nonverbal activity replaces the verbal message.

Reinforces Verbal Communication

A second function of nonverbal communication is seen when it *reinforces* verbal communication. Gestures energize our communication. Some people seem so animated you wonder if they could talk without their hands! To some extent, we all reinforce our verbal with our nonverbal messages. In a conflict setting, you may attempt to persuade a person that your position is viable, only to find she sits with arms folded in front of her and a scowl on her face. You know immediately you have a tough job ahead of you if you are ever to win this lady over to your side.

In the nonconflict areas of life it makes a difference how we say what we say. Picture a husband telling his wife he loves her with a flat, unemotional sound in his voice. Immediately, this man has problems because he has not reinforced the content of the message with the nonverbal aspects of the message. As we communicate, we expect that the verbal and nonverbal elements will agree. We are predisposed in this direction. Nonverbal communication reinforces the verbal message.

Contradicts the Verbal Message

Nonverbal communication also has the ability to *contradict* the verbal message. If, in the heat of a strong battle your enemy says, "Oh, I believe you," but the intonation of the voice tells you he or she really does not, you perceive a mixed message. Which will you believe—the content (verbal) or the relationship (nonverbal) message? Without fail, you will deduce the person does *not* believe you.

We witness much the same when a positive element marks the communication process. If a certain lady, of whom you are very fond, smiles and says, "You're terrible!" will you believe she thinks you are an awful, despicable person? Or will it register that you are a person she likes and is drawn toward because her smile belies her words? In such situations we reject verbal symbols (content) and accept the nonverbal message (relationship).

Reveals More than Nonverbal Communication

A fourth function of nonverbal communication is to *reveal* more than the verbal words disclose. In the third edition of *Group Processes* (1984), Joseph Luft compared and contrasted verbal and nonverbal communication in these words:

> Interpersonal communication takes place digitally and analogically (verbally and nonverbally) simultaneously. Verbal language is well adapted to the content part of communication, but is far less adequate for the relationship aspect. Nonverbal language conveys relationship information more adequately, but is less precise in defining the content of the relationship. Translation between these two languages is necessary but very difficult. Information may be lost or distorted, and curious inconsistencies may develop in relationships.[5]

If we rely more than we should on the verbal elements of communication, we miss the relationship messages being sent. We sometimes describe this function of nonverbal communication, to reveal more than verbal, as the "feeling" level or "intuitive" level of communication. It is a vast and perpetual arena where so many messages collide so quickly no one can totally process all that is happening. The nonverbal continues to filter into our communication grid as we search for congruency with the more easily received verbal messages.

How We Send Nonverbal Messages

Communication research has isolated ten ways we communicate nonverbally. All of these communication methods periodically surface in a conflict setting. Beside each method cited, a passage of Scripture will be listed to illustrate the nonverbal.

Proxemics

Proxemics means the study of distance or space used by people in the communication process. The research of Edward T. Hall has discovered four different distance levels we use to send messages in a nonverbal manner. In the culture of the United States, *public space* has been identified as twelve feet or more. A formal speaker or preacher illustrates the distance required for public space. *Social distance* runs from twelve feet to three feet. Most living rooms are designed to help us feel comfortable while not violating our need for social space. *Personal space* requires three feet to one and one-half feet. When another person does not honor this distance, we become uncomfortable. If a stranger moves in on you (closer than three feet), you will probably move away since he or she has invaded your personal territory.

In a very unscientific manner I have put this to the test. If I enter an elevator occupied by only one other person, I will stand next to her (clearly within the three-foot territory). Inevitably the person will move. Then I move next to her again. I have literally chased a person completely around an elevator on a long ride. We do not tolerate our personal space being invaded.

The fourth level Hall called *intimacy*. This refers to any distance less than eighteen inches. You must have a close relationship with another person to have the privilege of this closeness. The principle of immediacy reveals a general rule in proxemics: "The better we like a person the closer we want to be to that person." Conversely, the more we dislike a person the farther we desire to be from that person.

Perhaps this principle fits more appropriately when examining conflict and proxemics. The greater the hostility between conflicting parties, the farther apart they physically want to be. As a pastor I have observed couples coming for premarital counseling behaved quite differently than those one step away from divorce. The first could hardly be separated; the latter would seldom be close enough to physically touch each other.

Jesus gave Zacchaeus a clear invitation to a closer relationship when He said, "Zacchaeus, come down immediately. I must stay at your house today" (Luke 19:5). Jesus wanted a close relationship with this new believer. The message He sent by staying at the publican's house spoke volumes to the religious leaders of the day.

Facial Expression

Communication scientists report that we have over 250,000 ways we can express ourselves with the face. According to Birdwhistell, the eyebrows alone can be put into twenty-three positions. We send more nonverbal messages with our faces than any other means, and the face usually reveals the highest accuracy of all nonverbal messages. This may occur because we cannot see or control our faces to keep them in agreement with our verbal messages. In my work with fledgling preachers I have found facial expression to be the most difficult tool for them to use in communication. There must be a willingness to be vulnerable for the face to speak its language to the audience. Some people struggle with the risk of this vulnerability.

Within the last thirty years communicologists have discovered the facial phenomenon of "micro-momentary expressions" (MME's). In the 1960s two psychologists filmed interviews with their clients by means of a hidden sixteen-millimeter camera. The men would later study the visual record along with the words spoken to see if they could more efficiently help their patients. One day one of the doctors slowed the frames to about seven or eight per second. It was then he discovered the man's face was moving from a smile to a grimace faster than could be seen with the naked eye. Further investigation revealed that when the doctor spoke of a blonde woman, the man smiled. When a brunette lady was described, the man's face changed to the grimace. This all happened faster than natural vision could register. The doctors later determined that the client, while married to a brunette, was having an affair with a blonde. His nonverbal communication did not lie.

A scriptural example of facial expression can be seen in the account of the rich young man who came to Jesus with the question, "Good Teacher, what must I do to inherit eternal life?" (Mark 10:17). In the course of their conversation Jesus put His finger on the young man's area of need. The Bible tells us that Jesus looked at him and loved him. Then He told the man to sell everything, give it to the poor, and then come follow Jesus (Mark 10:21). The next words of Mark show us the message sent by the young man to Jesus. "At this the man's face fell. He went away sad, because he had great wealth" (Mark 10:22). His countenance and actions communicated his rejection of Jesus.

Paralanguage

Paralinguistics considers the tonal quality of the verbal message. The person receiving the message anticipates a match between the words that come in and the way in which these symbols arrive. Constantly we look for congruency. Does a close fit exist between the message content and the manner by which it enters? Smiles go with happy messages; a sad effect accompanies bad news. No content message is ever delivered independently of relationship communication.

This relationship information travels through nonverbal channels. When we register a divergence between the verbal and nonverbal messages, the receiver will opt for the nonverbal over the verbal. This may even defy logic. For example, if a close friend gives you words that do not match your relationship, you are likely to say, "Well, he is not himself," or, "She is having a bad day." We will find some way to excuse the verbal information since it does not fit with the association we have enjoyed with this friend. If this occurs over time, the relationship will be redefined.

We see a biblical example of paralanguage in the events that took place immediately after Pilate handed Jesus over

to the religious leaders who had been clamoring for His
death:

> Then the governor's soldiers took Jesus into the Praetorium
> and gathered the whole company of soldier's around him.
> They stripped him and put a scarlet robe on him, and then
> twisted together a crown of thorns and set it on his head.
> They put a staff in his right hand and knelt in front of him
> and mocked him. "Hail, king of the Jews!" they said. They
> spit on him, and took the staff and struck him on the head
> again and again. After they had mocked him, they took off
> the robe and put his own clothes on him. Then they led him
> away to crucify him (Matt. 27:27-29).

The mockery was evident in their tone of voice as they cried
out "Hail, king of the Jews!" They obviously did not regard
Him as a king since their immediate plans were to crucify
Him.

Eye Contact

In many ways the eyes provide the windows to the soul. We
actually listen with our eyes. Do you look at other persons
more when you speak or when they speak? Most of us look
more when the other individual speaks. We find it necessary
to pick up the nonverbal cues being sent so we look more when
listening than when talking.

Some self-image messages come through our ability to
make eye contact. Inferiority problems may first surface by a
person's inability to look you in the eye. Beginning preachers
often struggle with making eye contact, yet it is important to
make eye contact early in any communication experience. The
longer one waits, the harder it is to fix your eyes on another
person's eyes. In conflict the strong, steely gaze of an opponent
can have a "stare down" effect if that person is skilled in eye
contact. People communicate power through eye contact.

Power of a different sort was demonstrated by our Lord
Jesus Christ at the time of the crucifixion. Peter had boasted
that he would never deny his Lord (Luke 22:33). Jesus informed Peter that he would deny Him three times before the
rooster crowed (Luke 22:34). After Jesus prayed on the Mount
of Olives and had been arrested, Peter disowned his Lord

three times (Luke 22:54-60). At this point Luke described what happened: "The Lord turned and looked straight at Peter. Then Peter remembered the word the Lord had spoken to him: 'Before the rooster crows today, you will disown me three times'" (Luke 22:61). At this Peter went outside and began weeping bitterly. The look of the Lord to Peter was a powerful message that can be captured only by our imaginations, but it communicated straight to the heart of Peter.

Personal Attire

The fifth way we communicate concerns *personal attire.* Earlier we noted the robe and the crown of thorns put on Jesus before His crucifixion. His enemies used these symbols of mockery to dramatize the effect of their disbelief in Him as a King.

In our everyday living we select clothing that constantly makes a statement about us throughout a given day. A suit and tie still suggest the professional look. Occasionally, someone will seek to break the mode, but as a general rule we view rank and importance by what a person wears. A mink coat says more than a rabbit coat. Uniforms send messages every day. The policeman, the dentist, and the service station attendant—each has a distinct, recognizable garment.

People engaged in a battle wear uniforms. However, not all battles are on the battlefield. Still people make a statement by their dress. One man may attend the meeting in suit and tie with briefcase in hand. Another comes in casual clothes holding nothing more than the Bible. As they sit down to debate a given issue each has made a statement by how he has entered the foray. We send out messages continually by our attire.

In Jesus' parable of the lost son (Luke 15), personal attire played a large part in the recognition given when the wayward son returned. As the prodigal began to recite his prepared speech about being no more than a servant in his father's household, the father broke in and instructed his servants to bring the best robe, put a ring on the boy's finger, and sandals on his feet (v. 22). The father made a statement. No one could view the boy as a servant, but everyone instead must acknowledge him as reinstated son. Personal attire, in part, communicated this honored position.

Hand Gestures

The use of hand gestures varies greatly from one individual to another. Personality and upbringing help to determine how much or how little we use this medium. Even so, in times of crisis or conflict, gestures are exaggerated and accelerated. People who normally would never shake a fist at someone may do so if the argument becomes sufficiently heated. This non-verbal area is second in frequency only to facial expression. We use it to summon someone to come, to stop, to quiet down, or to hurry up.

When the Pharisees brought the woman who had been caught in adultery to Jesus, they tried to find some basis to accuse Him (John 8:6). The verbal communication forced the Pharisees to apply the category of sin to themselves before applying it to others. Jesus, using a form of nonverbal communication, stooped and wrote two messages in the sand. This non-verbal communication helped convince the accusers of their own sin and so they departed.

Body Position

The seventh way we send messages nonverbally is by *body position*. We can literally enfold or exclude a person next to us by how we position ourselves. The interest level of another person can be suggested by body position. An erect, edge-of-chair position usually signifies high interest. Conversely, when persons cross legs and arms, it frequently indicates we are being locked out of their lives.

In conflict situations, we usually find ourselves directly across the table or room from an adversary. We compete in this position much of our lives. Offense and defense find equal importance when we engage in war.

In the garden before the crucifixion, Jesus withdrew a short distance from His disciples, knelt down, and prayed. The body position sent the message of One who humbled Himself as the obedient Servant and demonstrated submissiveness even unto death (Luke 22:41).

Physical Environment

Research has supported the notion that our surroundings influence how we send out our messages. For example, books inhibit communication while flowers encourage dialogue. Perhaps we have been quieted so much in libraries that we carry this over in all communication contexts. Fresh air, warmth, and a spirit of informality can be established by how we design the environment. If we conduct conflict in an austere, cold, and formal setting, we will have greater difficulty managing it.

When the disciples saw Jesus transfigured on the mountain, they were at first terrified. Their normal experience did not include this environment God created for His Son. It communicated a message of such awesome power they could but wonder (Matt. 17:6). The physical setting of any communication event does send a nonverbal message.

Posture

We also send nonverbal messages by our *posture*. Deepseated feelings or even health matters can be conveyed by our stance. In the conflict arena the victory of one party over another can sometimes be sensed in how the losing party appears. We can exhibit defeat long before it is actually declared. Conversely, the chest thrust slightly forward with head held high usually shows us the posture of the victor.

The picture of our Savior on the cross just after saying "It is finished" included the posture of bowing the head in death (John 19:30).

Head Movement

The final way we express nonverbal messages is by *head movement*. If we agree, the head bobs up and down; if we disagree, it swings from side to side. This is a most universal use-of-head movement. Less frequently, but more powerfully, we can disconfirm a person by simply moving our heads to look in a different direction.

At the crucifixion some used their heads to mock our Savior. The Bible tells us they hurled insults at Him, "shaking their heads" at Him. Scorn and contempt were communicated by this nonverbal activity (Matt. 27:39-40).

What We Learn From Nonverbal Communication

Three outstanding principles emerge from studying nonverbal communication. First, *when verbal and nonverbal conflict, the receiver believes the nonverbal.* The verbal may be clearer as it travels through the communication channel but the nonverbal proves to be more reliable. Secondly, *nonverbal messages must be interpreted in light of verbal messages.* A faulty reading of the nonverbal can be common when only considered by itself. The third precept reminds us that *nonverbal messages best communicate a feeling, an attitude, or the relationship level.*

Since nonverbal communication is so much a part of life we dare not ignore it. The more skilled communicators we become for our Lord, the better we will use all verbal and nonverbal means of communication to glorify our God.

Notes

1. Charles T. Brown and Paul W. Keller , *Monologue to Dialogue: An Exploration of Interpersonal Communication*, 2d ed. (Englecliffe, N.J.: Prentice Hall, 1979), 156.

2. Randall P. Harrison, "Nonverbal Communication: Exploration into Time, Space, Action, and Object," *Dimensions in Communication*, ed. James H. Campbell and Hal W. Hepler (Belmont, Calif.: Wadsworth Publishing Co., 1965), 161.

3. Albert Mehrabian, *Silent Messages* (Belmont, Calif.: Wadsworth Publishing Co., 1971), 77.

4. Paul Watzlawick, Janet Helmick Beavin, and Don D. Jackson, *Pragmatics of Human Communication* (New York: W. W. Norton Co., 1967).

5. Joseph Luft, *Group Processes: An Introduction to Group Dynamics*, 2d ed. (Palo Alto, Calif.: National Press Books, 1970), 59.

8

INTERPERSONAL RELATIONS AND RECRUITMENT

The oft-quoted Alexis de Tocqueville, a Frenchman who visited the United States in its earliest days, once wrote, "These Americans are a peculiar people. In any local community a citizen becomes aware of a human need which is not being met; he thereupon discusses the situation with his neighbor. Suddenly, a committee comes into existence. This committee thereupon begins to operate on behalf of the need."

Thus David E. Mason introduced his strategic book *Voluntary Nonprofit Enterprise Management.* He reminded us that 52 percent of the American population is involved in some voluntary action and 31 percent in organized structured volunteerism on a regular basis.[1] Interestingly, volunteer involvement in religious activity outstrips every other form, including health and education. Yet we struggle in the church to find Sunday School teachers, deacons, and people to serve on various committees. Somehow in a society that prizes volunteerism as a social grace, people who need and practice it most are losing touch with the art.

This chapter emphasizes that most significant factor in recruiting volunteers in any activity—the quality of interpersonal relationship and the communication on which that relationship rests.

The purpose of human relations in the Christian organization differs from its purpose in business. In a profit-making organization, interpersonal relations serve as a tool or a means to accomplish the profit motive. In a Christian organization, it serves as an end as well as a means.

The major factor in effective recruiting of volunteers is the climate or environment in which we request participation. Their attitude toward response has been largely formed (perhaps unconsciously) even before the overt question of involvement has been asked. Consequently, recruiters (elders, pastors, Sunday School directors) who do not understand the processes and quirks of communication that we have discussed in this book are already at a disadvantage in approaching potential leaders.

Biblical Guidelines for Interpersonal Relationships

This segment launches with a heading borrowed verbatim from an article George Sanchez wrote some years ago in *Navlog*.[2] He suggested that one of the problems Christian organizations face stems from their neglect or ignorance of biblical guidelines for interpersonal relationships, and he offered four reasons for analyzing the ways Christians ought to relate to one another. Though not directly aiming at the recruiting process, Sanchez lays the kind of ground work that can help us in our understanding of this crucial skill.

The Goal and End of Interpersonal Relationships

Sanchez suggested first of all that "interpersonal relationships are foundational to all New Testament teaching regarding how to live as a functioning member of the body of Christ." Immediately I think of Philippians and Paul's *kenosis* hymn describing how believers respond to one another:

> If you have any encouragement from being united with Christ, if any comfort from his love, if any fellowship with the Spirit, if any tenderness and compassion, then make my joy complete by being like-minded, having the same love, being one in spirit and purpose. Do nothing out of selfish ambition or vain conceit, but in humility consider others better than yourselves. Each of you should look not only to your own interests, but also to the interests of others.
> Your attitude should be the same as that of Christ Jesus (2:1-5).

Concepts of unity, like-mindedness, humility, consideration, and a positive attitude permeate these dramatic verses.

Sanchez went on to note that "harmonious interpersonal relationships express what God wants to see in our everyday lives." Here again the Bible speaks: "May the God who gives endurance and encouragement give you a spirit of unity among yourselves as you follow Christ Jesus, so that with one heart and mouth you may glorify the God and Father of our Lord Jesus Christ" (Rom. 15:5-6).

The end result of positive interpersonal relations is the glory of God; that is also the primary goal.

Interpersonal Relationships and Reconciliation

George Sanchez expressed concern about interpersonal relationships as they serve the ministry of reconciliation (see 2 Cor. 5:19). Reconciliation is not just a vertical lifeline of spiritual vitality; it is also horizontal. God gives to us the ministry of reconciliation, and we use that as His ambassadors. Viewed in the light of the entire New Testament, these verses in 2 Corinthians 5 surely point to person-to-person as well as person-to-God relationships.

Finally, Sanchez noted that responsible interpersonal relationships are essential if the body of Christ is going to function as it should. Check out Romans 12 and 1 Corinthians 12 to review the entire development of the body concept. Every part takes on importance regardless of its beauty or seemingly obvious function. What is the church? Ordinary people energized by superordinary power in order to accomplish extraordinary tasks.

Wise leaders seek interdependence that sends the recruiter to the volunteer in an attitude of service and participative involvement together in the work of the Lord. Small wonder we use so many *ship* words in the church—worship, fellowship, stewardship, leadership. Perhaps we like to remind ourselves that when we serve the Lord Jesus Christ, we are all in the same boat.

Christian Analysis of
the Human Relations Movement

There might be some merit in first suggesting what we will not attempt to do in this section of the chapter. We do not wish to Christianize the research of Mayo, Roethlisberger, Dickson, and others. However, since we do so little administrative research in Christian organizations, and since administration *is* a single science, those of us interested in applying the findings of industrial and business management research to our work in the church, mission organizations, Christian schools, and other kinds of Christian organizations must learn to study the findings of secular administrative science with a carefully trained, theological eye.

We will learn to pour all information we find through the funnel of special revelation to see what comes out the other end for our use. Following are some conclusions in the form of principles that we have found coming out of our funnels.

Human Relations Is Both a Means and an End

The purpose of interpersonal relations in secular business can be very clearly stated: human relations is a tool, or means, for the achievement of the company's goals. Much of the literature in management science warns business executives to avoid the dangers of making human relations an end instead of a means. For example, when elimination of conflict becomes a primary goal of the organization, when an individual's expectations conflict with organizational goals, when human relations efforts center only on therapy with no contribution to the organization's goals, when human relations becomes a substitute for higher-level action—when any of these things happen, experts argue that human relations has gotten out of hand. The tool has become an end in itself rather than the means, which it must be.

Although clearly an organization, the church is also an organism. As an organism, it surely recognizes the necessity to create an atmosphere of unity and community. The very process of the functioning body centers in the relationship of people to one another, and the achievement of the best possible harmony and spiritual vitality in that relationship supplies one of the goals of the church.

To be more specific, loving one another, bearing one another's burdens, and putting others before ourselves are ends to be sought. As we move toward these goals, however, they also become a means of evangelism as an unbelieving world looks in, sees the love, and wonders about the Christ who can produce it (John 13). Herein lies Francis Schaeffer's "ultimate apologetic," with its emphasis on love and unity in the body.

Manipulation of People Is Wrong

When we view human relations as a means, it can become a tool in the hands of a totalitarian administration, using it to bludgeon workers into conformity with the organization's standards. Perhaps "bludgeon" is a poor word choice here, because the very nature of human relations implies a soft handling of people. Christians should be properly frightened by what they read in such books as B. F. Skinner's *Beyond Freedom and Dignity*. Control of other people in order to achieve some purpose desirable to the controller is manipulation of the first rank.

Over thirty years ago, B. F. Skinner stated:

> The hypothesis that man is not free is essential to the application of scientific method to the study of human behavior. The free inner man who is held responsible for the behavior ... is only a prescientific substitute for the kinds of causes which are discovered in the course of a scientific analysis. All these alternative causes lie *outside* the individual.[3]

In stark contrast to Skinner's animalistic behaviorism, the Bible teaches that Christians are free and dare not sell their souls to anything other than the lordship of Christ (1 Cor. 6:12). Because of the high view of human beings as images of the divine (marred by sin but restored in Christ), the Christian leader tends to see people as self-actualizing personalities. He or she values creativity and wants to discover and maintain the conditions that encourage rather than impede the self-actualization process and to set up these conditions with minimal power control. Although not all the concepts of Carl Rogers will coincide with biblical Christianity, he stands in positive contrast to Skinner with respect to his view of persons:

> We can choose to use our growing knowledge to enslave people in ways never dreamed of before, depersonalizing them, controlling them by means so carefully selected that they will perhaps never be aware of their loss of personhood.

We can choose to utilize our scientific knowledge to make man necessarily happy, well behaved, and productive, as Dr. Skinner suggests. We can, if we wish, choose to make men submissive, conforming, docile. Or at the other end of the spectrum of choice we can choose to use the behavioral sciences in ways which will free, not control; which will bring about constructive variability, not conformity; which will develop creativity, not contentment; which will facilitate each person in his self-directed process of becoming; which will aid individuals, groups, and even the concepts of science to become self-transcending in freshly adaptive ways of meeting life and its problems.[4]

Interaction Is Basic to the Human-Relations Process

In regard to interaction and human relations, Christians find themselves in wholehearted agreement with the research of the Hawthorne studies (see chap. 5, "Lesson from the Hawthorne Studies"). In formal or informal interaction between counselor and counselee, through daily contact with workers as a group, the strategic nature of interpersonal communications cannot be overemphasized. We may contend that the pastor's primary role lies in proclamation and exposition: he is God's prophet and teacher. However, in the role of prophet and teacher, he must also remember his social functions and the effect of his verbal and nonverbal behavior in the process of interaction.

Sunday School directors would do well to strengthen the inner emotional balance of the workers. We applaud quality curriculum and well-equipped classrooms. However, adding all these and a host of other external improvements is like increasing the lighting at the Hawthorne plant. What counts, in the final analysis, is a leader's relationship to her departmental directors and teachers.

Recruiting Volunteers

Volunteers are simply persons who do not get paid for their work, who are not required to do it, and who can quit at anytime. David Mason claimed: "Voluntary organizations have deep taproots because of their noble and profound purposes. As such, they often elicit great commitment and loyalty. The challenges faced by the voluntary sector today are as great as or greater than those at any time in history."[5] Therefore, professional leaders and lay leaders (who are themselves volunteers) must be convinced that interpersonal communication stands vital to the recruitment and retention process. Objectives, job descriptions, and training will occupy our attention in the next chapter. Here we are concerned about that gentle art of contact that involves a person in some form of productive ministry.

Here are six guidelines describing the role of interpersonal relations (IPR) in the recruitment process.

1. *Align recruitment to informal friendships.* This first guideline could be construed to mean that recruiters find it easier to twist the arms of their friends than those of acquaintances or strangers. That is not our connotation. Instead, consider the relationship cultivated between Paul and Priscilla and Aquila. They were genuine friends who enjoyed spending time together. They shared a like vocation (tentmaking) as well as Christian faith and interest in theological discussions. We should hardly be surprised, therefore, that Paul could enlist the help of this wonderful Christian couple in going ahead of his ministry in several cities and hosting the gathering of believers in their home.

Followership and friendship seem like difficult roles to mix, but when properly blended they make for an outstanding working relationship. Luncheons, visits in the home, and social events for couples can establish a cordial relationship that will solidify ministry contacts.

2. *Accept no substitute for dialogue.* Ministry disagreements have to be worked out together, eyeball-to-eyeball. Never threaten to go over somebody's head or, worse yet, threaten to quit if you do not get your own way. When we begin to understand each other's perceptions, meanings, and contexts, the chances that we can work out a mutually satisfactory settlement of our problems increases dramatically. Sometimes those problems stem from some incident in the recruiting process, and Matthew 18:15 must be applied immediately.

3. *Assume vulnerability in leadership.* Sometimes when we recruit someone for ministry we may be treated badly by that

person. Rejection is as common in recruitment as it is in free-lance writing. Yielding graciously at such times preserves the opportunity to return another day to ask again and, perhaps that time, to enlist the individual.

4. *Always keep your word.* As a recruiter you probably represent a larger group of people on a committee or a board. Make sure you can deliver what you promise the potential volunteer; it is your responsibility to produce what you agree on in terms of equipment, training, personal attention, evaluation, and all the other good things that keep people on the job. Integrity in leadership represents as significant a dimension in the modern church as anything we might discuss or describe.

5. *Acknowledge rejection gracefully.* Soft answers *do* turn away wrath, and grievous words *do* stir up anger (Prov. 15:1). Good recruiters do not argue, arm twist, or agonize over a person's response—they accept it. Such a confidence assumes the working power of the Holy Spirit in both lives, and it assumes you have adequately communicated everything that needs to be said (in the way it needs to be said) before you have (at some later point) asked for a response.

6. *Avoid clashes of authority.* Recruiters do not "pull rank" on volunteers, nor do they drop little hints about how displeased the elders or pastor will be if the candidate says no. The organization committed to participative management learns to support the recruiter's efforts and avoid authority clashes with other officers in the bureaucracy. Mason was surely right when he said:

> I believe the answer [to meeting the challenges facing the voluntary sector] lies in applying management skills to the task. Superior management can do for the voluntary sector in the years ahead what it has done for the private sector in the years past. It can take the resources of our culture of cooperation, while the heart for it is still beating, and apply those resources to the task with efficiency and effectiveness. It can—if we *adapt* the best of what the world has learned about management in business and industry and use it to elicit and apply the energy of voluntarism toward a rejuvenated society.[6]

Interpersonal Relations and Participatory Management

Steps Toward Team Leadership

Research from Fortune 500 companies as well as numerous small businesses suggests several practical ways to make participatory (participative) administration work especially in voluntary nonprofit organizations (like a church). The underlying axiom here is that *leaders are not persons who can do things better than others in the organization; they are persons who can help others in the organization do things better than they themselves can.* Patricia Dean-Rogers suggested the following seven steps toward better team leadership:

- Make employees confident of their abilities.
- Realize that intrinsic rewards are stronger motivators than extrinsic ones.
- Provide necessary information on issues requiring employee response.
- Provide reaction at critical stages of a program.
- Follow up and acknowledge the validity of employee contributions.
- Establish an atmosphere of mutual trust.
- Communicate! Ambiguity hinders progress.[7]

Dean-Rogers does not deal with voluntary organizations, but the principles certainly cross the line. Notice how many of them deal with communication and interpersonal relations. How do we make employees confident? How do we provide necessary information? How do we acknowledge validity? How do we establish trust? We find the answer to all those questions in her seventh point—communicate!

One more paragraph from Dean-Rogers before we leave the article:

So participative management is more than indiscriminate delegation; it is sincere caring—caring for the results, for the company's image and certainly for the employees. Companies perceived favorably in terms of participative management are active in nurturing employees, allow for growth on the job with adequate reinforcement, maintain a respected corporate image (with no record of cover-ups for public relations' sake), and even offer assistance in the job search when cutbacks dictate layoffs. Participative management, then, is seen as a holistic approach to management by successful and concerned organizations.[8]

Facilitating a Shared Vision

Leaders recruit other leaders. Their behavior sets the standard and the model for the behavior of the volunteers. According to James Kouzes and Barry Posner (*The Leadership Challenge*), such people spend considerable effort gazing across the horizon of time, imagining what it will be like when they have arrived at their final destination. They understand and can communicate a shared vision. Then they enable others to act. They do not just bring them on the team and expect the work to get done, but they carry out that crucial function of administration: facilitating the effectiveness of subordinates. According to Kouzes and Posner:

> If there is a clear distinction between the process of managing and the process of leading, it is the distinction between getting others to do things, forcing them in a way, and getting others to want to do them. Managers get other people to do, but leaders get other people to want to do.[9]

According to Theodore Levitt of Harvard University, "The natural tendency of relationships, whether in marriage or business, is entropy—the erosion or deterioration of sensitivity and attentiveness."[10] When such entropy threatens, the leader alert to interpersonal relations and communication reviews those crucial processes, renews attentiveness to their quality, and does whatever is necessary to repair the relationship. He or she understands that in volunteer nonprofit organizations, recruitment and retention of volunteers is the very lifeblood that enables the organization to continue its work.

Notes

1. David E. Mason, *Voluntary Nonprofit Enterprise Management* (New York and London: Plenum Press, 1984), 4-5.
2. George Sanchez, *Navlog*, July 1977, 7.

3. B. F. Skinner, *Science and Human Behavior*, (New York: Macmillan Company, 1953), 447-48.

4. Carl Rogers, "The Place of the Person in the New World of Behavioral Sciences," monograph.

5. Mason, *Enterprise Management*, 11.

6. Ibid., 12.

7. Patricia Dean-Rogers, "Participative Management," *Inflight*, July 1988, 103.

8. Ibid., 105.

9. James M. Kouzes and Barry Z. Posner, *The Leadership Challenge* (San Francisco: Jossey-Bass Publishers, 1987).

10. Theodore Levitt, *Royal Bank Letter*, March/April 1989, 2.

9

————→»»» «««←————

INTERPERSONAL RELATIONS AND TRAINING

Almost twenty-five years ago, William J. Dickson and F. J. Roethlisberger published *Counseling in an Organization: A Sequel to the Hawthorne Researches, 1966.* According to their own statements, the book was designed to evaluate the counseling program that grew out of the historic Hawthorne Studies. In part 2 of that significant volume, the authors treated "employee concerns at work" and gave five chapters to what they called "Five Basic Concerns of Employees":

1. Keeping a job;
2. Friendship and belonging;
3. Felt injustices;
4. Authority;
5. Job and individual development.

While not specifically related to training for ministry, these elements deal precisely with the kinds of things that concern us regarding performance and retention of volunteers in Christian ministry of all kinds.

One stimulating recent study explored the issue of "Shared Accountability" with respect to coordinating Christian education programs in local churches. Dr. Eileen Starr pinpointed the problem:

> Unfortunately, some clergy who fear a loss of power and control are reluctant to allow the laity to function as coworkers in a mutual ministry. They view the laity as not only lacking in ministry skills, but also in motivation. However, it must be recognized that God has called all Christians to minister (Eph. 4; 1 Cor. 12). Each member of a church shares some of its power and its responsibility for ministry. When undue emphasis is given to the use of power

and authority in the church, it diminishes the importance of all members working together for the edification of the body of Christ.[1]

Starr went on to draw five principles from those two passages, principles that emphasize the kind of organization that postures itself appropriately for the recruiting, training, enlistment, and retaining of volunteers.

1. The function of church leaders is primarily to equip believers for spiritual ministry.
2. Believers are given spiritual gifts that are intended to build up other believers.
3. The use of the gifts of all believers is equally important. Within the church there is no place for a hierarchy of gifts or ministries.
4. Believers are dependent on other believers for spiritual growth in addition to the ministry of the Holy Spirit and the Word.
5. The unity, stability, and spiritual maturity are all fruits of the process of mutual spiritual accountability among believers.[2]

How all of this relates to training should be immediately obvious. The desire for and willingness to undergo training holds a much greater problem for Christian ministries than does methodology or programming. In order to produce a viable quality of interpersonal relationships in which training can take place, the organization must have identified a philosophy of ministry that emphasizes shared service and team leadership. In that tone, we will direct our attention in this chapter to three facets of that approach to training: designing interpersonal relationships, relating roles and needs, and developing retention qualities.

Designing Interpersonal Relationships

Some leaders think that distance from subordinates enhances the leadership role. They shun intimacy, avoid non-business contacts, and elect to keep all conversations cold and sterile. Yet such behavior fails to recognize how crucial interpersonal relationships are to effective training. To some extent that applies to short-term training programs (weekend, a week, or several sessions over a month). Training goes on continuously between leader and follower and at all points the communication spotlight shines on encounter and interchange, either facilitating or hindering the training process.

Modes of Analysis

Abraham Zalesnik did some work in attempting to identify what he called "modes of analysis," defining how institutional supervisors approach and utilize gathered data. For example, *description* is an analysis mode that seeks to detail the processes of interaction over time. *Explanation* states causes, asking why interpersonal behavior proceeds as it does. *Consequences* tends to formulate the outcomes of interpersonal behavior, asking how interpersonal relations proceed differently under permissive or authoritarian leadership.

On the one hand we do not wish to get too technical in dealing with this subject. Yet, it may be worthwhile to review some structural theories of interpersonal relationships. Irvin Goffman viewed interpersonal behavior as performance, pointing to the analysis of what people will do in face-to-face encounters. George Homans, on the other hand, developed a theory of exchange whose general framework emphasizes two or more individuals interacting on a social-psychological transaction, exchanging valuable commodities—their words, ideas, and feelings. Zalesnik's and Roethlisberger's combined efforts develop the theory of equilibration, emphasizing "balanced states" and "congruence."

We could go on, but perhaps the chief point is to recognize how varied and kaleidoscopic professional studies have been in treating interpersonal relationships in organizations.

Guidelines for Communication Flow

Interpersonal communication in organizations is constantly influenced by internal characteristics of organizational environment. People do not accept or reject training in a vacuum. Training programs in one church do not necessarily look like training programs in another since the environments differ dramatically. When we talk about a "communication system," we mean those patterns of transmission and interpretation of messages among and between various persons within the organization's environment. So when we approach people before, during, and after training programs, we do well to keep several guidelines in mind:

1. The flow of communication between (among) individuals is conditioned by a multiplicity of sources, the sequentiality or simultaneity of the flow, and the durability of the messages.

2. As communication within the church or organization stabilizes, specialized networks form that interpret messages on the basis of authority, information, expertise, friendship, status, and other views.

3. Since interpersonal-relationship networks differ, we need to create institutional mechanisms that keep us in touch with one another. For example, within a Sunday School there must be some designed system for teachers to stay in contact with one another both intradepartmentally and interdepartmentally. In a church using miniflocks or house churches, communication networks usually develop very well within individual groups but the groups tend to lose touch with each other.

In thinking about training programs, we want to pull together the unity of the body in functional as well as theological terms so that we understand what, why, and how others serve Christ within the congregational setting.

Relating Roles and Needs

In thinking through leadership styles, the wise executive recognizes that each subordinate has a set of expectations about how the boss should relate to him. The better a leader understands these factors, the more accurately she can determine what kind of behavior on her part will enable the subordinates to act most effectively. At times a semiautocratic style of leadership may seem called for because of factors in the subordinates or the situation. On the other hand, there may be groups with whom the effective leader will pursue an exclusively participatory or even egalitarian leadership style.

Identifying Participatory Groups

A classic article in *Harvard Business Review* by Robert Tannenbaum and Warren Schmidt identifies certain "essential conditions" in describing groups that can be effectively led through a free democratic and human-relations-centered administration:

- If the subordinates have relatively high needs for independence.
- If the subordinates have a readiness to assume responsibility for decision making.
- If they have a relatively high tolerance for ambiguity.
- If they are interested in the problem and feel that it is important.
- If they have the necessary knowledge and experience to deal with the problem.
- If they have learned to expect to share in decision making.[3]

Leaders coming into a new situation must recognize that groups that have been led to expect "strong leadership," then are suddenly confronted with the opportunity to share in decision making and experience wide freedom in the work, tend to become upset and frustrated. The reverse, of course, also holds true. A group that has been led by a very participatory leader will resent and perhaps even retaliate against a boss-type autocrat who moves in to take control.

What People Want from Work Groups

What specifically are the needs of people in groups? When we head up training teams or attempt to keep an ongoing personnel development program in place, what kinds of things do people tell us they need? J. Donald Phillips and Laurence Taylor spent fifteen years asking groups that precise question. Their findings were reported in an issue of the *Hillsdale College Leadership Letter.* This is what individuals said:

1. I need a sense of belonging. (People need to be wanted, welcomed, and genuinely needed for themselves—not just for their brains and skills.)

2. I need to have a share in planning group goals. (People

are motivated toward improvement and quality control only when they feel their ideas have had a fair hearing.)

3. I need to feel that goals are within reach and that they make sense to me. (People are not satisfied when goals only make sense to management.)

4. I need to feel that what I am doing has real purpose and value beyond the group itself. (People need to see their place in the wider scheme of ministry.)

5. I need to share in making the rules of the group. (People are much more loyal to things they help create and can therefore understand.)

6. I need to know in some clear detail what is expected of me. (People want a positive assessment of what they can and should achieve.)

7. I need to have responsibilities that challenge my abilities and interests. (People need to be mentally and spiritually stretched and allowed a reasonable amount of creativity.)

8. I need to see that progress is being made toward the goals we have set. (People must be kept from boredom and fatigue, a common dysfunctional problem in organizations.)

9. I need to be kept informed. (People regard reasonable communication as a recognition of their status as individuals and their importance to the organization.)

10. I need to have confidence in the leadership. (People base that confidence on assurance of consistent fair treatment, recognition, and security.)[4]

Developing Retention Qualities

All the effort we put into recruiting and training people is useless if they fade away after two or three months of service. This complex problem haunts the evangelical community. Churches now seem content to settle for Sunday school teachers or children's church leaders who will stay in those ministry posts for far too short a tenure to be effective. Once again, interpersonal relations and interpersonal communication emerge.

R. Lofton Hudson wrote about developing an understanding of people (a six-part reprint from *Church Administration*). He emphasized honesty in human relationships—calling for an abandonment of phony strength, hiddenness and closedness, the inauthenticity of the oversell, and an open confession of limitations. Said Hudson:

> It seems obvious that honesty is basic good human relations. Without it we may send out signals which distort reality for the other person. Without honesty we are forced into the habit of suspecting and having to screen everything another person says. Without honesty we feel maneuvered and manipulated, and resentment looms. Love and fairness require that we try to be and say unto others as we wish to have them be and say to us.[5]

Finding Flexible but Stable People

Hudson called for emotional maturity and described the maturing process in four dimensions: "What it enables you to do, what you can do without, what you can do with others, and what you can do for others."[6] He argued also for leaders to be flexibile. He described the kind of people we need directing our training programs. We like his descriptions of that kind of leadership:

- Flexible but stable people do not allow themselves to get uptight when they are discussing issues.
- Flexible but stable persons can state firmly their own convictions without forcing all others to agree.
- Flexible but stable people will constantly seek new ways to be in this world without giving up old ones until better ones are found.[7]

Developing Loyalty That Lasts

Obviously one quality we also want to see developed in the people we train is loyalty to Christ, to the church, and to the specific ministries they have agreed to undertake. Loyalty is vital, a biblical concept that becomes a way of life. Whatever one thinks of President George Bush, his eight years of loyal service to Ronald Reagan certainly represented a high quality virtue in our covenant-breaking society. We want people who are willing to say, "This is my appointed ministry, and this is my group. I must work in and with it until the Lord releases me."

That kind of loyalty should not be viewed as servitude, blind following of leaders, or organizational dogma. Let us link it instead with honor, duty, responsibility, and accountability.

Consider two dimensions of loyalty. The first produces devotion to great causes or personalities, an excitement which quickly rises and often rapidly abates. The other, though not exciting, appears the more important because we face it everyday. It is inherent in the hundreds of duties we must do, and it becomes the lifeblood of team work. It embraces adherence to duty, keeping promises, and faithfulness to ideals.

Establishing Quality Control

One of the great blights on the church in recent years has been its failure to establish strong and adequate systems of quality control. Somehow we have assumed that because our work is being done by volunteers it must therefore be of an inferior quality, and we dare not expect high standards of performance. The result has been an offering to God of shoddy workmanship and programming that often does not pass the most elementary tests of adequacy.

Christian organizations should be genuinely interested in quality control. Quality control begins and ends with the people in the organization. It is not a question of better programs or machinery (as industry has spent millions of dollars to learn) because the performance of the human element in an organization remains beyond the influence of computer processing or statistical techniques. Richard A. Kaimann said it well: "Since it is the worker who builds quality, an attitude of quality mindedness must be developed within him." Kaimann suggested four essential control checks to help a leader who genuinely wants to see quality work among the persons whose performance he or she supervises:

1. The operator knows what he is *supposed* to be doing;
2. The operator knows what he is *actually* doing;
3. The operator can regulate the process if he fails to meet specifications; and
4. The operator has determination to use every measure to produce conforming products.[8]

From a leadership point of view, several things are involved here. The first is a *commitment to the power of quality*. No church or school can throw off the strangling fingers of mediocrity until it first decides that quality is possible. Second, a *commitment to a Theory-Y view of the worker.* What Kaimann called "quality mindedness" is not an option unless we can really excite the individual Sunday School teacher, youth worker, and board member about the potential of really *good* work. The third point stresses *training for the task.* And finally, there is the *building-in of incentives,* even nonmonetary incentives, to stimulate the kind of interest in the power of quality that must be a part of the worker's life-style.

So we come right back to an idiographic leadership style and the kind of motivation that is needed to achieve quality:

> The Christian organization which, unwittingly, glosses over deficient performance, or pretends it does not exist, is performing an ultimate disservice....
>
> Perhaps the responsibility for such a situation lies with the management and a lack of comprehension of management principles, Biblically based, which secular organizations seem to be using far more effectively than our Christian organizations.[9]

The human ingredient remains the key issue in quality control. Pastors who function as ineffectual leaders are hardly candidates to direct leadership training programs. Churches in which intrastaff quarreling is a way of life can neither develop strong lay leaders nor emphasize the qualities of biblical eldership. Like almost any other phase of the church's ministry, *good programs administered by poor leaders will fail while poor programs administered by good leaders can succeed.*

Recognizing Spiritual Power

In Christian leadership, human ability provides a poor substitute for spiritual power. Unfortunately, it is frequently used in much church ministry today. The Greek word *dunamis* identifies the supernatural dynamic of the indwelling and filling Holy Spirit. Paul wrote to the Roman Christians, "May the God of hope fill you with all joy and peace as you trust in him, so that you may overflow with hope, by the power of the Holy Spirit" (Rom. 15:13); and he reminded Timothy that evidence of the Spirit-filled life was exhibited in spiritual power, love, and a sound mind (2 Tim. 1:7, KJV).

Second Corinthians 4:7 offers one of the key New Testament passages with respect to the power of the Spirit in ministry: "But we have this treasure in jars of clay to show that this all-surpassing power is from God and not from us." This dynamic verse, when studied in context, issues a clarion call for competence in Christian service and leadership—a competence that makes use of all possible resources discussed in earlier verses. Yet Paul reminded us that all of them exist, as it were, in an "earthenware" pot (NEB), a most unglamorous view of self!

In the final analysis, we dare not allow spiritual power to be paralleled with the power of authority, competition, or position. Rather, we continually use all legitimate sources of power for leadership, but each source must be totally impregnated by this last, all-encompassing power: the power of God's Holy Spirit in the life of the believer. He produces a ministry that is not self-initiated but God-given, not self-centered but Christ-centered, and dependent not on human ability but on supernatural power. "Because we have the grace of God to carry on our service for Him, we don't have to quit" (2 Cor. 4:1, author's paraphrase).

Notes

1. Eileen Starr, " Shared Accountability: A Fresh Look at Coordinating Christian Education," *Christian Education Journal* 9 (Winter 1989): 73-74.

2. Ibid., 75.

3. Robert Tannenbaum and Warren Schmidt, "Choosing a Leadership Pattern," *Harvard Business Review* (March/April 1958): 99. (Bullets added by editor.)

4. J. Donald Phillips and Laurence Taylor, *Hillsdale College Leadership Letter* 1 (October 1962):2

5. R. Lofton Hudson, "How to Understand People," *Church Administration,* Reprint, n.d., 5.

6. Ibid., 9.

7. Ibid., 11. (Bullets added by editor.)

8. Richard A. Kaimann, "Quality Control: The Man, Not the Machine," *Management of Personnel Quarterly* (Winter 1968): 8-12.

9. Ted W. Engstrom and R. Alec Mackenzie, *Managing Your Time* (Grand Rapids: Zondervan Publishing House, 1967), 108.

10

INTERPERSONAL RELATIONS AND SUPERVISION

During the 1961-62 NBA season, Wilt Chamberlain led the league with an average of 50.4 points per game, established a never-broken season record of 45 games in which he scored 50 or more points, and, in a single game on March 2, 1962, scored 100 points while playing for the Philadelphia 76ers.

No one has ever doubted Chamberlain's individual ability; he stands as the NBA season scoring leader in each season from 1959 through 1966. Nevertheless, during that span of time he did not play on a championship team. In each of those seven seasons the Boston Celtics became the world champions.

A climate of participative leadership and team spirit offers the only satisfactory environment in which interpersonal relationship and communication can adequately develop the recruitment, training, and supervision of volunteers. In their outstanding book *The Leadership Challenge,* James Kouzes and Barry Posner encourage leaders to "strengthen" others and suggest numerous ways that can be done, including the supervisory process of sharing information and increasing subordinates' discretion and visibility.

> Empowering others is essentially the process of turning followers into leaders themselves. The process of building and enhancing power is facilitated when people work on tasks that are critical to the organization's success, when they exercise discretion and autonomy in their efforts, when their accomplishments are visible and recognized by others, and when they are well connected to other people of influence and support. There are several strategies that you can use to build more power for yourself and create more power for others.[1]

Those strategies, developed in some detail by the authors, are simply listed below:

1. Get to know people.
2. Develop your interpersonal competence.
3. Use your power in service of others.
4. Enlarge people's sphere of influence.
5. Keep people informed.
6. Make connections.
7. Make heroes of other people.[2]

Leadership and Relationship

Repeatedly we have stressed in this text the importance of interpersonal relations to leadership style and administrative process. Biblical ministry is impossible without effective personal relationships. It follows, therefore, that adequate supervision is likewise impossible without this foundational ingredient.

Decentralize Authority

A leader gives away "power" by increasing the autonomy and decision-making capability of subordinates. The leadership team pulls together, delegation becomes a reality, and the authority for running day-by-day operations moves constantly closer to the trenches in which those operations must be carried out. In a word, good leaders *decentralize.*

About decentralized authority Kouzes and Posner said:

> The increased sphere of influence also ought to be over something relevant to the pressing concerns and core technology of the business. Choosing the color of the paint may be a place to start, but you had better give people influence over more substantive issues. If quality is top priority, then find ways to expand people's influence and discretion over issues of quality control. If innovation is a priority, then increase people's influence over the development of new products, processes, or services. The same applies for all the critical issues of the business.[3]

The Bible contains a major doctrinal foundation for all of this. Leaders who have grasped the teaching of the New Testament understand that God calls and gifts *all* His servants, not just those who have been through Bible college and seminary, nor those who are ordained or commissioned. Spiritual gifts are given for the benefit of the community of faith without a hierarchy of importance (1 Cor. 12). We may discover differences in function and role but not in rank. Ministry is the work of the whole body, the responsibility and privilege of every believer. Professional staff leaders equip and enable other workers to carry out their ministries in the body.

Encourage Dialogue

Mutual ministry reflects the need for dialogue more clearly in the process of supervision than in any other activity. Supervisors must interact with those whom they lead. They must establish some kind of relationship or the ministries of both become impossible. James Reed called for *"Dialogue not monologue"* in such relationships:

> One reason for the discord among some church staffs is that some members of the staff don't know how to listen. Few ministers have mastered the art of listening. They are given more training for speaking than for listening. Monologue or one-way communication often leads to one-sided relationships where one or more parties are injured. Dialogue is communication. Good teamwork demands communication.[4]

Communication and Hierarchy

Organizational communication is a two-way process in which facts and information travel between the parties in interpersonal relationship so that adequate decisions can be made, tasks carried out, and goals achieved. Unfortunately, facts threaten many leaders, making them defensive about their positions in the organization.

Sometimes supervisors' natural psychological reaction is to reject incoming information and go with "gut instinct." Many times in leadership (particularly in decision making) gut instinct is important. However, rational managers trained in the processes of leadership only resort to that level when necessary. Otherwise they understand how the flow of communication literally makes possible their leadership roles.

Hierarchy and Decision Making

Leaders do not need the ability to select the facts they want to hear but rather the ability to discern facts they receive. Obscure or inaccurate information leads to ambiguity and inaction in decision making. These behaviors in turn lead to a stagnated or dysfunctional leadership style.

Hierarchy makes chief executive officers (and many other leaders in the larger organization) ready prey for miscommunication and distancing from the real functions of the organization. A pastor who remains aloof from his people, for example, will soon watch his preaching degenerate into general-principle proclamation rather than life-changing practical application of God's Word. He will also watch his decision making take the form of detached dicta, pronounced from an isolated office and uninformed by the wealth of valuable knowledge he could have solicited from members of the leadership team.

Hierarchy (a statement of how the organization is arranged) often slips into bureaucracy (a description of how the organization functions). This separates clergy and laity, divides leaders and followers, and fails to instill in people we supervise a confidence in their own potential.

Effective supervisors transcend stagnation by staying alert to how subordinates think and feel while at the same time keeping those subordinates totally informed on everything that is happening above them in the organizational chart— policies, procedures, and any decisions affecting their work. They express themselves clearly and effectively and encourage subordinates to share their own ideas and opinions freely and frequently.

Supervisory Communication

In the chapter on supervision and evaluation in *Feeding and Leading*, I offered a few paragraphs regarding the role of communication in the supervisory process. I reproduce them here:

> The supervisor must keep his people informed. That means he must guarantee himself a way of getting the proper information from the higher echelons of the organization. For example, the Sunday school superintendent should be

an *ex officio* member of the board or committee of Christian education because it gives him access to information about the total church program so he can keep all teachers and workers in tune with what is going on.

But communication also means a willingness to have subordinates come to their supervisor with suggestions, expecting that he will have a sympathetic ear to their points of view. Let me just add a few simple suggestions describing what should be happening when a supervisor listens to a subordinate:

1. Rephrase in your own words anything you hear which really sounds important.
2. Avoid exaggerating the good points—you might miss something the subordinate is really trying to tell you.
3. Learn to concentrate—especially in long conferences or meetings.
4. Listen for the unfamiliar. If you're an experienced supervisor, so much of what you hear sounds like so much of what you have heard before. So listen carefully for some new item.
5. Be extra careful when you disagree. Think before you speak and possibly, don't speak at all.

In communication you always want to be careful with the nonverbal area, what Ross Snyder calls "the feeling strand." My personal preference calls for following up any significant employee conference with a memo which establishes in writing the things you have agreed on so there is no question weeks or months later.[5]

Self-Realization and Creativity in Supervision

An awareness of one's uniqueness is not just some idea that randomly appeared on the drawing boards of social psychologists. An analysis of history seems to indicate that outstanding leaders throughout the ages have had a clear grasp of themselves as persons. Sometimes there was an emphasis on their own importance, even to the point of developing a Napoleonic complex or a neurosis similar to that of Alexander the Great. Apparently, however, some inherent power that I call *self-realization* existed in the lives of most of them that moved them to achieve beyond the average level.

The Power of Personal Goals

It is unthinkable that a composer could continue to work after he had become deaf, but Beethoven did just that. John Milton did not allow blindness to interfere with his writing. Michelangelo, who wanted to sculpt so badly, fought against any odds to achieve. Winston Churchill bounced back from defeat and public humiliation, with an uncanny sense of personal and national destiny, to lead his nation again. These persons demonstrate the power of personal goals.

Part of the study of psychocybernetics indicates that thrusting ahead to personal goals and imagining the kind of behavior one would employ in those expected goal situations are sources of power common to many successful leaders. The vision of the goal carries its own empowering motivation. This sense of growth and self-expectation allows people to search for unrealized resources—and to find them.

The difference between an effective leader and a lifetime follower may not be only an overt ability, a keen intelligence, or even drive. Sometimes ambitious people get nowhere. The secret may lie in the power of self-realization and self-concept: How do I view my life? What do I believe God wants to do with me? What are my values? My spiritual gifts? My lifetime goals? What does God have to change in my life in order for me to realize those goals?

The Dynamic of Spiritual Achievement

Does self-actualization sound like so much religious humanism? Self-actualization can be an analysis of the realization of God-given gifts and capacities exercised through the power of the Holy Spirit by means of the grace of the Heavenly Father. Achievement does not have to be for selfish ends, nor does it have to be attained through fleshly efforts.

The apostle Paul provided a shining example of the power of self-realization. A man who had achieved far beyond most of his peers, yet perennially dissatisfied with those achievements, he pressed on to higher levels of spiritual growth, wider outreach for the cause of the gospel, and a more significant and lasting impact on the lives of others (Phil. 3:10-14).

People scold the church from all sides today because of an alleged commitment to tradition and an unwillingness to be creative and flexible when new forms and ideas are so desperately needed. Quite obviously, "the church" is people, and when we make (or agree with) this kind of criticism, we suggest that somebody, somewhere, is too tradition bound to allow the church to shed its shackles of ultraconservatism in practice.

The contemporary church must attempt to maintain equilibrium between two polarized groups. The younger group pulls toward change, and the older pulls against it. Each must share its strengths with the other, and both must recognize the inherent power and importance of creativity to an institution and its leaders.

The Creativity of Cooperative Ministry

Creativity seeks new solutions to old problems as well as new ones. It is not always as rational as it might be, but then, the creative process has never been clearly marked by rationality. On the other hand, traditionalism is rational. It documents with scientific precision and generally works only with the known, proven, and measurable. Many leaders prefer traditional solutions, suspicious of change. They fail to see that a cooperative team ministry actually promotes their own self-realization rather than stifling it.

Creativity also brings with it an aura of flexibility. An institution cannot remain rigid if it allows its leaders to be creative thinkers. When the equilibrium of the organization shakes, the creative pole may attract too strongly, and productive energy can be dissipated down blind alleys. That is precisely what Albert J. Sullivan has called "The Right to Fail," and he argued this is essential if we would enjoy the power of the creative process in our institutions:

> The right to fail is of the essence of creativity (just as the prevention of failure is of the essence of conservatism). The creative act must be uninhibited and marked by supreme confidence; there can be no fear of failure—nothing inhibits so fiercely, or shrinks a vision so drastically, or pulls a dream to earth so swiftly, as fear of failure.[6]

If individual leaders want to experience the power of creativity in their own administrative style, they must live with the right to fail. Their church or institution will have to give them the right to fail, not all the time, but at least occasionally. In research and experiment, self-realization cannot really know failure because in such activities we measure the *striving*, not the *reaching*.

Generally speaking, in churches and Christian institutions of education at all levels, traditional administrative processes, reinforced by the desperate financial crisis of the past two decades, have all but crushed the right to fail. And with it, a great deal of the potential power of creativity has also perished.

Evaluation—Giving and Receiving

Perhaps the most important thing we can say about evaluation is that it must be mutual. Indeed, we can probably go back and apply our three key words of interpersonal relationship (mutuality, presentality, and simultaneity) to the supervisory process, particularly the evaluative segment of that process. While we evaluate subordinates on a continuing day-by-day basis, they also evaluate us. Both evaluations may be informal most of the time, but the informality does not negate the reality of the process.

Evaluation provides an opportunity for increasing positive interpersonal relations or for destroying whatever we have built in earlier weeks and months. Every leader must understand that evaluation only proceeds on the basis of clear-cut job descriptions and specific objectives for each role in the organization. Standards must be set and evaluation linked directly with those standards, not some whim of the supervisor.

Evaluative Measures

Effective evaluation employs a variety of measures. Some may seem informal and highly subjective like a supervisor's casual observation of a worker. Others are formal and considerably more objective. Consider a carefully designed questionnaire which measures the goal achievement of a group of Sunday School teachers over a given year. Leaders should understand the jobs they supervise and be able to speak competently about quality or the lack of quality in the carrying out of those jobs. *Evaluation aims at improving the quality of ministry.*

The personal sessions following a formal evaluation period can be very positive if the evaluations are mutual, and both agree on the goal of the evaluation. They have nothing to do with hiring or firing (virtually nonessential terms among volunteer employees anyhow). In Christian organizations, evaluation debriefings should aim at mutual encouragement, helping people be better teachers and leaders. But the key lies in multiple measures and knowing in advance what we are looking for.

Evaluative Questions

Questions must be asked in the evaluative process, and the quality of those questions may be the key to success or failure.

1. *Use open questions, not closed questions.* Invite people to freely express what they think rather than boxing them into a certain point of view. Example: "Bill, how do you feel about the effectiveness of your teaching?" Not, "Bill, don't you think that all of our teachers ought to attend the staff meeting?"

2. *Use leading questions rather than loaded questions.* We want to give direction to the reply but not restrict it. Example: "How did you go about arriving at this solution to the problem?" Not, "What makes you think your solution to the problem was the only right one?"

3. *Use cool questions rather than heated questions.* Let us appeal to reason in the evaluation process and keep the emotion level as low as possible. Example: "What kind of goals would you like to set for yourself for the next year?" Not, "Don't you think I have the right and responsibility to set goals for your ministry?"

4. *Use planned questions rather than impulsive questions.* Think out a sequence of questions for each individual worker rather than just going with the flow. Example: "What kinds of things would you like to see changed in our office over the next year?" Not, "Do you think our personnel is content with present procedures?"

5. *Use treat questions, not trick questions.* Let people know they can make a real contribution, a real change in the organ-

ization by expressing their views. Example: "You know as much about this as I do Mary, how would you handle it?" Not, "Which of the members in our office has been least helpful in getting your work done properly?"

6. *Use window questions, not mirror questions.* You need to see into the staff member's mind and feelings, not just hear a point of view. Example: "That's an interesting observation, why do you feel that way about the problem?" Not, "Here's the way it looks to me; do you agree?"

Evaluative Guidelines

Larry Osborne has suggested several helpful guidelines to keep in mind when you yourself are being evaluated by a supervisor. First of all, he says, choose the time carefully. That is not always possible, but when we can we want to avoid being reviewed during times of personal failure or unusual stress.

Secondly, said Osborne, "Avoid anonymous responses." Here we have a standard rule of wise evaluation. Some forms of evaluation may of necessity be anonymous—student ratings of faculty at the undergraduate level, general all-staff ratings of company management, etc. Among people in leadership levels of ministry, written evaluation should lead to eyeball dialogue. Speaking as a pastor, Osborne argued:

> I've come to the conclusion that people who won't say something to my face have no right to be heard. If I can't get an honest answer without anonymity, I'm left with serious questions about their integrity and courage. And if, on the other hand, people are too intimidated by my presence to respond openly, I probably have bigger problems than any pastoral review will be able to solve.[7]

Evaluative Tools

Osborne mentioned several evaluative tools that readers may wish to track down for further study.

Communicating Styles Inventory
Training Associates Press
1177 Rockingham
Richardson, TX 75080

Your Style of Influence
Center for Church Renewal
P. O. Box 863173
Plano, TX 75086

Scales for the Measurement of Attitudes
Marvin E. Shaw and Jack M. Wright
McGraw-Hill, 1967

The Experience of Work:
A Compendium and Review of 249 Measures and Their Use
ed. John D. Cook
Academic Press, 1981

Let's conclude this chapter by remembering that the attitude of the supervisor is primary in developing positive interpersonal relations. Never assume, for example, that a cause is lost or an employee must be dismissed until you really understand the problem. Assume God works in His people and you need to find out how He wants to use you in continuing that changing, growing pattern.

Remember, too, that you are not singularly responsible for the effectiveness of your subordinates. Responsibilities have been diffused throughout the body, and you facilitate the unleashing of appropriate motivation to make goal achievement possible. Leadership finds its fulfillment when all God's people exercise their gifts, and supervision puts you in an enabling position to structure opportunities for ministry. The unity of the body is crucial in all supervisory processes. We want to build that unity and maintain it, never tear it down.

Notes

1. James M. Kouzes and Barry Z. Posner, *The Leadership Challenge* (San Francisco: Jossey-Bass Publishers, 1987), 179 180.

2. Ibid., 180-85.

3. Ibid., 182-83.

4. James Reed, "Working Together as a Team," *Church Administration* (September 1987): 21.

5. Reprinted from *Feeding and Leading* by Kenneth O. Gangel, published by Victor Books, (1989), SP Publications, Inc., Wheaton, IL 60187.

6. Albert J. Sullivan, "The Right to Fail," *Journal of Higher Education* 34, no. 4 (April 1963): 191.

7. Larry Osborne, "Performance Reviews: Avoiding the Pitfalls," *Leadership* (Summer 1988): 63.

11

CONFLICT DEFINED AND CLARIFIED

Carefully consider the following twelve words. As you examine each word ask yourself if you closely associate any or all of these words with conflict.

anger	adversary	battle	challenge
criticism	disgruntled	fight	pressure
struggle	tension	trouble	warfare

Identifying Conflict

People have many understandings of *conflict*. Here are seven common misconceptions of what conflict means.

1. *Conflict is abnormal.* Some people seek to completely rid relationships of all struggle. They consider it improper, if not deviant, to expect conflict to be part of the human experience. "Normal people do not fight." Unfortunately, life does not agree with this viewpoint. As long as we live in this earthly body, conflict must be considered as a normal part of our day-by-day living. To expect otherwise demonstrates an unrealistic view.

2. *Conflict and disagreement are the same.* Here we face a problem of intensity. Severe conflict can and does occur where little disagreement exits. At the ideological level two armies may do battle (conflict), but the individual soldiers do not find themselves in disagreement at all.

Even in Evangelical Christianity some well-meaning people leave terrible destruction in their wake due to poorly managed conflict. Yet they do not perceive disagreement with anyone. On the other hand, "disagreement" may be a cop-out when the conflict is far more serious. It may not be a simple misunderstanding but rather a momentous clash of values between two equally influential groups. To call this a simple disagreement understates and minimizes the importance of the issues involved.

3. *Conflict is pathological.* Some believers view conflict as evidence that people are frustrated, psychologically maladjusted, or neurotic in their behavior. From this viewpoint conflict becomes a disease which must be cured. Joyce Frost and William Wilmot have cogently observed:

> This view ignores the reality that many times people are indeed angry and frustrated, and legitimately so, when they are unable to progress toward the goals they desire.... Teaching people that conflict is dysfunctional does not make conflicts go away—they simply continue, but participants think *they* are abnormal.[1]

To view conflict as pathological merely clouds the picture and makes management of the particular conflict situation more difficult.

4. *Conflict must be reduced or avoided.* When a person views conflict from only a negative perspective, it is a short step to making it imperative to subdue conflict at all costs. Someone with this misperception seeks to eliminate any and all conflict. He cannot appreciate any positive values which conflict may bring to the conflict encounter. "Peace at any price" often becomes the slogan of those who seek to stop conflict. They demonstrate discomfort whenever conflict comes their way.

5. *Conflict is a personality problem.* This excuse frequently appears so that the conflict cannot be probed to any significant depth. All personalities have problems with other personalities at some point in time. Conflict usually involves much more than the "smoke screen" of the personality problem.

6. *Conflict is linked only with anger.* No one would deny that conflict often carries strong emotional messages with it. At times conflict conveys a faulty concept when we link it *only* with anger. People can engage in strong conflict with others and not demonstrate anger. When philosophies conflict or values dramatically differ, conflict ensues, but anger may not be present.

7. *Conflict is the admission of failure.* Here we face a misguided understanding of conflict. Conflict management may call for an admission of failure, but to be occupied in the conflict process does not guarantee either success or failure. The tacit message sent by this misconception implies conflict is always bad and wrong for God's child. The option of working through conflict and becoming stronger from it seems foreign to this false view of conflict.

Now that we know what conflict isn't, we will seek to define conflict and to examine it in a positive way.

Essential Elements in Defining Conflict

How should we define conflict? Numerous individuals have attempted to give us the basic ingredients. Consider these:

> A conflict is "a situation in which two or more human beings desire goals which they perceive as being attainable by one or the other *but not by both.*"[2]
>
> Conflict is two or more objects aggressively trying to occupy the same space at the same time.[3]
>
> [Conflict is] a struggle over values and claims to scarce status, power and resources in which the aims of the opponents are to neutralize, injure or eliminate their rivals.[4]

1. *Interdependency.* One irony linked to an accurate view of conflict is that the participants must be connected. For example, think about a church member couple who find themselves in conflict with the pastor. They solve the problem by leaving the church and taking their ministry across town to another church where they get along better. They would no longer be in conflict with the first pastor since the relationship was severed. Some link must still connect the conflicting parties for conflict to be present.

2. *Interactive Struggle.* As children playing the game "tug-of-war," a person in conflict feels tension from the opponent. A sense of "I can't let up!" marks the relationship. The sensation makes us believe sincerely that our adversary is attempting to take us in a direction we don't want to go. The process offers no relief until we have observed the opponent crossing over to our side.

The word *struggle* is an excellent synonym for conflict. Scarce resources prove to be the "stuff" over which conflict occurs. Time, people, and money represent the kind of fixed commodities over which we struggle.

3. *Incompatible Goals*. As the process of conflict wears on, it can often become obvious that our antagonist plans to end up at a different location than we do. The goal may be for us to be totally supportive of his agenda. This means we must absolutely abandon our plans to stop the warfare. Capturing us as prisoners does not interest him. He wants us enlisted as his soldiers. The depth of conflict can be better understood when we recognize the issue of incompatible goals.

4. *Perceived Interference*. This definitional element adds the dimension of hindrance. What I am trying to do is thwarted by your attitude or action. I cannot progress in my ministry because you are slowing or stopping my efforts. The block may be perceived rather than actual, but the conflictual interference is no less real.

5. *Interface of opposition and cooperation*. In addition to the interdependency of the relationship, a symbiotic element emerges in true conflict. At the same time the conflicting parties engage in fighting, they find themselves in positional agreement since they hold membership in the larger body, the church. This positive/negative, agree/disagree, accept/reject, in favor of/against element characterizes genuine conflict.

Conflict and the Communication Process

Conflict does not occur as an isolated event. It functions as part of an ongoing process. An accurate picture of conflict requires a holistic view of the communication process. What happens before, during, and after the conflict episode merits our careful attention. The following chart emphasizes a process approach in examining conflict. The model considers that conflict causes changes when it occurs. The ten topics represent the more significant subjects related to conflict management.

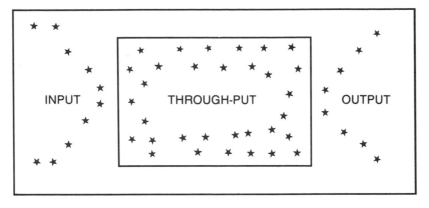

Key: * = Conflict

BEFORE	DURING	AFTER
Predisposition to fight or not	Management vs. mismanagement	Assessment Evaluation
Perspective more idealistic	Perspective more realistic	Perspective revised (new)
Role definition assumed	Role definition by you vs. others	Role definition modified
Relationship anticipated	Relationship experienced	Relationship adjusted (+ vs. -)
Communication skills previously learned	Communication skills employed	Communication skills sharpened
Power inherent	Power displayed	Power clarified
Values of others unknown	Values of others revealed	Values of others codified
Style more personality determined	Style more process determined	Style more product determined
Coalitions vague	Coalitions surface	Coalitions permanentize
Problem solving planned	Problem solving attempted	Problem solving measured

We will look at this chart part by part. This will help us to understand the process in handling conflict and the changes that occur.

BEFORE	DURING	AFTER
Predisposition to fight or not	Management vs. mismanagement	Assessment Evaluation

No conflict occurs in a vacuum. Every individual brings an attitude and/or a bias either for or against each potential conflict situation. What we observe in those who share a close relationship with us contributes a strong influence over us. Past experiences in conflict management or mismanagement help to establish what predisposition we bring to the conflict situation.

One authority defined conflict management as "the process of influencing the activities and attitudes of an individual or group in the midst of disagreement, tensions, and behavioral actions which are threatening the relationship and or the accomplishment of goals."[5]

During the actual conflict our previous disposition is tested again and again. "Am I handling this situation rightly?" "What should I be doing differently?" "What emotions surface?" "Should I speak with more force or less intensity?" Constantly we consciously or subconsciously register the feedback when we find ourselves in a conflict context.

When the immediate conflict episode ends, we discover a new idea of how we should approach the next conflictual circumstance. We may choose to take the necessary steps so that a similar confrontation will not occur. We do not have the option to change the past, but we can alter the outcome of some future conflict.

BEFORE	DURING	AFTER
Perspective more idealistic	Perspective more idealistic	Perspective revised (new)

Before we engage in conflict, our viewpoints tend to be more idealistic. It may take the form of perceived victory or a conviction that the other party in the conflict will agree with us if she thinks more about this problem. Solutions to conflictual problems do not usually resolve with just additional thinking. Before the actual "fight" we may be tempted to view the conflict as more severe or less severe than it actually is.

As we experience conflict, our view of the issues, parties, and potential outcomes has a way of adjusting to realism. Compromise can become more attractive when conflict continues beyond what we initially expected. The give and take between the parties usually becomes more focused on primary issues. Secondary matters are stripped away as we realistically see what can and cannot be obtained.

After an incident involving conflict most people revise their perspective. We never undergo a conflict without some change being effected in our lives. It may reinforce our original stance or radically overhaul our perspective.

BEFORE	DURING	AFTER
Role definition assumed	Role definition by you vs. others	Role definition modified

Before conflict begins, the participants define their roles according to personal assumptions. At times a mixed or conflictual definition could be the source of future conflict. This stage may sometimes be ignored or minimized. Since the conflict has yet to be experienced, we do not take the time to anticipate how we will respond when the actual conflict occurs. In some instances we may not even be aware that conflict is coming.

The struggle itself clarifies our definition of conflict and how it may differ from other parties engaged in the conflict situation. We can experience surprise, frustration, and disbelief when we begin to realize how someone else defines our roles, his or her roles, or even the issue which brought about the conflict. The more we communicate, the clearer our differences become. This type of communication intensifies the conflict. As we understand each other, the differences assume even sharper contrast. At times the conflict never receives proper management because we cannot agree on a mutual definition of roles.

When conflict is efficiently managed, some modification in role definition usually occurs. The parties in conflict change some facet of the role description previously held. The exercise of the conflict process effects some degree of change when the outcome of the fight is determined. It may be a minor adjustment to the role definition before conflict. Or it could be a major adjustment if the conflict was intense over a long period of time.

BEFORE	*DURING*	*AFTER*
Relationship anticipated	Relationship experienced	Relationship adjusted (+ vs. -)

When we experience conflict, we can best measure the relationship we share with another person. The smooth waters before a conflict may provide clues as to how we will manage conflict, but at best we can only guess. The energy used during the struggle of the fight brings about a depth of relationship which normal dialogue cannot approach. The strength of the relationship is greatly enhanced when it properly harnesses the stout winds of conflict.

Conversely, the negative assessment of the relationship may be damaged beyond repair. No one ever comes out of conflict the same way one entered. The process of doing conflict causes us to make adjustments either positively or negatively with the relationship. How we experience relationship during the conflict to a great extent determines what sort of adjustment we make in the output. The occurrence of conflict usually does not indicate the outcome as much as *how* we perceive conflict both during and after the conflict episode.

BEFORE	*DURING*	*AFTER*
Communication skills previously learned	Communication skills employed	Communication skills sharpened

Our ability to ask questions, listen, evaluate, and read nonverbal cues is largely the product of life up to the point of a particular conflict. We either feel adequate with these skills or suffer from a sense of deficiency as we anticipate a given conflict. This assessment does not apply to all conflict situations. The issue under debate, the parties involved, and the risks we are willing to take all play an important part in how well we project what we will do in the coming battle.

Once the conflict begins we find out if our predictions about our skills were valid or not. Some abilities in communication may appear to be stronger than other skills as we clash with an opponent in the arena of conflict. We tend to take quick readings when under the fire of the enemy. Judgment accelerates in the give and take of conflict.

Once the conflict episode concludes, we usually assess the damages and the victories. Part of this process helps evaluate what communication skills we have utilized. For example, we may find our listening skills sharpened. We hear the verbal and the nonverbal better than before the conflict encounter. We may also find some areas where we expected competency but found it lacking. This can create territories where we schedule improvement as desired, if not necessary.

BEFORE	DURING	AFTER
Power inherent	Power displayed	Power clarified

Influence in conflict situations carries a strategic message with it. Usually the more power one party possesses, the more likely the outcome will be in his or her favor. Power may not reside in an individual as much as in the relationship. The issues, the context, and the background of the participants— these all serve to influence how we use and misuse power during conflict. Prior to the actual conflict, power is more latent and inherent.

As we experience conflict, power becomes crystal clear. The influence one person has over another quickly comes to light. Previous "debts" are called in as the battle wages. Like a knife, conflict severs the group or individuals so sides can be vividly seen. Power serves as the unseen dynamic responsible for much of this activity. Who has not felt the hammer of influence as persons we thought were with us proved they were not on our team? Power does much to clarify the opposing factions in any given conflict circumstance.

When the skirmish ends, power is redefined. It may still be in the hands which held it before the battle began. If so, it is almost always stronger having gone through the conflict. Power may be distributed to those who had little or no influence. Seldom is power equally shared as individuals emerge from conflict. The picture of who has it and who does not seems clearer after passing through the furnace of conflict.

BEFORE	DURING	AFTER
Values of others unknown	Values of others revealed	Values of others codified

A certain mystery hangs over the values our adversary holds prior to the actual conflict. Our own values may not be as sharply defined before we engage in conflict. The mutual values between conflicting individuals exist but will probably be unknown before conflict is experienced.

The values our opponent holds, those we hold, and shared values should come to light during the conflict if we make progress toward productive management of conflict. This revelation of values is vital to creating multiple alternatives which should help to direct the conflict toward a positive outcome. When we know values, more options can surface when both parties energetically seek a satisfying result for all concerned.

Once the values are clear, the postconflict time is given to codifying those values. Sometimes we do this because future battles are sure to come. In our purer moments we codify to find those workable areas where we can mutually minister without the fire of conflict being ignited again.

BEFORE	DURING	AFTER
Style more personality determined	Style more process determined	Style more product determined

Conflict management style varies as it travels through the process. "How will a person respond to conflict?" This question looks for patterned behavior which gives us a clue as to what a conflict style might be. The individual's personality influences conflict before the episode begins. In addition to personality, the age factor, family background, and previous conflict experience help to determine the initial conflict style.

How our adversary relates to the conflict becomes a potent influence on us during the episode. We all have an amazing ability to flex under fire. If I am to negotiate, the motivation to do so is not so much my personality now as it is the behavior of my antagonist.

The adjustments made after confrontation serve as the dominant force for what our anticipated style will be when encountering conflict of this type again. If a win-win outcome was possible, the style will not usually change. If the battle was bloody, with more losers than winners, we may want to plan radical changes in style for future confrontations.

BEFORE	DURING	AFTER
Coalitions vague	Coalitions surface	Coalitions permanentize

A study of coalitions examines how we align with one another when we anticipate or experience conflict. Since coalitions relate to values, it is difficult to forecast how these will form before the confrontation. Who has not counted the votes for a project thinking we had enough to approve it, only to find some members switched? When the conflict includes many people, we can be sure coalitions will form, but we cannot always predict how this formation will occur.

As conflict develops we choose sides. Coalitions usually form because the individual desiring a coalition can gain something he or she could not achieve alone. Coalitions form as an antithesis of power. They help to keep power honest. Weaker parties unite so that the common adversary will listen to this new more significant voice. Some amount of conflict needs to be experienced so that we can identify weakness and strength.

After the confrontation a coalition may cement into a newer and more powerful relationship. If the coalition helped to achieve worthwhile gains for each of its members, this new relationship will often permanentize. If the coalition was unsuccessful, it will usually disband after the conflict experience.

BEFORE	DURING	AFTER
Problem solving planned	Problem solving attempted	Problem solving measured

Before a confrontation we plan how we will solve this conflict problem. We gathered the evidence and arranged it to support our cause. Since conflict seems to always involve a problem, we design what we perceive as the best solution for this predicament. Usually both parties go through these preliminary steps preparing for the eventual confrontation.

When the conflict occurs, our problem-solving abilities are put to the test. The strategies and tactics so carefully prepared either work or fail to accomplish what we intended. The weapons brought to the conflict encounter vary with each party. Some people fight according to accepted rules of warfare, others do not.

When the conflict episode concludes, we measure how well our problem-solving ability worked. Adjustments and fine tuning usually occur. We repair what calls for our attention and wait for the next skirmish.

To understand conflict we must view it as an expressed struggle where opposition and cooperation exist within the same relationship. This interdependent association surfaces as an ongoing process. If we see the battle from a holistic perspective, we can comprehend the total picture with greater accuracy and position ourselves for more effective conflict management.

Notes

1. Joyce Hocker Frost and William W. Wilmot, *Interpersonal Conflict* (Dubuque, Iowa: William C. Brown Co. Publishers, 1978), 6-7.

2. Larry L. McSwain and William C. Treadwell, Jr., *Conflict Ministry in the Church* (Nashville: Broadman Press, 1981), 25.

3. G. Douglass Lewis, *Resolving Church Conflicts* (San Francisco: Harper and Row, 1981), 73.

4. Lewis A. Coser, *The Functions of Social Conflict* (New York: The Free Press, 1956), 8.

5. Norman Shawchuck, *How to Manage Conflict in the Church* (Irvine, Calif.: Spiritual Growth Resources, 1983), 21.

12

CONFLICT MANAGEMENT AND RELATIONSHIP LEVELS

Communication not only imparts information but also reveals a relationship. Every communication experience contains both a "content" aspect and a "relationship" aspect. The "content" feature provides the data sent and received. How we receive this information and what we do with it is more determined by the "relationship" feature.

Relationship statements sound like this: "This is how I see myself"; "This is how I see you"; "This is how I see you seeing me." In any ongoing communication we experience both the content and the relationship aspects (often seen as nonverbal cues), and they work together in simultaneous fashion. The relationship level gives us instruction as to information being received. Since it provides us information about information, we call it "meta-information."

Every message sent and received should actually be viewed as metacommunication. All our past experiences influence every relationship definition. Paul Watzlawick, Janet Beavin, and Don Jackson state in their book, *The Pragmatics of Human Communication*, "Any communication implies a commitment and thereby defines the relationship."[1]

Communication Patterns

If we find that certain behaviors work well with certain messages, we will repeat those behaviors. For example, if a child discovers a cute smile and baby talk obtain the desired outcome, he or she will use it until it no longer works. Small children are very pragmatic in their approach to communication. They seem to intuitively understand how the relationship aspect of communication functions.

Among adults, research indicates that "the more spontane-ous and healthy a relationship, the more the relationship aspect of communication recedes into the background."[2]

Relationship Levels: An Old Testament Example

The relationship between David and Jonathan points to the validity of this principle. As David became increasingly popu-lar, King Saul became increasingly suspicious of him. On one occasion David asked Jonathan, Saul's heir apparent:

> "What have I done? What is my crime? How have I wronged your father, that he is trying to take my life?"
> "Never!" Jonathan replied. "You are not going to die! Look, my father doesn't do anything, great or small, without con-fiding in me. Why would he hide this from me? It's not so!"
> (1 Sam. 20:1-2)

The account continues as these young men devise a plan to reveal if Saul was in fact dedicated to the task of taking David's life. David would absent himself from a feast. Jona-than planned to defend David's absence. If the king spoke kindly of David's absence, Jonathan would shoot arrows short of a given target. However, if Saul was irritated and angry over David's absence, Jonathan was to shoot arrows beyond a given spot. In this way both David and Jonathan would share the message of Saul's intent as to the elimination of David.

They were able to focus on the content of the symbolic message Jonathan sent because their relationship level was so healthy it did not need attention. Jonathan, as Saul's son, was the next, presumed king of Israel. Would he turn David in if his father actually did desire to kill him? Was the relation-ship between David and Jonathan stronger than the one be-tween a father and son?

These questions of betrayal and strength of relationship do not appear to have entered David's mind. He seems not even to have considered any risk in this strong trust of Jonathan. The trustworthiness of genuine friendship far overshadowed any such doubt or uncertainty. The account concludes with David and Jonathan weeping because they both understood Saul's murderous intent.

Conversely, *the more a struggle over defining the relationship occurs, the less importance is attached to the content in communication.*

The relationship between Saul and David became more and more unpredictable. After David spared Saul's life the second time (1 Sam. 26), the king declared, "I have sinned. Come back, David my son. Because you have considered my life precious today, I will not try to harm you again. Surely I have acted like a fool and have erred greatly" (v. 21).

On the surface this sounds like a great confession: Saul admitted his sin. He promised in front of many witnesses not to try to harm David again. He extended what appeared to be a warm, heartfelt invitation for David to come home to his palace. Did David go? No. The last few words of this chapter declare, "So David went on his way, and Saul returned home" (v. 25). The content of Saul's message could not be accepted because the relationship between him and David ruled against the acceptance of the normal meaning of the words. David found himself concerned with the relationship to the extent the content of the message could not be trusted.

Each of us have some individual(s) whom we would trust with our very lives. The friendship is so strong that risk just does not seem to exist. We believe that such persons have only our best interests at heart. We do not worry about duplicity, secondary meanings, or false motives. We probably have been exceedingly vulnerable with these persons and found over a period of time that they have demonstrated reliability. This is the David-Jonathan relationship.

You could probably list some "King Sauls" in your life also. Your repeated exposure to them has caused you to seek verification of everything they say. Experience has proven communication may or may not be true. It has to be validated by someone more reliable than the source.

In such settings a very negative atmosphere develops. Discouragement can move in and lead us quickly toward spiritual defeat. Over time King Saul so discouraged David that he temporarily sought refuge with Israel's enemy (1 Sam. 27). But joining the enemy may not provide an answer to the conflict problem. It simply creates a new set of difficulties for us.

Conflict can easily become confused here. If we are more concerned with identifying the relationship, we may miss some of the data coming through at the content level. We can become so preoccupied with the message content that we misread the relationship.

Relationship Levels and Courtship

The American institution of dating gives us a more contemporary illustration of content messages versus relationship messages. From content messages a young man receives, he may misread the relationship with a young lady as more serious than she intends. As he continues down this false road he may travel all the way to an engagement proposal, only to find she rejects the idea. He has obviously not understood the level of the relationship the same way she interpreted it. In the irony of content versus relationship messages however, he might discover that she expected the diamond ring six months before he offered it! We constantly assess relationships on the basis of the data we possess.

Clarifying Content and Relationship Levels

Relationship clarifies content. The relationship you sustain with other individuals will govern how you classify the content of any message they send and you receive. Our problems begin when ambiguity clouds the communication so that we find ourselves uncertain as to what information we should believe. Ambiguity characterizes the communication episode when both content and relationship aspects allow for multiple meanings.

For example, a sign in a restaurant reads: "Customers who think our waiters are rude should see the manager." The meaning this message imparts is not clear. Will you receive help if you see the manager? Or will you be treated more rudely? Both meanings could be legitimate. Since the sign is written, we do not benefit from nonverbal cues. However, if we know the restaurant owner to be a bit of a joker, the relationship level would govern what meaning we attach to the sign. *The greater the ambiguity created by unclear content or rela-*

tionship messages, the greater the potential for conflict to be present.

Problems become more complicated when we fail to recognize both the content and relationship levels of communication. Consider the following story about a married couple:

> The husband was greeted by the excited wife who had just purchased a much-needed chair for the living room. The new chair fitted perfectly into the decor of the room, and she paid only half price. She knew if her husband had been with her he would have made the purchase. However, the husband was upset with the purchase of the chair, and a bitter quarrel arose. As the problem was explored, both the husband and wife agreed that to purchase the chair was the most appropriate and natural thing to do. They were perplexed to find that on the one hand they agreed and yet "somehow" disagreed on what seemed to be the same issue.

At the content level they agreed—the purchase of the chair was the appropriate course of action. At the relationship level the question—"Does one have the right to take the initiative without consulting the other?"—was unresolved. As long as they fixed just the content level, they had an imperfect management of the conflict. The more crucial question—"Does one have the right to take the initiative without the other's knowledge?"—had to be answered for the conflict to be adequately governed.

Symmetrical Versus Complementary Relationships

Our association with each other takes the form of a symmetrical or complementary relationship. The discussion will center first on the symmetrical relationship, then on the complementary one.

Symmetrical Relationship

This term describes an interactive pattern that *mirrors* the other party in the communication event. What you perceive you are receiving is what you give. It may be weakness or strength, goodness or badness. Your response simply reflects the other communicator. When this characteristic dominates a relationship, the parties usually experience a destructive escalation of conflict. One insult deserves another insult. Your opponent defends his or her position as correct, so, therefore, you defend yours. Such escalation simply drives the communicators further apart and makes conflict far more difficult to manage.

The strong, divisive controversy between Paul and Barnabas over whether to have John Mark accompany them on their second missionary journey (Acts 15:36-40) pictures the destructive force of a symmetrical relationship. Each man stood adamant in his position. Barnabas was set on taking John Mark. He evidently felt everyone deserved a second chance. After all, "failure is not final" was probably his major argument.

Paul, on the other hand, was convinced it was not wise to take with them someone who might again desert them as he had done previously. "Quitters never win" may have been Paul's major contention. Paul insisted that the trip be made without John Mark, and no creative solution seemed available. The sharp disagreement became an either-or situation. Whenever we reduce all options to a clear either-or outcome, a relationship runs a high risk of being broken. This is exactly what happened to this first missionary team. They split and went their separate ways.

God in His grace used both men to spread the message of Jesus Christ and His salvation, but the interpersonal black eye is permanently recorded in God's record. Later, Paul realized and recognized John Mark's value in ministry when he asked that Mark be brought to him shortly before his death (2 Tim. 4:11). Had John Mark changed? Had Paul changed? Scripture provides no answer.

Unfortunately, we do not need to travel back to biblical times to see examples of how an escalation of symmetrical relationships displays destructive power. The American home abounds with examples. Consider the relationship of a teenage boy with his father. The conversation might sound like this:

Boy: But, Dad, you don't understand. None of my friends have to be in at midnight on weekends!

DAD: In this house all children will be in by midnight.

BOY: I don't understand why you insist on being so inflexible! Why can't I phone you and tell you at midnight where I am and what time I will be home?

DAD: You will be expected to be home no later than 12:00, midnight!

BOY: And what if I'm not! Am I going to find my car turning into a pumpkin or something?

DAD: The hour is set, and if you disobey it you know the consequences!

BOY: Oh sure, you'll take away my car keys and treat me like a child. I'm not in the sixth grade anymore!

DAD: If you act like a sixth grader, you will be treated like a sixth grader.

BOY: I just don't see why you are so strict about a midnight curfew.

DAD: I just don't see why you want to rebel against my parental authority.

This conversation goes nowhere. Neither the son nor the father has moved his opponent one inch. High symmetry characterizes the relationship and, if continued over time, could have powerful destructive consequences as to the father-son relationship. More pain comes since neither person plans to even try to see the situation from the other's viewpoint.

The boy's suggestion to phone at midnight may indicate an interest to see if any possible compromise existed. However, the dad in no way intended to flex. No possible discussion could dent his position. He simply went through the motions of a conversation. He had fixed his mind as to what possible outcome would transpire. The boy requested some rationale as to why the twelve o'clock curfew was so rigid. No answer came other than the curfew would not change.

Symmetrical relationship built frustration in both parties. The boy wanted to know the father's reasoning; the father could not understand why his son did not want to accept the inevitable. The battle lines were clearly drawn for future conflict. If this definition of "family" was maintained, ultimate ill-will and broken hearts were inevitable. Tragically, both son and father continued to believe that "truth" resided with each of their personal positions. Scenes like this can be multiplied over and over. The individual issues may change, but the process continues on.

Complementary Relationship

Maximization of *difference* describes this concept. Superiority marks one person in the relationship; inferiority brands the other. One individual occupies the "one-up" position while the other operates from the "one-down" position. Both accept this one-up/one-down relationship as valid. We see it in the interlocking nature of the relationship.

Sometimes such an attitude is set by the social or cultural context. When students enter a new level of schooling, they usually view themselves in a one-down position. The "lowly freshman" concept is no myth. The seniors have been in the institution longer, gaining experience and wisdom as they make their pilgrimage through the hallowed halls of education.

We have many ways to reinforce the importance of seniors over freshmen. The location of the lockers will usually be designed to give greater prestige to the senior, if possible. Freshmen rarely, if ever, get elected president of the student council. Varsity athletes predominantly are juniors and seniors. We reserve the more exotic electives in a school for those closer to graduation.

This dictation of status also occurs in other social contexts. If a young but poor girl marries a young but rich boy, the natural consequence will find her in a one-down position. Her family just does not have the wealth and status of his family. One can overcome such an initial complementary position, but it will not happen unless both parties make a conscious effort to do so.

When a young person marries a mate significantly less intelligent, the one-up and one-down positions usually occur. Absolute equality is seldom experienced in a relationship so intimate as marriage. When repeated behavior etches the complementary pattern indelibly into our experience, we lose optimal efficiency in the relationship.

If in conflict we want both parties to emerge as winners, a prolonged model of complementarity will not achieve the desired result. The person in the one-down position tends to become satisfied with losing. A possible exception occurs when the one-down individual becomes skilled in the fine art of indirect manipulation. Then we have a case of "underdog" winning over "top dog." Valid evidence supports the notion that over the long haul the "underdog" strategies will prevail over "top-dog" strategies.[3]

The complementary relationship may occur in a single communication event. We find an illustration of this when the Samaritan woman in John's Gospel viewed herself in a one-down (complementary) relationship. She responded to Jesus' request for a drink of water by saying, " 'You are a Jew and I am a Samaritan woman. How can you ask me for a drink?' (For Jews do not associate with Samaritans.)" (John 4:9). How interesting that even before Jesus spoke, the message of relationships was present. She had sized up the situation and did not expect this man to speak to her. He hardly would request a drink from her! The woman's comment reveals both a racial and sexual difficulty that existed in her culture. She first predetermined that Jews do not associate with Samaritans. She also seems to have accepted the fact that asking for a drink was a form of association. The history of these two peoples would give credence to her question. Every orthodox Jew made great effort to avoid any sense of fraternization with a Samaritan. A genuine contempt existed between these nations.

Her second presupposition taught her that men did not request a drink from women. Her inclusion of the obvious fact that she was a woman lends support to this presupposition. By all measurement she entered the dialogue in a one-down position. As the events of the account unfold, Jesus revealed her instability in the marriage bond and then gave her the satisfaction of eternal life so that she might never thirst again. She moved from a strong complementary position to a position of sharing eternal life. This became a clear win-win situation, in part, because God elevated her from a rigid one-down relationship.

If, over time, the complementary relationship continues, rigidity will develop in the relationship. In times of conflict very predictable behavior will occur. The person in the one-down position simply learns to tolerate people in the one-up position. An unfortunate example of this is when the pastor (one-up) continues to try to minister after he has relegated all lay leaders into a one-down position. The church endures his ministry while nothing significant for God is accomplished. The best management of conflict becomes difficult, or perhaps impossible, in this situation.

A Communication Axiom

"All communicational interchanges are either symmetrical or complementary, depending on whether they are based on equality or difference."[4] Since exclusive symmetrical or complementary interchanges produce negative results, how should we use these relationship realities?

As we measure how we relate to others we need to make sure that neither symmetrical nor complementary interchanges dominate the communication process. When a relationship becomes either rigidly symmetrical or complementary, greater problems develop. In the conflict domain this imbalance hinders us from finding creative alternatives which could yield reconciliation or, at least, an accepted truce in the battle.

As you process the messages from others around you, seek to understand as clearly as possible how they define the relationship. Is it consistently symmetrical? Is it mainly complementary? The answer you obtain should help you in all your communication, but it will prove invaluable as you attempt to work through conflict you experience with a brother or sister in Christ. We should also exercise care as to how rigidly we approach a conflict experience. Our predisposition about the relationship may inaccurately lead us into greater destructive conflict than is necessary. We seem to suffer from a "labeling" syndrome. Allow for change to occur in yourself and in those with whom you regularly have communication.

When we do not recognize the changes God makes in each of our lives, we develop a prejudice which kills effective interpersonal relationships.

We must identify content and relationship messages if we expect to have healthy associations with one another. We will determine *how* we receive a message by the relationship we sustain with the person giving the message. If we consider the relationship healthy, we spend more time on the content and less time on the relationship. Since the concept of a symmetrical or complementary relationship identifies all communication, we must make every effort to keep these balanced. For if the relationship becomes exclusively symmetrical or complementary, the result works against developing a healthy relationship with people.

Notes

1. Paul Watzlawick, Janet Helmick Beavin, and Don D. Jackson, *The Pragmatics of Human Communication* (New York: W. W. Norton and Company, 1967), 51.

2. Ibid., 52.

3. Everett Shostrom, *Man, the Manipulator: The Inner Journey from Manipulation to Actualization* (Nashville: Abingdon Press, 1967).

4. Watzlawick, *Pragmatics*, 70.

13

CONFLICT AND
THE OLD TESTAMENT

From Genesis to Revelation God tells us about conflict. Originally, Adam and Eve were created without conflict as a part of their experience. By Genesis 3, sin had become a part of the human dilemma. Conflict immediately surfaced on at least five levels:

1. No longer could Adam and Eve fellowship with their Creator. The divine appointment in the "breeze" time of the evening was gone.
2. The seeds of interpersonal conflict came to harvest very rapidly as Adam quickly shifted responsibility to Eve.
3. Creation or nature would not be productive as it was in the past. "Sweat of the brow" (v. 19) suggests a strong conflict between the human beings and their environment.
4. The spiritual conflict between human beings, Satan, and his organization was set into motion. This will not terminate until Satan is finally consigned to his place in the lake of fire.
5. Perhaps the most insidious conflict was the internal one. Now Adam, Eve, and all their offspring would face the struggle or conflict on the inside created by sin. A sinful nature would become ingrained in each individual fathered and mothered by this first couple. Each of these five levels of conflict would greatly influence the history of humankind.

The confrontation between sin and righteousness provides a foundational perspective for understanding the history of the Old Testament. From the time God selected Israel to be a special people—through their entrance and exit from Egypt, the conquest of the promised land, the earthly kings who ruled, the captivity and return—the record consistently reveals the message of conflict. Often this conflict was mismanaged, but at no time did God fail to control it. The wisdom literature of the Old Testament illustrates how God provided for a people who demonstrated conflict at the different levels mentioned previously. (See ch. 11.)

Conflict Used Constructively

The confrontation experienced in a rebuke can and should have a positive response. "A rebuke impresses a man of discernment / more than a hundred lashes a fool" (Prov. 17:10). Negative feedback or criticism indicates that nature of the one who receives this data. The "rebuke" in and of itself is not bad or wrong, but rather a vital part of life. God commanded the Israelites to practice the activity of rebuking (Lev. 19:17). When they failed to confront a neighbor frankly, two problems developed. First, they ran the risk of hating a brother in their hearts. Second, they might share the guilt of the person needing the rebuke.

At times even a rebuke was not strong enough in confrontation. For example, Eli did rebuke his evil sons for their sins (1 Sam. 2:25) but he did not restrain them from these sinful practices (1 Sam. 3:13). The Lord held him accountable saying, "The guilt of Eli's house will never be atoned for by sacrifice or offering" (1 Sam. 3:14). The Lord expected strong confrontation in this conflict and judged Eli when he did not do it. The issue then, as now, concerned the management of the conflict. The Book of Proverbs consistently reinforces this *positive* concept of conflict management.

In this book the term *rebuke* closely relates to instruction or teaching:

> Do not rebuke a mocker or he will hate you;
>   rebuke a wise man and he will love you.
> Instruct a wise man and he will be wiser still;
>   teach a righteous man and he will add to his learning.
>   (Prov. 9:8-9)

Confronting or rebuking is a positive ministry we have with one another. In the fascinating story of King Ahab and the prophet Micaiah (1 Kings 22:1-28), Ahab revealed his true nature when Micaiah finally gave him the accurate message from God. At issue was the wisdom of going to battle with Jehoshaphat against the Arameans. Ahab could have received the message of sure defeat in the coming battle, but instead he dismissed the lone prophet's rebuke by saying, "Didn't I tell you that he never prophecies anything good about me, but only bad?" (v. 18). How one receives a rebuke indicates the type of person one is.

A rebuke is sometimes the avenue whereby a discerning person gains knowledge: "Flog a mocker, and the simple will learn prudence; / rebuke a discerning man, and he will gain knowledge" (Prov. 19:25). David understood this positive concept of conflict:

> Let a righteous man strike me—it is a kindness;
>   let him rebuke me—it is oil on my head.
> My head will not refuse it.
>   Yet my prayer is ever against the deeds of evildoers.
>   (Ps. 141:5)

The "kindness" mentioned is the familiar word *hesed,* meaning "loyal love." David realized that when a righteous man engaged in conflict against him to the point of physical violence, it should be welcomed as one welcomes the refreshing application of oil to the head. An authentic friendship processes conflict and accepts the positive function it plays in developing a deeper relationship. "Faithful are the wounds of a friend, / But deceitful are the kisses of an enemy" (Prov. 27:6, NASB).

Conflict Used Destructively

In God's wisdom He understands and helps us when we manage conflict poorly. Proverbs serves as a microcosm of negative management of conflict. The frequent use of words such as *quarrels, dispute, strife,* and *anger* exhibits how much we need the clear counsel of God in conflict management.

While not exhaustive, the following representative principles emerge from Proverbs to help us handle our conflict
situations:

1. *At times conflict is best managed by avoiding it.* Strife
linked to our sin must be confessed and corrected. This type of
conflict is best avoided by living a loving and faithful type of
life. As the wisdom of Proverbs puts it, "Through love and
faithfulness sin is atoned for; / through the fear of the Lord a
man avoids evil" (Prov. 16:6).

Frequently, the foolishness of destructive conflict is of our
own making. When we miss the fear of the Lord in life, we find
it difficult, if not impossible, to avoid evil. Embracing evil can
bring a destructive experience with conflict.

From the first chapter of Proverbs, God's counsel about
avoiding evil rings out loud and clear. The folly of evil which
produces destructive conflict has been revealed and should be
avoided. Read the wise words of a father to his son:

> My son, if sinners entice you,
>   do not give in to them.
> If they say, "Come along with us;
>   let's lie in wait for someone's blood,
>   let's waylay some harmless soul;
> let's swallow them alive, like the grave,
>   and whole, like those who go down to the pit;
> we will get all sorts of valuable things
>   and fill our houses with plunder;
> throw in your lot with us,
>   and we will share a common purse"—
> my son, do not go along with them,
>   do not set foot on their paths;
> for their feet rush into sin,
>   they are swift to shed blood.
> How useless to spread a net
>   in full view of all the birds!
> These men lie in wait for their own blood;
>   they waylay only themselves!
> Such is the end of all who go after ill-gotten gain;
>   it takes away the lives of those who get it.
>   (Prov. 1:10-19)

How long will you simple ones love your simple ways?
How long will mockers delight in mockery
and fools hate knowledge?
If you had responded to my rebuke,
I would have poured out my heart to you
and made my thoughts known to you.
But since you rejected me when I called
and no one gave heed when I stretched out my hand,
since you ignored all my advice
and would not accept my rebuke,
I in turn will laugh at your disaster;
I will mock when calamity overtakes you—
when calamity overtakes you like a storm,
when disaster sweeps over you like a whirlwind,
when distress and troubles overwhelm you.
Then they will call to me but I will not answer;
they will look for me but will not find me.
Since they hated knowledge
and did not choose to fear the Lord,
since they would not accept my advice
and spurned my rebuke,
they will eat the fruit of their ways
and be filled with the fruit of their schemes.
For the waywardness of the simple will kill them,
and the complacency of fools will destroy them;
but whoever listens to me will live in safety
and be at ease, without fear of harm.
(Prov. 1:22-33)

The senseless battle associated with destructive conflict shows up in how quickly a person wants to fight. "It is to a man's honor to avoid strife, / but every fool is quick to quarrel" (Prov. 20:3). How swiftly we seek to go into battle may reveal if we have much skill in daily living. So many battles simply do not merit the efforts we give them. When the clash appears to be turning into a warfare with destruction written all over it, we do well to ask: "Is this really worth it?"

Do not rush into conflict. Honorable people avoid strife. Somehow we have missed this point in much of our living. If I avoid strife I might be viewed as weak or wimpy, but according to God's assessment, it may be the honorable method of dealing with the fight. Fighting becomes very difficult for one person to do alone.

We do not deny that battles, at times, are most appropriate. Our plea focuses on making certain that the worth of conflict justifies the demands of so much expended energy. Not every attack merits retaliation. Avoidance of conflict may be the most expedient way to cope with the contention of another believer.

The writer of Proverbs suggested the avoidance of conflict in the family context. We read, "Better to live in a desert than with a quarrelsome and ill-tempered wife" (Prov. 21:19). As much as a man needs a wife and a woman needs a husband, it is better to be isolated, living in a dangerous desert than to subject oneself to an ill-tempered mate. Charles Bridges in *A Commentary on Proverbs* said:

> It is better to be destitute altogether of the communion of social life, if it must be purchased at so dear a rate as the companionship of one, whose *contentions* will turn every comfort into bitterness.[1]

2. *When God's children reduce their conflict with the Lord, they find even their enemies are at peace with them.* "When a man's ways are pleasing to the Lord, / he makes even his enemies live at peace with him" (Prov. 16:7). At first one might have some trouble with this. How could anyone be persecuted if this verse was really normative for God's child? Bridges helped to clarify these words:

> The best way for *our enemies* to be reconciled to us, is for us to be reconciled to God. All our danger lies in his wrath, not in their anger. No creature can touch us without his permission. Laban followed Jacob as *an enemy,* but was constrained to be *at peace with him.* Esau when about to execute his long-brooded threat, was melted down into brotherly endearment. . . . And such will be the ultimate victory of the Church over all opposition.[2]

Our sovereign God can and often does overrule in the affairs of humankind. Perhaps the strongest principle suggests we should make sure all is well between us and our God when we experience conflict. If our Lord fights the battle for us, the chances of victory are overwhelmingly better than if we attempt to fight the war without His help. Our vertical relationship with God does affect our horizontal association with men and women.

3. *We are personally responsible to control our tempers.* "Better a patient man than a warrior, / a man who controls his temper than one who takes a city" (Prov. 16:32).

In the heat of battle we often find it easy to blame destruction caused by conflict on an adversary. "I yelled at him because he deserved it!" "She was asking for it so I lost my temper!" We seem to blame our opponents when we allow temper to rage out of control. Whether we want to admit it or not, God holds us personally responsible for our words and actions in times of fighting. This verse in Proverbs speaks of contrast: a warrior versus a patient man; taking a city versus controlling our tempers. Most of us would honor the warrior over the patient man or woman. We would view conquering an enemy more desirable than controlling our own tempers. But God reverses the priorities. It is not the outward demonstration of power or strength but the inward demonstration of power or control which He described as better.

4. *Wisdom dictates that we manage conflict in its early stages.* "The beginning of strife is like letting out water, / So abandon the quarrel before it breaks out" (Prov. 17:14, NASB).

When we find ourselves engaged in conflict, we need to determine if we are traveling down a destructive path. If so, the sooner we abandon the quarrel the better. Tension will always be a part of our earthly human experience, but is it building in a certain relationship? If so, we need to confront the other party with the desire to move the conflict toward a win-win solution for both parties. Conflict, like most cancers, can be treated in the early stages. However, our aversion to confrontation lulls us into thinking that maybe it will go away on its own. It will not. If we can adjust the tension in the early phases of conflict, we have a much greater potential for productive management of the conflict.

5. *In any conflict situation hear all sides. Guard against formulating an opinion too early.* "The first to present his case

seems right, / till another comes forward and questions him"
(Prov. 18:17).

Controversy is by nature dialogical. Its existence requires
two antagonistic sides. If we concentrate on just one side of the
issue, we are likely to have a distorted picture of the conflict
experience. In any fight when we hear only one side, it sounds
very persuasive. In the marriage context, either a husband or
a wife can appear totally innocent when only one side of the
conflict is heard. In the chapter entitled "Soul Oneness: II—
Communication, or 'What do I do when I'm angry?'" Larry
Crabb resurrected several common communication problems.
Here are two:

> • "Whenever I try to tell her how I feel, she seems disinter-
>   ested and sometimes critical."
> • "He simply avoids all conversation about us. We can
>   discuss vacation plans, where to send the kids to school,
>   and what car to buy, but he refuses to talk about our
>   relationship."[3]

If you heard only his side of her disinterest and critical
demeanor, you could find yourself quite compliant to his
cause. On the other hand if you listened only to the wife whose
husband avoided any and all conversation about their relationship, you might find yourself totally sympathetic to her
dilemma. Both experience and Scripture demand the hearing
all sides of any conflict situation.

6. *A mutually agreed upon third party or (method) can help
manage the conflict.* "Casting the lot settles disputes / and
keeps strong opponents apart (Prov. 18:18)."

The casting of pebbles (lot) to determine an outcome served
as an objective method to decide what a given solution should
be. The lot was not a chance conclusion since God's sovereign
choice determined the outcome. "The lot is cast into the lap, /
but its every decision is from the Lord" (Prov. 16:33).

The value of a mutually agreed upon third party can assist
in trying to help adversaries work through the conflict process. Compromise in long-standing battles may be best settled
by negotiation regulated by this neutral third party.

7. *Some conflicts are not worth the fight. If it is a win-lose*

situation, and what is being lost does not really matter, then why fight? "A man's wisdom gives him patience; / it is to his glory to overlook an offense" (Prov. 19:11).

Too often in times of contention, we elevate a sense of justice higher than it ought to be. Our cause becomes so noble that we must set the record straight! After all, we do have a reputation to protect! Overlooking "an offense" is more difficult when we are innocent, and our accusers have misrepresented the facts. Somehow we feel compelled to "protect the truth" so that justice prevails at all costs! But maybe we should reexamine an event in David's life.

Absalom had successfully turned the hearts of the people and led a rebellion against his father David who was running for his life. As he left Jerusalem, a man named Shimei pelted David and his men with stones and called down curses upon them. One of David's men wanted to solve the conflict by removing Shimei's head. David illustrated the truth of over-looking this offense:

> David then said to Abishai and all his officials, "My son, who is of my own flesh, is trying to take my life. How much more, then, this Benjamite! Leave him alone; let him curse, for the Lord has told him to. It may be that the Lord will see my distress and repay me with good for the cursing I am receiv-ing today" (2 Sam. 16:11-12).

We would do well to emulate the attitude and action of David as he showed himself gracious to a man who was defi-nitely in the wrong. Patience is part of the fruit of the Spirit God promised us when IIis Spirit controls our lives (Gal. 5:22-23).

8. *By doing something good (nice) for the person we are having conflict with, we reduce destructive conflict.* "A gift given in secret soothes anger, / and a bribe concealed in the cloak pacifies great wrath" (Prov. 21:14).

In general, bribes were condemned in Old Testament time (Deut. 16:19; 1 Sam. 12:3; Eccl. 7:7). Fallen, sinful people appear to have the power to soothe anger by appealing to avarice. How sadly this comments on our human relation-ships.

On a more positive note, generosity and kindness can alleviate the destructive power of great wrath. When we generate more heat than light in any relationship, it is time to try gentleness that the Holy Spirit produces when He takes control of the situation.

9. *Be slow to involve yourself in a quarrel that is not your own.* "Like one who seizes a dog by the ears / is a passer-by who meddles in a quarrel not his own" (Prov. 26:17).

A strong part of every conflict revolves around who defines the relationship. The health of some relationships requires working through conflicts periodically. When an uninvited third person crashes the conflict, usually both adversaries will turn on this intruder. One may mean well and seek to help, but if one has missed the subtle way in which this relationship exists, one's efforts will be futile and perhaps even resented.

An example of this principle may be seen in the family context. Two young brothers may be pounding on each other with as much energy as possible. If someone outside the family attempts to break up the scuffle, both boys could easily turn on this stranger who does not understand how their family communicates. As certainly as grabbing a dog by his ears will create an immediate disturbance, so an intruder entering a conflict episode will experience surprising hostility. We keenly feel our sense of ownership in conflict encounters. Here is the unwritten rule: if it is not your conflict, don't butt in.

10. *Destructive conflict must be fed to continue its existence.*

> Without wood a fire goes out;
>> without gossip a quarrel dies down.
> As charcoal to embers and as wood to fire,
>> so is a quarrelsome man for kindling strife.
>>>> Prov. 26:20-21)

Fuel keeps the interpersonal fire crackling just as dry twigs keep a physical fire burning. Yet, in a conflict someone often stands to gain by maintaining the fight. The primary thought in "quarrelsome" is *contest, discord,* or *brawling.* These persons live to fight. They are not happy unless they have strong contention with someone; they work hard at keeping the destruction of conflict going. They enjoy fighting so much they become warriors for hire. Persons in conflict find help in understanding the adversary if their opponents consistently thrive on the continuation of a destructive battle.

Conflict entered the human experience when sin entered the garden of Eden. The Old Testament record consistently reveals conflict as a reality. Since conflict permeates our lives, the issue becomes constructive or destructive management of conflict in specific instances. Proverbs illustrates both the positive and negative facets of managing conflict. The wisdom of Proverbs guides us toward a constructive use of conflict in addition to warning the reader about the deadly destructive power of mismanaged conflict.

Notes

1. Charles Bridges, *A Commentary on Proverbs* (1846; reprint, Carlisle, Pa.: The Banner of Truth, 1983), 381.

2. Ibid., 231.

3. Lawrence J. Crabb, Jr., *The Marriage Builder: A Blueprint for Couples and Counselors* (Grand Rapids: Zondervan Publishing House, 1982), 63.

14

CONFLICT AND THE NEW TESTAMENT

Opposition and conflict filled the earthly life of Jesus Christ. The religious leaders of His day strongly resisted what Jesus did and who He claimed to be. His teaching of righteousness directly clashed with the message taught by the religious leaders. The Sermon on the Mount provides numerous conflict examples (Matt. 5—7). Repeatedly, Jesus declared, "You have heard that it was said," and, "But I tell you." Both religious leaders and Jesus agreed about the law's value. The conflict became severe when they considered the interpretation and application of the law.

Conflict and the Gospels

Instead of examining the conflict between Christ and the leaders of His day, we will turn our attention to some of the conflict episodes which existed among Christ's followers.

In each of the following accounts we will identify (1) the conflict issue, and (2) what we learn about conflict.

Luke 22:24-27

Also a dispute arose among them as to which of them was considered to be greatest. Jesus said to them, "The kings of the Gentiles lord it over them; and those who exercise authority over them call themselves Benefactors. But you are not to be like that. Instead, the greatest among you should be like the youngest, and the one who rules like the one who serves. For who is greater, the one who is at the table or the one who serves? Is it not the one who is at the table? But I am among you as one who serves.

Conflict issue. On the surface the disciples debated who was the greatest. They attached importance or worth to position. The higher the position, the more importance they granted to it. The question was: "Who would determine greatness?" Did the world around them decide greatness, or were they to use a different standard?

What we learn about conflict. This conflict revealed a deeper problem—role definition. Each wanted his own position viewed as more significant than those of his fellow disciples. Jesus redirected their role definition to servanthood rather than kingship. He clarified for them the definition of leadership-by-servanthood concept.

Conflict frequently helps us unveil a deeper area needing resolution. What pastor has not felt the pangs of watching a fellow minister lead a church which outgrows its facilities while he continues to struggle with the same few people? By what standard do we assess greatness? If we use faithful servanthood criterion, we need to be careful not to confuse "bigness" with "greatness."

On the other hand, smallness may not indicate quality. A small ministry may remain small until God desires it to grow. The closer our leadership parallels that of Jesus Christ, the less we need concern ourselves about largeness and smallness. He calls us to perpetually serve Him in our ministries.

Luke 10:38-42

> As Jesus and his disciples were on their way, he came to a village where a woman named Martha opened her home to him. She had a sister called Mary, who sat at the Lord's feet listening to what he said. But Martha was distracted by all the preparations that had to be made. She came to him and asked, "Lord, don't you care that my sister has left me to do the work by myself? Tell her to help me!"
>
> "Martha, Martha," the Lord answered, "you are worried and upset about many things, but only one thing is needed. Mary has chosen what is better, and it will not be taken away from her."

Conflict issue. The narrative of Mary and Martha shows us conflict over goals. Both women had good objectives in mind. We would commend Martha's untiring service. But we should also applaud Mary's desire to hear the Lord teach and be with Him. The conflict entered when Martha wrongly determined that Mary had made a bad choice. After all, considerable work had to be done, and Mary was doing nothing. The behavior we exhibit exposes the goals we possess and sometimes creates strong conflict. This account shows us the conflict issue of perceived poor choices and incompatible goals.

What we learn about conflict. Role definition and role expectation can be a battle zone for conflict. Each woman read the situation differently. Conflict existed at the assumption level. Martha assumed since what she was doing was correct behavior, Mary ought to do this also. Sometimes we transfer our own goals and objectives to other believers. We see the behavior, but the conflict lies at a far deeper level. When we engage in such unspiritual thinking, we force our set of goals, values, and attitudes on other believers. This can create a deep conflict which we do not easily manage.

Opponents often carry emotional baggage as part of the conflict experience. This surfaces more regularly when combatants on either side of the issue hold legitimate positions. Both Mary and Martha desired a good thing. It would be difficult to criticize Martha's serving heart. Who would tell Mary she ought not to listen to the Savior's teaching? Like Martha, we become more zealous when we know what we are doing is right.

Part of Martha's problem surfaces when she started faulting Jesus. "Don't you care...?" she complained. She felt even Jesus did not seem to understand the burden she carried. Since He said nothing to Mary about working, Martha felt He was not showing adequate concern. At times we can all quickly identify with Martha. Overworked and underpaid we can tolerate, but to be underappreciated calls for more than we can endure. Remember, Martha's solution to get Mary to work was not the direction Jesus took in this conflict. Jesus wanted Martha to realize it is better to *listen and understand* the Lord than to merely *labor and not hear* the Lord.

John 12:1-8

Six days before the Passover, Jesus arrived at Bethany, where Lazarus lived, whom Jesus had raised from the dead. Here a dinner was given in Jesus' honor. Martha served, while Lazarus was among those reclining at the table with him. Then Mary took about a pint of pure nard, an expensive perfume; she poured it on Jesus' feet and wiped his feet with her hair. And the house was filled with the fragrance of the perfume.

But one of his disciples, Judas Iscariot, who was later to betray him, objected, "Why wasn't this perfume sold and the money given to the poor? It was worth a year's wages." He did not say this because he cared about the poor but because he was a thief; as keeper of the money bag, he used to help himself to what was put into it.

"Leave her alone," Jesus replied. "[It was intended] that she should save this perfume for the day of my burial. You will always have the poor among you, but you will not always have me."

Conflict issue. Judas Iscariot raised the question of values. He put high value on the potential money this perfume could bring. Judas attempted to hide his avarice by referring to the poor. However, the Gospel writer revealed Judas as a thief who concerned himself more about wealth than worship. Values and scarce resources emerge as the issues.

What we learn about conflict. Jesus defended the individual who revealed the better set of values. Conflict sometimes has a right side and a wrong side; we do not always experience a win-win situation. Being in tune with God's program compels a person to associate with a definite position. Not to identify with this side would clearly be wrong.

Conflict often reveals a hidden agenda. To Judas the poor represented little value. But if less money were contributed, then he had less to steal. Conflict, like a knife, can cut through superficiality to the essential elements involved. Conflict is dynamic, never static. Hidden agendas quickly appear when conflict drives the communication. If the hidden agenda of a powerful board member aims to place his future son-in-law in the newly created minister of youth position, no other candidate will have the right stuff. Some call this church "politics," and it should be avoided at all costs. Conflict benefits the process by unmasking the dishonesty of the person who tries to implement his or her secret plans. This account also shows us that conflict usually stems from scarce resources. A fixed amount of money, time, people, or space provides the source of the struggle. We may rejoice when someone gives $10,000 to the church with no strings attached. Usually conflict will arise over where, how, and when the money should be used. Immediately our values start to surface. Do we appreciate our relationship with God's people more than our desires for missionary funding?

Matthew 20:1-16

"For the kingdom of heaven is like a landowner who went out early in the morning to hire men to work in his vineyard. He agreed to pay them a denarius for the day and sent them into his vineyard.

"About the third hour he went out and saw others standing in the marketplace doing nothing. He told them, 'You also go and work in my vineyard, and I will pay you whatever is right.' So they went.

"He went out again about the sixth hour and the ninth hour and did the same thing. About the eleventh hour he went out and found still others standing around. He asked them, 'Why have you been standing here all day long doing nothing?'

" 'Because no one has hired us,' they answered.

"He said to them, 'You also go and work in my vineyard.'

"When evening came, the owner of the vineyard said to his foreman, 'Call the workers and pay them their wages, beginning with last ones hired and going on to the first.'

"The workers who were hired about the eleventh hour came and each received a denarius. So when those came who were hired first, they expected to receive more. But each one of them received a denarius. When they received it, they began to grumble against the landowner. 'These men who were hired last worked only one hour,' they said, 'and you have made them equal to us who have borne the burden of the work in the heat of the day.'

"But he answered one of them, 'Friend, I am not being unfair to you. Didn't you agree to work for a denarius? Take your pay and go. I want to give the man who was hired last the same as I gave you. Don't I have the right to do what I want with my own money? Or are you envious because I am generous?'

"So the last will be first, and the first will be last."

Conflict issue. Perceived injustice marked the question: Why didn't we receive more? The workers did not anticipate the outcome. They reasoned, if the person working only one hour received "x" amount of money, then the person who worked eight hours ought to receive "8x" the amount of money. But the owner assured them he could do whatever he wished with his own money. The issue focused on felt injustice. The workers assumed their expectations were in agreement with the owner, but such mutual understanding did not exist.

What we learn about conflict. Conflict often resides in our perspectives. We view the issue from our limited frame of reference. Unfortunately, we make little attempt to understand how someone else might view the same "facts." This produces a deep-seated conflict since it exists at the level of definition and involves a basic value we call justice.

Conflict also revealed the character of those who complained. Their contract was a legitimate one. If the owner decided to be generous to the latter workers, that was his decision. The conflict existed because some workers made the whole payroll their business when only their checks were legitimately their business.

We live in a society which overemphasizes personal rights. The words *I deserve* fall from nearly everyone's lips. Because our culture exhibits so much "me" consciousness, we can easily lose sight of the facts of any situation. The issue of ownership gets lost in our zeal for perceived justice just as it did for these first-century laborers. Conflict forces us to think more clearly in the vital areas of living.

John 21:15-19

When they had finished eating, Jesus said to Simon Peter, "Simon son of John, do you truly love me more than these?"

"Yes, Lord," he said "you know that I love you."

Jesus said, "Feed my lambs."

Again Jesus said, "Simon son of John, do you truly love me?"

He answered, "Yes, Lord, you know that I love you."

Jesus said, "Take care of my sheep."

The third time he said to him, "Simon son of John, do you love me?"

Peter was hurt because Jesus asked him the third time, "Do you love me?" He said, "Lord, you know all things; you know that I love you."

Jesus said, "Feed my sheep. I tell you the truth, when you were younger you dressed yourself and went where you wanted; but when you are old you will stretch out your hands, and someone else will dress you and lead you where you do not want to go." Jesus said this to indicate the kind of death by which Peter would glorify God. Then he said to him, "Follow me!"

Conflict issue. Peter's commitment to the Lord emerges as the theme of this repeated questioning. Christ seems to regularly restore Peter. After Peter denied his Lord, he never again lived with the previous arrogance. He did not continue to boast about his ability to be faithful. The issue appeared to be one of commitment and restoration so that Peter could be the tool God had planned for him to be as we learn in the Book of Acts.

What we learn about conflict. Conflict keenly focuses on past performance which we cannot ignore or slight. We cannot live in the past, but we must recognize what has transpired to make sense of the present and future. Jesus seemed to reinstate Peter to a leadership position. Individual responsibility springs from this narrative. When engaged in conflict, we must personally own our words and behavior.

In this dialogue, notice that the stronger person (Jesus) came to the level of the weaker person (Peter). We should not deem it as weak or wrong when we move to the other person's level. Christ's instructional purposes with Peter focused on the process, not necessarily with the product. Too often in conflict we are blinded by the desired outcome (a win for me), and we miss the value of the process (a learning experience for both).

Conflict and the Epistles

Romans 12:9-21

The following five points flow from this Romans passage:

1. *We find in this passage an environment where destructive conflict would less likely occur.* The commands of this passage

will produce strong relationships among believers. If the alliances suggested in the passage were allowed to develop, we
would not eliminate conflict, but it would help us manage it
more effectively (vv. 9-13).

2. *Each believer has a personal responsibility for being at
peace with all men (vv. 16-18).* Our ability to identify (v. 15)
with other believers will help us establish a position of harmony. Some have confused harmony with unanimity. Music
would be very dull if all we could play were middle C. In
music, harmony represents difference without discord. For
example, one accepted musical key consists of a *C*, an *E*, a *G*,
and another *C*. This sound expresses difference without discord. Some people fail to comprehend that one can differ with
another, yet need not go to war. We should educate our leaders
to expect differences if we want healthy, harmonious relationships.

3. *This passage also focuses on persecution.* Even when
faced with those who persecute you, "bless and do not curse"
(v. 14). The imperative mood tells us no options exist here, God
expects obedience. But when He commands, He also provides
the power to help us obey the command. How much we desire
His purposes to be lived out in our own lives may be the issue.

4. *The passage tells us that God's children must govern their
behavior by doing right, not practicing revenge (v. 17).* The
ugly side of conflict must not be evident in God's child. We are
constantly tempted to fight using the same tactics as the
ungodly, but right behavior still should regulate our conflict
relationships. Our God presents Himself as the Creator, the
Builder of the universe. The Bible pictures Satan as the de-
stroyer, the one who attempts to tear down what God builds.
When engaged in conflict, we need to consider whether we
identify with the actions of God or Satan!

5. *God desires that goodness will continually motivate His
children.* Since the Lord repays vengeance, we cannot take
matters into our own hands. God's ability to set the record
straight far surpasses our puny efforts. We must conquer the
evil around us by the goodness God enables us to do (vv.
19-21). We must depend on the Holy Spirit to produce this
goodness. He must energize us if this goodness will extend to
those who seek only our ruin.

1 Corinthians 6:1-8

This passage highlights two basic truths about conflict.

1. *The issue of conflict in Corinth surfaced in many different ways.* One conflict experience involved going to law before unbelievers when they should have judged their own earthly matters. The proper context was inside the body of believers— not outside before the unbelieving world. Churches today seldom think of themselves as courts. Yet, a legitimate judicial function does exist in any body of believers. We need to be careful how quickly we abandon the collective judgment of the family of God. Conflict should not drive us to outside arbitration, but it should serve as an opportunity for believers to adjudicate their own problems.

2. *The conflict was deeper than the Corinthian believers imagined.* Not only should one of the least of the brethren have been able to judge the disputes, but Paul questioned: "Why not rather be wronged? Why not rather be cheated?" (1 Cor. 6:7). They failed to realize their relationship with a brother was more important than the issue leading them to secular legal proceedings. Conflict's intensity can cloud our judgment and cause us to operate with confused value systems. A well-established priority system must be in place before entering the conflict arena.

Galatians 2:11-21

Six principles about conflict emerge from this passage.

1. *Paul wrote of Peter, "I opposed him to his face" (v. 11).* Paul made the confrontation in person. Correction sometimes demands a face-to-face encounter over wrong behavior. Conflict with Cephas over this issue was the right behavior. While most people do not enjoy face-to-face confrontation, it must be done when needed. Our attitude and manner of approaching the confrontation must include "speaking the truth in love" (Eph. 4:15). If we have truth apart from love, we will be overly harsh with others. If we possess love independent of truth, we will not see the issue correctly. We must balance these two concepts in the time of confrontation.

2. *Peter was not preaching a spurious message, but he had been behaving in a hypocritical manner (v. 12).* Conflict does not always arise because of distinct, doctrinal issues. Most of

the situations we encounter are related to behavior more than belief or doctrine. Peter's inconsistent activity drew the rebuke Paul gave him. The issues with which we grapple today usually relate to something someone said or some unwise act that upsets another believer.

3. *Cephas was a leader.* His behavior was noted and followed by other believers (v. 13). His action distracted others from accepting the full grace of God, even negatively influencing Barnabas. Conflict served as a pointing device to Peter and this group that included Barnabas. Their behavior had to be corrected because the privileged position of leadership could not be taken lightly. God expects more from one who has been entrusted to function as a leader. No one rises to a standard above submission to God and His Word.

4. *Paul demonstrated the value of confronting with others present (v. 14).* The issue of conflict spread beyond a personal confrontation between two first-century leaders. All people involved in any conflict should be present when we manage the conflict. No parties who have valid input should be denied the opportunity of the conflict process.

5. *Paul's question clarified the issue.* "If you, being a Jew, live like the Gentiles and not like the Jews, how is it that you compel the Gentiles to live like Jews?" (Gal. 2:14, NASB). In any conflict situation we must make the issue *clear.* Fighting battles at nonimportant or wrong levels wastes time and energy. Both parties in any conflict circumstance must agree on the essence of the struggle. If the agreed conflict issue possesses perceived potential management, the conflicting parties usually have a clearer picture of where the differences exist.

6. *Paul provided a clear answer to the problem which caused the conflict (v. 20).* The believer relates to Christ on the basis of grace (not law). Righteousness comes from what Christ did on the cross. Our faith in this same Christ who lives within us provides the dynamic for living day by day. Paul did not stop by just pointing out Cephas's wrong. He also desired to correct the wrong behavior in such a way that repeated problems of this nature would not reoccur.

Philippians 1:12-18; 4:2-3

Two significant concepts relevant to conflict surface in the Philippian letter.

1. *Paul admitted that some were preaching Christ out of envy and strife (v. 15).* But the greater issue overshadowed the lesser, personal issue, and Paul determined not to make it a fight (v. 18). Some conflicts we should avoid. The fight is not worth the energy and time that would be demanded. We need the wisdom of the Lord to know when to do battle. As a rule, the issue and the people involved will help us decide if a conflict is worth the time and energy to see it to a workable outcome.

2. *Paul's "true comrade" was to help Euodia and Syntyche live in harmony (4:3, NASB).* Their present conflict was not worthy of the effort they put into it. Paul's plea to confront these ladies was based on past mutual struggles they had experienced in proclaiming the gospel. This "true comrade" was designated as a conflict manager to help reconcile the ladies.

Sometimes we find ourselves embroiled in a conflict not of our own making. As referees we may be drawn into the battle. As distasteful as this may sound, we can have a worthwhile ministry by helping two opposing parties manage their conflict. Your ability to help them come to creative alternatives may be just what God desires. Do not shy away from the ministry of a "loyal yokefellow."

Conclusion

In this chapter we examined some conflict believers of the first-century experienced. Our goal was to whet your appetite so that you can better comprehend what God says about conflict in the New Testament. We discussed the importance of role definition, the level of the conflict issue, values clarified by conflict, scarce resources, and perspectives. Past events can significantly influence our current conflicts.

God's counsels us through these early New Testament believers to manage our conflicts with the Holy Spirit's help so that healthy and spiritual interpersonal relationships will result.

15

ORGANIZATIONAL CAUSES OF CONFLICT

When asked by *Leadership* journal what church people fight about, conflict specialist Speed Leas first responded by identifying four areas of "significant value conflict": social action, liturgy and worship, theology (charismatic verses noncharismatic or conservative versus liberal), and the life-style of the pastor. Pressed for the most significant issue Leas noted:

> The biggest single category—46% of the total cases—involved the pastor's interpersonal *competence*. And this 46% divided equally into two situations. In one (23% of the total), the clergy were withdrawn, apathetic, not taking initiative, not providing any kind of leadership. And the other 23% involved pastors who were contentious and authoritarian.[1]

In their book *Church Fights,* Speed Leas and Paul Kittlaus distinguish three kinds of conflict: "intrapersonal, interpersonal, and substantive."

1. *Intrapersonal conflict:* The contest that one has when different parts of the self compete with one another. (I want to be a beloved pastor, but I also want to be a preacher who speaks the truth.)

2. *Interpersonal conflict:* Personality differences between people that are not related primarily to issues. (I like to think of myself as a strong, independent person, but my administrative board chairperson treats me like an incompetent who must be told what to do.)

3. *Substantive conflict:* Disputes over facts, values, goals, and beliefs. (I think we ought to put a new roof on the church, but the social concerns committee wants to open a clothes closet for the poor).[2]

Conflicts come from every possible sector and from numerous causes. Leadership style itself offers a prime source of conflict since an autocratic leader locates decision making primarily within the self. But organizational fuzziness also creates conflicts. People who do not understand the objectives and direction of the organization experience indifference and a lack of involvement. Richard Patterson wrote:

> Fuzziness is also a culprit in conflict regarding the organization's structure. When line and staff relationships are unclear or when the formal structure is not the way the organization operates (the informal being more effective), considerable chaffing will occur. Ambiguity in the real or perceived structure, tolerance of the informal power to function over the formal power, or too wide a span of control will all produce their own particular conflict difficulties. The professor who is on several committees with various functions may find significant conflict as he attempts to function within an ambiguous organization.[3]

We can get more specific. Certain behaviors in an organization seem to produce interpersonal conflict, and that is precisely that kind of conflict we want to deal with in this chapter.

Confrontation as Conflict

We need to be careful here because confrontation and conflict can be viewed from both negative and positive dimensions. If one Sunday School teacher is unhappy with something said by another, she or he may choose to confront that second person with a defensive spirit thereby creating or at least aggravating conflict. On the other hand, that confrontation might be carried out in the spirit of Matthew 18:15-20 and actually alleviate conflict. Which comes first: conflict or confrontation? That is precisely the point: it could be either, and the careful leader will analyze a given situation to see where the episode stands in its outworking.

Purposeful Deviation

Paul showed us in Philemon that confrontation is also a biblical behavior on the part of leaders. It sometimes becomes necessary because of purposeful deviation on the part of subordinates. The altering of reports or the distortion of events may meet the letter of the law but fail in the spirit of the law. Sometimes subordinates create different power centers in order to seek refuge from the pressure of conflict. Avoiding or ignoring the conflict provides no solution. Ultimately confrontation needs to focus on the source of conflict and deal with it rather than with personalities. Eugene Habecker wrote:

> Confrontation is one of least glamorous and most difficult facets of leadership. It is, however, one of leadership's most necessary and important responsibilities. Failure to confront produces negative results for both persons and the organization. Only as the art of confrontation is carried out under the divine leadership of the Holy Spirit will the kind of personal and organizational results desired by leaders be accomplished.[4]

Levels of Conflict

Wise leaders understand that conflict operates at different levels and that confrontation may very well be best carried out through compromise. Some conflict seems strictly personal (a dad and a daughter debate when she should return from a date) while others spread across the organization and could be called "societal" (a search committee turns down a popular candidate for youth pastor against the wishes of a majority of the congregation). Patterson drew several conclusions from these two levels of conflict.

1. Discern conflict level input.
2. Determine the level at which conflict can best be resolved.
3. Defend for the consequences.
4. Decide whether the issue is worth escalating to a higher level.[5]

Keeping Groups Healthy

In all of this, effective leaders understand their role. Drawing from material by James MacGregor Burns, Speed Leas argued for transforming leadership that raises the level of human conduct and the ethical aspirations of both leaders and subordinates. He suggested that leaders must carry out four functions to keep their conflicting groups healthy:

1. Empower individuals to use their best efforts in the conflict
2. Arouse confidence in the group and its leadership
3. Provide or help the group discover common goals
4. Provide or help the group discover the means of achieving the goals[6]

Criticism and Conflict

We have dealt quite a bit with criticism throughout this study, primarily because it seems such a major part of communication and conflict in leadership roles. Seasoned leaders understand both the give and take of criticism.

Giving and Receiving

Even in criticism (giving and receiving) we keep that central goal clearly in focus. More than ten years ago, John Alexander reminded us:

> Actually, practicing the principles of practical criticism is ultimately a matter of discipleship. God has called us to unity. We really are "one in the spirit" and "one in the Lord." By developing an ability to give and take criticism, we can more fully express that unity before God and reveal that unity before men.[7]

In the present context, it may be necessary to emphasize that either the give or the take may lead to conflict. In giving criticism it is certainly essential to be as objective as possible: speak to the person directly, avoid nagging, deal only with behaviors that can be changed, and avoid the dangerous words *always* and *never*, and, of course, avoid *sarcasm*.

When you become the target of criticism, the practice of Proverbs 15:1 and the exercise of the utmost maturity is crucial. In response we practice Matthew 18:15 and take ourselves immediately into a confrontational mode as described in the paragraphs above.

Irrational Ideas About Leadership

Part of our problem with receiving criticism is that we nourish and cherish false ideas about our leadership roles. In the *Creative Leadership Series,* Speed Leas reviewed Albert Ellis' list of ten most irrational ideas about leadership:

1. It is a dire necessity for an adult to be loved or approved by almost everyone for virtually everything he does.
2. One should be thoroughly competent, adequate, and achieving in all possible aspects.
3. Certain people are bad, wicked or villainous and they should be severely blamed and punished for their sins.
4. It is terrible, horrible, and catastrophic when things are not going the way one would like them to go.
5. Human unhappiness is externally caused and people have little or no ability to control their sorrows or rid themselves of their negative feelings.
6. If something is or may be dangerous or fearsome, one should be terribly occupied with and upset about it.
7. It is easier to avoid facing many life difficulties and self-responsibilities than to undertake more rewarding forms of self-discipline.
8. The past is all-important and because something once strongly affected one's life, it should indefinitely do so.
9. People and things should be different from the way they are, and it is catastrophic if perfect solutions to the grim realities of life are not immediately found.
10. Maximum human happiness can be achieved by inertia and inaction or by passively and uncommittedly enjoying oneself.[8]

Dogmatism and Conflict

People, even leaders, find difficulty in separating words and ideas from their own persons. Everyone in the organization ought to be courteous and practice all the rules of good listening every time they speak; but they do not, nor do we. Furthermore, we may not only waste organizational time but create organizational conflict by insisting on the correctness of our own opinions.

Accurate Assessment

We are not talking here about life-changing theological issues like the doctrine of salvation; we are referring to conversations or reviews of something that has happened in the past: an event, a statistic, or an interpretation of something that was said. Our Western mentality traps us so much into thinking about reasons and motives we convince ourselves that accurate assessment is essential to the ongoing of the organization. Most of the time, of course, it is not.

"The Wrongness of Being Right"

The accuracy of the argument, the designation of who was right and who was not, probably does not make any major difference at the present time or for the future health of the ministry. Ted Engstrom and Edward Dayton have argued the wrongness of being right:

> Being right can be a losing proposition. If you are right all the time, you will intimidate people, and make it all the harder for them to remember the facts or attempt to share them with you. "No sense in telling old-So-and-So. He has his mind made up before you begin." People don't really believe old-So-and-So is right all the time. They just believe that that is what he thinks about himself. People in this situation easily become isolated. And the tragic consequence is that they continue to believe that they are right (most of the time), when in fact the number of opportunities they have to interact with important events become fewer and fewer.
>
> Another problem with a discussion about someone's attempt to be right is that it easily cuts off the creative juices. Remember the rules of brainstorming sessions?: Anything goes. No judgments. Build on one another's ideas. No idea too big or too small or too far out. In other words, no arguments, no concern about being right, just a concern to contribute to the dialogue.[9]

Conflict and Efficiency Breakdown

Earlier in this chapter we mentioned briefly the problem of fuzziness in organizations, particularly with respect to structure and goals. That fuzziness can often result in efficiency breakdown and conflict among the troops. This is particularly problematic among organized people who really care about the organization and therefore it hurts our best people the most. It may help us to remember that "the purpose of the church isn't efficiency; it's developing closer relationships with God and one another. Churches deal in a hard-to-describe and hard-to-measure commodity called spiritual growth. The process of personal growth can rarely be seen as an efficient operation."[10]

Efficiency in Leadership

In such a setting, leadership must explain the deficiencies and take responsibility for them. That is to say, even though the church does not exist to achieve efficiency, efficiency and particularly effectiveness make possible the kind of spiritual growth that Stephen Board described. He went on to correctly observe that:

> All problems are management problems. That doesn't mean they can always be solved by management, but they land on management's plate. Leadership then is the most important clement of any organization. So I believe we find the balance when we give our leaders—whether pastors, Sunday school superintendents, or head ushers—some skill and authority to do their jobs with a heart for people.[11]

Conflict Episode Model

It may be useful here to inject Gerald Wilson's explanation of a conflict episode in which he brings together the issues of "felt conflict," "latent conflict," "perceived conflict," and "manifest" conflict. This is actually the Pondy model, made up of a sequence of conflict episodes following a specific pattern of development. The model begins with the *aftermath* of the preceding conflict episode. Obviously, somewhere along the line there was a first, but each subsequent episode builds on the history of those before it.

Latent conflict is potential conflict which makes its way either to perceived conflict or felt conflict. When we perceive that our goals and intentions fall at cross purposes with the boss or subordinate, we recognize that the potential of conflict

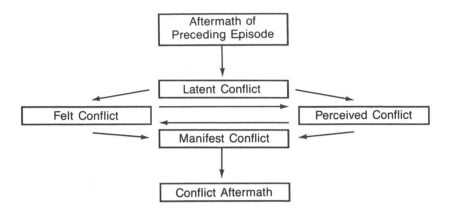

Reprinted from "Organizational Conflict: Concepts and Models" by Louis R. Pondy published in Administrative Science Quarterly (vol. 12, No. 2) by permission of Administrative Science Quarterly.

exists, but we do not necessarily act upon it. In other words, *perceived conflict* is unexpressed and could end right there in the mind of the preceptor.

Felt conflict is personalized. Now we have made the problems our own, and that influences our feelings for the other person. "The double arrow" according to Wilson, "suggests the possibility of movement in either direction." We might perceive conflict and then internalize it, or feel it and depersonalize it to the level of perception only.

The real culprit, of course, is *manifest conflict* which takes feelings and perceptions to the interpersonal level. Now it has become communication behavior and probably communication breakdown. Gerald Wilson described the situation as either-or:

> Conflict can be expressed either with or without language. For example, you may hotly or cooly disagree with another in the context of some meeting. The expression, in this case, is verbal. You are able, also, to state, "I don't want to talk to her about the matter. In fact, I don't want to talk with her at all. Please tell her I am not in." Your friend would certainly get the message that you are expressing conflict with her— especially if she knows and believes that you are, in fact, in your office.[12]

The *aftermath* can be positive or negative—breaking up or making up. Obviously, wise leaders have redemptive goals. They understand conflict management strategy and the consequences of using it. They attempt to center the issue on goals and behavior rather than feelings and emotions. They allow all concerned people to speak as openly and forcefully as they wish. They avoid forcing strategies like manipulation, nonnegotiation, personal rejection, and emotional appeal. They avoid lose-lose or win-lose methods and focus on win-win methods which center in understanding and a mutual agreement to solve the problem.

We have drawn generously on Speed Leas in this chapter, and that may be a good place to end. He describes the importance of the leader serving as model in conflict settings:

> The way you are aware of yourself in conflict will profoundly affect your ability to manage yourself and work with others in the midst of a conflict. . . .
> The power of this kind of leadership is twofold. Part of the power is in the long-term effects it has on the decisions being made—where the office will be, who stays on the staff, and what the program will be—and the other part of the power is the profound effect it has on others [who watch the modeling behavior of the leader].[13]

Notes

1. Speed Leas, "Inside Church Fights," *Leadership,* Winter 1988, 14-15.

2. Speed Leas and Paul Kittlaus, *Church Fights: Managing Conflict in the Local Church* (Philadelphia: Westminster Press, 1973), 29-32.

3. Richard Patterson, "Leadership Conflict in Higher Education," unpublished resource paper, October 1977, 5.

4. Eugene B. Habecker, *The Other Side of Leadership* (Wheaton: Victor Books, 1987), 102.

5. Patterson, 14.

6. Speed B. Leas, *Leadership and Conflict* (Nashville: Abingdon Press, 1982), 29.

7. John Alexander, *Practical Criticism,* IVP, 1976, 30.

8. Leas, *Leadership and Conflict,* 56-57.

9. Ted W. Engstrom and Edward R. Dayton, "The Wrongness of Being Right," *Christian Leadership Letter,* March 1980, 2.

10. Stephen Board, "Why Isn't the Church Efficient?" *Lay Leadership,* premier issue, 26.

11. Ibid., 27.

12. Gerald L. Wilson, et al., *Interpersonal Growth Through Communication* (Dubuque, Iowa: William C. Brown Publishers, 1985), 261.

13. Leas, *Leadership and Conflict,* 82-85.

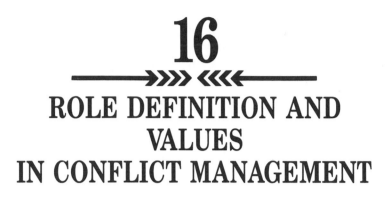

16

ROLE DEFINITION AND VALUES IN CONFLICT MANAGEMENT

This chapter focuses on two primary areas. The first centers on conflict and role definition. The second area features values as they relate to conflict. These areas are not mutually exclusive. How we define our roles in conflict depends on what we value. Put another way, what we value shows through the roles we see as viable in any communication context.

A high value attached to "peaceful relationships" certainly dictates what role a person will assume in the conflict process. Some hostility may be expressed by those fighters who simply enjoy a good fight. They value a healthy debate and will argue an opposite point just for the sake of argument. They reveal values through the way they define their roles.

Conflict and Role Definition

To understand the connection between conflict and role definition we must first comprehend at least three definitions:

"A role is a set of norms that applies to a specific subclass within the society."[1] Please note this definition does not tell us who establishes the "set of norms." It simply states that they exist. The second implication of this definition suggests that a role has a bearing on a "specific subclass" within society in general. We can identify both the subgroups and their appropriate set of norms.

"Interrole conflict is when two (or more) roles representing contradictory expectations about a given behavior are expected."[2] This definition reveals three implications which focus on the words *two (or more) roles, contradictory expectations,* and *a given behavior.* At times multiple roles have conflict built into them. Picture a boy who does not get along with his mother but relates well to his father. Add to the scene a husband who has a fine relationship with his wife. This man will have interrole conflict. At some point in time his role as husband will conflict with his role as father.

A biblical example of interrole conflict surfaces in the small letter Paul wrote to Philemon. When we think of Philemon and Onesimus, we remember Onesimus, the runaway slave, had escaped from his master and probably stolen something as he departed (Philem. 18). Paul led Onesimus to the Lord and then sent him back to Philemon, his master.

Philemon could have struggled with an interrole conflict. On the one hand, he viewed himself as Philemon the slave owner while on the other hand he was Philemon the believer. Paul made his appeal for Onesimus on the basis of Philemon's defined role as a believer. As such, Philemon would receive Onesimus, not as a runaway slave but as a fellow believer in Jesus Christ.

"Intrarole conflict comes when there are conflicting expectations concerning a single role."[3] The implications of this definition are twofold. First, it involves a single role instead of multiple roles. Second, clear conflicting expectations exist in this single role. More than one child has faced this problem early in life. The father says one thing while the mother says another. The role for this little girl is a daughter in either instance, but she has intrarole conflict since the expectations disagree.

A biblical example of intrarole conflict can be seen in the life of Jesus Christ. As He performed His many miracles, He gave adequate evidence of His role as the promised Messiah of the Old Testament, the sovereign Ruler the people had long awaited. But as Messiah, His role also included the suffering Redeemer. In both instances He fulfilled the role of the promised Messiah. The conflict came when the people did not recognize that the sovereign One would also suffer. They missed the suffering element in their expectations.

Role Definition as a Control

A role exerts certain pressure on the individual. Expectations come from what the group defines as your role. If the people of a church view the role of youth pastor as less experienced, less knowledgeable, and less spiritual, the facts will not matter. The youth pastor may have been in the Lord's work for 15 years, hold a master of theology degree, and demonstrate clear godly character. Yet the pastor who has only 10 years of experience, a Bible school diploma, and a glaring deficiency in his prayer life will still be considered the better man when role expectations determine the viewpoint. The controls are built into the system. The situation can change, but initially the definition of the role governs the perspective.

William Brooks and Philip Emmert underscore the power of the perceived role by saying:

> This is an outgrowth of a person's interaction with his or her culture and his or her peer group in which the group, the culture, the individual's sex, his abilities, and so forth, create a role for the individual just as an actor has a role in a play. Our role defines what we can and cannot do. The role defines what we can and cannot say. The role defines what we are and what we might become. When we act outside of our role, society brings pressure to bear to cause us to go back to that role and engage in the proper behaviors appropriate to it.[4]

As early as Genesis, biblical examples show us how society brought pressure causing a person to live inside the expected role behavior. At age seventeen Joseph dreamed of his brothers' sheaves of grain bowing down to his sheaf of grain. His second dream revealed the sun, moon, and eleven stars bowing down to him. His brothers hated him when he shared these dreams with them. Even his father rebuked him and questioned Joseph, "What is this dream you had? Will your mother and I and your brothers actually come and bow down to the ground before you?" (Gen. 37:10). The society around Joseph did its utmost to bring him back to reality.

From a human point of view the fulfillment of this dream appeared extremely remote. Brothers who hate us just do not bow down to us! Or do they? History reveals Joseph's dream was God's revelation in advance. When a sovereign God arranges the circumstances, the unlikely becomes likely. Joseph's brothers did journey to Egypt and bow before Joseph because God ordained it to happen. But the point of introducing this account is to note the strong effort by Joseph's family to bring him back to "normal" role expectations.

Role Definition as a Predictor of Behavior

Role definitions condition us to look for consistency within our set categories. Our interaction with others establishes whether we perform a role appropriately or not. We then set a category after repeated observation of role behavior. For example, if a child's observation and life experience indicate firmness in a "father," when he becomes a father, he will probably demonstrate firmness. Admittedly, the supernatural work of the Holy Spirit and the Word of God can temper firmness with tenderness. From the human perspective, one will perform the role one has learned.

When we apply this to conflict, then family, environment, and history become quite important. If one's spouse grew up in a house where the person who shouted the loudest won the fight, this type of behavior is likely to surface when conflict issues arise. If a wife watched her mother pout to get her way and the father always acquiesced, it will come as quite a surprise when this strategy does not work with her new groom. A congregation may be baffled when they withhold affection from their pastor, and he continues to serve them. This is especially true if this always worked before when the leaders wanted to rid the church of a pastor.

How do we set up these categories in which we look for consistent behavior? Past research has indicated our process of categorization:

1. Role response linked to family context 70%
2. Role response linked to occupation 68%
3. Role response linked to marital status 34%
4. Role response linked to religion...........................30%[5]

Notice that family and occupation lead the field in establishing our role responses.

Role Definition as Mutually Defined

In communication conflict a sense of interdependency exists. How one person defines a role may vary greatly from how one's opponent defines the role. Over time, each party in the potential conflict may change the definition of the role each brings to the battlefield.

This is complicated further by the fact that each may understand perfectly one's own role and the role of the other individual, yet the conflict may still exist. For productive management of conflict, each person involved must exhibit minimal agreement in this area of role definition. Note the following three principles:

1. If we are in conflict, the closer my role definitions and your role definitions agree, the greater the possibility for effective management of the conflict. Note the plural in "definitions." I must be clear in my part and in my definition of your part while at the same time you must be clear in your definition of your part and how you define my part. In conflict we may not agree on many things, but clarity is required at the definition level.

2. The more congruent my actual behavior and the mutually defined roles, the greater likelihood of beneficial management of the conflict. Conflict is tough enough to work through by itself. Surprises brought about when one member does not agree with role expectations will complicate the process.

3. The older we become, the closer our actual behavior is expected to match our role-defined behavior. Children can experiment with many acceptable behaviors, and society will describe them as funny or cute. Adults are not given this freedom. Predictability becomes more expected with the passing years.

Conflict and Values

Since conflict activity usually revolves around scarce resources, a reading of values (yours and your opponent's) surfaces rapidly when conflict is present. It may focus on money, people, or space, but the struggle requires you to validate why you hold your position. Therefore, what you value rises to the top. The clearer the honest communication about your values, the greater potential for positive management of conflict.

Values Revelation

When we play games or choose to hide our values, they become difficult to read and have a harder time surfacing in our conflict experience. Even when we do decide to allow others to see a clear picture of our values, we label the choices "good," "better," or "best." If we have difficulty sorting the good from the better and better from the best, we may not initially be as honest and open as we should. For example, if I value a youth program over a music program, I am not consciously opposed to music. But when limited money is available, I will cast my vote for camp scholarships and not for new choir robes.

Comparison strikes at the heart of values. Many different degrees may exist in this comparison. For example, when conflict occurs between the youth people and the music people, a person may vote 51 percent of the time for youth and 49 percent of the time for music. However, the individual will be perceived by the music people as against music. If our fictitious church leader had voted 95 percent of the time for youth endeavors and 5 percent of the time for music projects, he would still wear the labels "Pro-youth" or "Anti-music." The person will probably not perceive self as against music but rather making difficult decisions between two good values.

This can be further complicated by the size of each conflict issue. For a leader to vote five percent of the time for music may appear quite different when everyone considers the issue important. If the decision centers on hiring a music person before a youth person, a positive vote would carry far more weight than a conflict over which group will use the gym Friday night.

This could also reveal a problem of consistency in any leader's value system. It would be wonderful if we always made our decisions on solid, logical interpretations of the needs and resources of the local body of believers. However, at times decisions are motivated by the emotional forces within us rather than cognitive consideration.

Values Clarification

All communication has some clarification of values. We cannot communicate without illuminating our value system to some extent. Both the verbal and nonverbal cues communicate how much or how little value a person attaches to the communicated message. The question in most instances deals with how well we clearly communicate our values. Conflict functions to put the values into sharper focus.

Our value of security goes on display when we find ourselves in a fight. While under attack, we will look quickly for a haven if we highly prize personal security. Our value of security influences the conflict management style we employ. If we appreciate the communication processes which govern the conflict episode, we will likely be more patient during the struggle demanded as we seek to manage the conflict.

On the other hand, if we have less regard for the communication process, the other party, or the conflict issue, impatience will probably characterize our approach. When one of the conflicting individuals repeatedly supports his or her arguments with how much money the other party's ideas will cost, it soon becomes obvious that one highly values money. In most conflict episodes, values surface clearly when the dialogue is examined closely.

An Exercise in Value Clarification

As you review the following conversation, what values do you hear? The scene will picture two men: (1) a pastor and (2) a layman we will call "Mr. Brown." The setting is the pastor's office. Mr. Brown and the pastor will reveal some shared values. Some values will be unique to the pastor, and Mr. Brown will unveil some values he alone holds. So you should be looking for (1) shared values; (2) the pastor's values; and (3) Mr. Brown's values.

The imaginary conversation looks like this:

PASTOR: Won't you come in, Mr. Brown? May I hang up your hat and coat? I have some fresh coffee on the table: Would you like a cup?

BROWN: No thank you, I'm trying to cut back on my coffee intake.

PASTOR: I've really appreciated your faithful attendance during these cold winter months. How's the family doing?

BROWN: Oh, they are doing fine. We all dearly love this church. The kids would put up a fuss if we didn't come every week. The Sunday School teachers seem to be doing a great job.

PASTOR: When you phoned me you said there was a matter troubling you that you needed to talk to me about. How can I help you?

BROWN: Well, Pastor, my wife and I are quite upset with the way the morning services have been conducted. We just don't seem to do things the way we used to do them. Why, I remember when every Sunday morning worship service started with the Doxology. We never sing it anymore.

PASTOR: I know; lately the music director and I have tried to vary our corporate worship service so that we don't find ourselves in a rut. We want to lead our people in expressing meaningful worship rather than falling into a routine.

BROWN: Well, Pastor, it is not just the Doxology. The wife said just the other day that we don't seem to know anybody who attends church anymore. We have so many strangers coming it doesn't seem like our church now.

PASTOR: Our attendance has been increasing. The Lord has really been blessing us with new people. Have you noticed our overall attendance is up about 50 people in our services the last few months? We have a lot to be thankful for.

BROWN: I know it is good to grow, but the wife and I have also noticed the sermons rarely teach us anything new. What about the 150 people who have been attending all along? Shouldn't we be fed something from the pulpit too?

PASTOR: Yes, of course, you should. I feel badly that you don't think you are obtaining any spiritual food from our Sunday worship service. But surely you would agree that we do have to explain the basics of the Bible to these new people, wouldn't you?

BROWN: Sure, they have to be fed too. But couldn't they come to a special class designed just for them?

PASTOR: Well, we've had so many coming lately, I haven't been able to schedule a time when I could meet with all of them. Since our other adult workers are loaded to the limit, we haven't been able to get a class started either.

BROWN: It seems like we ought to have some changes made on Sunday mornings. My grandparents, my parents, and now the wife and I have faithfully put our money in this church for years. Now it seems we are supporting something we receive very little benefit from. Frankly, we are unhappy about it all!

Shared Values

Did you notice some mutual values the pastor and Mr. Brown expressed? (1) Both thought regular attendance was important. (2) The good of the church seemed to be shared by both men. (3) Concern for Mr. Brown's family was a common value. (4) How the morning service was conducted appears to have been mutually important. (5) Each man admitted the Sunday morning service had changed from what it was. (6) The pastor and Mr. Brown both spoke positively about growth. (7) Both men agreed that all people attending should be spiritually fed from the pulpit.

The Pastor's Values

(1) From the beginning of the appointment the pastor valued Mr. Brown's comfort. He hung up his visitor's coat and offered him coffee. The pastor appeared to desire that this meeting be as informal as possible. (2) The pastor valued the extra effort the Browns had put forth to attend the church. (3) The pastor valued Mr. Brown's coming to him. He took the initiative so Mr. Brown could express what was troubling him. (4) Clearly, both the pastor and music director valued change and "meaningful worship" rather than the routine. (5) He saw benefit to having more people attend the worship service and considered it important to meet their needs in this service. (6) The pastor attached value to qualified persons who would lead these new people.

Mr. Brown's Values

(1) He apparently believed some good could come from bringing this problem to the pastor's attention. If he saw the situation as hopeless, he would not have bothered to make the phone call and keep the appointment with the pastor. (2) He valued his health. At least he was trying to "cut back on" his "coffee intake." (3) He valued what his kids thought about the church. This was interpreted as "the Sunday School teachers" doing a great job. (4) He valued the way the morning service was conducted in the past. He could be called a protector of the status quo. History was important to him. (5) He wanted to know those with whom he worshiped, though he may not have been skilled enough in interpersonal relationships to progress

very far in this direction. Even so, he did not want to worship with strangers. (6) He desired a pulpit ministry that would teach him new truths. He assumed the other 150 people felt as he did. (This may or may not have been true.) (7) He associated money with what he thought he deserved. In so many words, he did not sense a return on his investment. He did not ask what he could do to minister; he looked for the pastor to minister to him and his wife.

In this chapter we discussed two concepts vitally related to communication conflict. We defined role definition; we viewed it as a control, a predictor of behavior, and examined the worth of mutual definition. If we understand the role each person brings to the battle, we will find the positive management of conflict more likely.

We also linked conflict to the concept of values. We looked at how they surface, what they clarify, and introduced an exercise in value clarification. Since conflict frequently occurs at the level of values, we need to probe beneath the surface if we want to skillfully manage conflict.

Notes

1. Stewart L. Tubbs and Sylvia Moss, *Human Communication: An Interpersonal Perspective* (New York: Random House, Inc., 1974), 177.

2. Ibid., 178.

3. Ibid.

4. William D. Brooks and Philip Emmert, *Interpersonal Communication* (Dubuque, Iowa: William C. Brown Company Publishers, 1976), 23-24.

5. Michael Argyle, *Social Interaction* (New York: Atherton Press, 1969), 133.

17

POWER IN CONFLICT MANAGEMENT

You may immediately find the words *power* or *conflict* negative expressions which ought not to be part of a believer's life. Before you toss them aside, an examination of what they represent might be in order.

The Concept of Power

Power should be viewed as the ability to influence the other person(s) with whom we experience conflict. At the heart of power in conflict situations, we discover the persuasive ability of discussion and argument. Since power may be used positively or negatively, it becomes neither morally right nor wrong. Joyce Frost and William Wilmot have noted, "Power is necessary to move a conflict along to some kind to productive management."[1] The desire and opportunity to influence other individuals with whom we struggle must be present, or conflict has become nothing more than two independent monologues.

It helps to remember that power or influence constantly permeates the conflict process. How we use this influence in the conflict encounter becomes the critical issue. This chapter gives attention to six conflict and power areas: (1) the denial of power; (2) the definition of power; (3) how power operates; (4) types of power or influence; (5) the measurement of power/influence; and (6) the sharing of power/influence.

The Denial of Power

The person who claims to have the least amount of influence may not, in fact, be exercising the lesser amount of power. The subtlety of claiming less power may be more effective than the strategy of openly acknowledging the possession of power. Research indicates that manipulation by the use of covert power will usually prevail over the opponent who overtly seeks to display power.[2] Denial of power or influence in conflict situations usually occurs in one of four ways:

1. *One denies responsibility for communicating something.* Examples of such statements are: "That is not what I said," or, "You never heard that from me!" This person makes the point that the data belongs to someone else, not him.

2. *One denies that something was communicated.* This sounds like: "He is just making that up," or, "I never heard of such a thing." Such a denial pertains to the information itself, claiming it does not exist.

3. *The message sender denies that the message was intended for the person who received it.* A person using this denial might verbalize it as: "Sure I said it, but I wasn't referring to her," or, "I didn't have him in mind. I was speaking of people in general." The other approach may try to clarify another specific target or may try to generalize the facts in question.

4. *One denies the context in which it was communicated.*[3] This may find expression as: "But you don't understand what we said right before and after that comment," or more generally, "You had to be there to understand." This denial focuses on information marked as missing to the person who has been offended by certain words.

Power Is Defined Within the Relationship

At times we may refer to power as located within an individual (for example, "Paul is a powerful person"). But Joyce Frost and William Wilmot have correctly observed that influence is "a property of the social relationship rather than a quality of the individual."[4] The context of the conflict remains the determining element in understanding the meaning of the power variable. The influence of an elder who possesses the highest status will carry a considerable amount of value in the meeting of the elders. But, if he also happens to be the poorest volleyball player in the church, his influence during a game of volleyball at a church-wide picnic will be radically reduced. *When the context changes, the variable of power also changes.*

How Power Operates

Six primary elements summarize the role of power in conflict:

1. *The conflicting parties are interdependent.* This is basic to our understanding of conflict. Each needs the other and cannot survive without the other. If for no other reason, each needs an enemy to attack.

2. *Each person possesses resources upon which the other person is dependent to reach his or her goals.* These resources vary widely. It could be someone's influence on somebody else. It could be money, expertise, experience, status—the list goes on. But my goal cannot be reached unless I obtain this resource from you. Somehow I must persuade you to cooperate and give me what is needed to achieve my goal.

3. *When one person can influence the goal attainment of another, he or she has power over that person.* When Nabal belittled David after he protected Nabal's flocks free of charge, David established a clear, achievable goal to kill every male of Nabal's household as swiftly as possible (1 Sam. 25:34). Abigail's ability to influence David against this goal pictures the power she had over him. She was literally able to stop David from vindicating himself by the words she said and the gifts she brought him. She acted swiftly and decisively to avert David's sure revenge which would have exterminated her family.

When we study this scriptural account (1 Sam. 25:23-31), certain facts stand out. (1) Abigail does not appear powerful as we usually think of power. She bowed down, fell at David's feet, called him lord, and pleaded for David to listen to her. (2) She assumed responsibility for the *faux pas* of a wicked and foolish man. Many people think a powerful person would have distanced herself as rapidly as possible from Nabal, instead of taking responsibility for his actions. (3) She was generous with her praise and tangible gifts and pleaded for forgiveness from David. So often, we think of powerful people as receiving, not giving. (4) She recognized God had tremendous plans for this man named David: "a lasting dynasty for my master, because he fights the Lord's battles" (1 Sam. 25:28). Abigail seemed to be the only person in Nabal's family who understood what God was about to do through this David whom many in Israel must have considered to be only an outlaw.

4. *Each person in conflict has some degree of power.* No one is totally powerless. If one party has no power, the conflict does not and cannot occur. Certainly, one party may have *more* power when compared to the other, but each of the conflicting parties possesses some influence. When we see great disparity of power, it may appear as if one of the opponents has very little. But even when a dictatorial nation totally suppresses a revolt or rebellion, history indicates that the seeds will germinate and come to life again.

Power bases can and often do shift during the course of a conflict. People take constant readings during the actual struggle of a given conflict. The ebb and flow changes the power bases as some grow stronger while others weaken.

5. *People in conflict make choices which define power either as equal or unequal.* Those with more influence can decide to share power by changing the structure of the relationship. This usually must come from the top down if any sharing of power is to be meaningful. At times "token" sharing or a false indication of sharing may be nothing more than a strategic ploy until our opponents can fire their big guns and wipe us out.

6. *The productive use of power to achieve both individual and relational goals requires a skill which we can learn.* When others insist that the power structure cannot be changed, usually we will find them gaining something from the present power structure which they do not intend to lose. Most conflicts do not develop so rigid a structure that change cannot occur. We should remember that changes during conflict situations reveal an incremental pattern which takes more time than we originally plan. The deeper and more ideological the conflict, the slower the process of change. This may help to explain why churches split rather than work through deep-seated conflicts.

Power and *dependence* are closely connected. *The power or influence* one person has over another person *is equal to the dependence* the latter has on the first. Power requires dependence, and dependence finds power a necessary part of the equation. One additional refinement is important. The person in conflict depends upon the other person to the extent that (1) *the other person can influence* the first person's goals, and (2) *other avenues are available* for the first person to realize personal goals or objectives.[5] If you find yourself in conflict with someone who holds the *only* key to completing your goal, you may find yourself rechecking the importance of that goal.

For example, we may assume a wife has a goal of staying married till death, but conditions became so ugly and unlivable she opts for a divorce. She has changed her original goal (staying married) since her husband held the exclusive key to her seeing that goal fulfilled. Any dependent person may find life so difficult that goal changes occur in order to relieve the dependency.

We also reduce power when other avenues appear to achieve our personal goals. The elementary school football coach loses influence if Johnny's personal goals can be adequately fulfilled by playing trumpet in the elementary band.

Types of Power or Influence

R. P. French and B. Raven (1960) have isolated five types of power.[6]

Reward Power

With reward power something valued by A is held by B. Therefore B holds "reward power" over A.

We find one of the first examples of reward power when Esau despised his birthright and sold it to his brother for a bowl of soup (Gen. 26:29-34). Esau held reward power over Jacob since he possessed the birthright which Jacob wanted. Through Jacob's cunning behavior, he received the reward of the birthright because Esau treated it as insignificant compared to his physical needs. Esau, described as godless (Heb. 12:16), did not appreciate the power he possessed. The coveted birthright channeled the covenant promises of God through Abraham, Isaac, and now Jacob.

A more contemporary picture of reward power might be seen when a nominating committee member holds the power to place or not place a certain name on an election ballot.

Coercive Power

This is the opposite of reward power. Some punishment could be given to A by B. Thus B holds influence over A.

In a sense the Lord used coercive power over Israel. In the conditional covenant concerning their stay in the land God had promised, Moses solemnly warned them of the lethal destruction which disobedience would bring:

> The Lord will drive you and the king you set over you to a nation unknown to you or your fathers. There you will worship other gods, gods of wood and stone. You will become a thing of horror and an object of scorn and ridicule to all nations where the Lord will drive you (Deut. 28:36-37).

> The alien who lives among you will rise above you higher and higher, but you will sink lower and lower. He will lend to you, but you will not lend to him. He will be the head, but you will be the tail (Deut. 28:43-44).

> Because you did not serve the Lord your God joyfully and gladly in the time of prosperity, therefore in hunger and thirst, in nakedness and dire poverty, you will serve the enemies the Lord sends against you. He will put an iron yoke on your neck until he has destroyed you (Deut. 28:47-48).

God used the powerful motivation of impending punishment for disobedience if His people did not cooperate with His expectations of what their behavior should be in the land.

In our current day, coercive power is exercised when sinning believers persist in their sins after the process of Matthew 18:15-17 has been completed. Leadership within a biblical church must act in loving discipline and exclude the persistent sinning brother from the assembly of believers.

Legitimate Power

Here both A and B agree that B has authority or power over A. Some other external considerations have established the ranking or hierarchy which both have accepted.

In the last few chapters of Genesis, Joseph had risen to the highest possible position under Pharaoh. The "external" government had invested him with this supreme standing. Joseph's brothers now admitted and recognized Joseph as their ruler. We see the convincing evidence of Joseph's legitimate power in their coming to him after the death of Jacob and presenting what they said was a last request of their father: " 'I ask you to forgive your brothers the sins and wrongs they committed in treating you so badly.' Now please forgive the sins of the servants of the God of your father" (Gen. 50:17).

Legitimate power can be seen in the leader's role in the local church (Heb. 13:17). The member who understands submission and practices obedience to godly leadership demonstrates awareness of God's design.

Referent Power

This influence arises when A strongly desires to be like B. B holds an inherent power over A who thinks of B as a more godly, mature, spiritually successful person.

The Paul-Timothy mentor relationship provides us with a good picture of referent power. What Timothy saw and learned from Paul he was to reproduce in other men who could reproduce it in others (2 Tim. 2:2).

In many ways each individual recorded in Hebrews 11 would serve as a person with referent power to the growing spiritual believer today.

When one leads a person to Jesus Christ, a certain amount of referent power seems inherent in the relationship. The new believer (A) strongly desires to spiritually grow and develop into the man or woman of God (B) that the witness is. The believer who models the life of a Christian to a new convert demonstrates referent power in excellent fashion.

Expert Power

Some special skill or ability is possessed by B but not by A. Therefore, A is dependent upon B.

The Old Testament connection between Abram and Lot seems to illustrate the principle of expert power. Abram's reliance on God set him apart from other people living in his day. Lot found himself dependent on Abram even after they had separated and gone different ways. In Sodom, Lot was captured by a federation of kings (Gen. 14:1-16) who defeated the people of Sodom. Abram, taking his 318 trained men from his own household, rescued Lot by defeating these powerful kings who had devastated Sodom.

In a less obvious fashion Lot's dependency on Abram can be seen as Abram pleaded for the sparing of Sodom. Perhaps Abram believed that Lot's presence surely would account for ten righteous individuals. But ten could not be found, and Lot barely escaped with his life and two daughters. Lot was dependent on Abram who had the special skill or ability to believe God and be used by Him.

Today, expert power may best be noticed by individual church members who lack homiletical skills or language proficiency. They find themselves dependent upon Christian leaders who may be the author, the raditelevision preacher, or individual scholar skilled in languages or people skills.

The Measurement of Power or Influence

If we are to productively engage in conflict, it helps to correctly assess our power in any given relationship. No magic formula exists to determine this estimate. Even so, the following questions may prove beneficial:

1. *Who appears to be the most powerful?* The designated leader often is not. To understand how power functions we need to observe the communicative patterns which emerge from actual interactions during conflict. Does one person rely on the other to reach a final decision? Quantity of comments does not always influence the final outcome of a discussion. Are more questions targeted to one person than the others? This may help clarify who has the power to move the group forward.

2. *Who accommodates the most?* Usually the more accommodation, the less the influence or power. This must be true accommodation, not just a temporary ploy to survey the enemy.

3. *What are the patterns of power in the relationship?* Look for relational patterns. This means we focus on the "interacts" not just the "acts" in the conflict situation. We do not just examine a message sent and received. We also consider the receiver of the message as a sender. We focus on communication as a two-way street. In each interaction the sender de-

clares a message which affects the receiver who, in turn, transmits a message back to the sender. This loop forms the "interact" and establishes a pattern. Whoever sets the pattern usually exercises the more power.

4. *Who can best predict changes in power relationships?* To be able to anticipate what the opponent will do or say gives one a relational awareness advantage that allows for more power to be exercised. Effective predictors quickly obtain the upper hand in most conflict struggles. They have so well anticipated our arguments, they are not only ready for them, but they have formulated excellent answers to them.

5. *What decisions reveal a complex ritualized pseudopower relationship?* This occurs when we perceive the decision has been made in advance. Decision making becomes more of a ritual that has no significance to the actual problem since the solution was determined long before the conflict occurred. When we fall victim to this, we sense we have been cheated because the opponent fought unfairly. The conflict experience became a game of pretend rather than an actual conflict. When we overuse this strategy we usually create greater, more difficult conflict problems.

6. *Who is invested in maintaining the power relationship at its present status, and why?* Here we are seeking to discover who benefits most from things remaining as they are in the relationship. The importance of this question may best be seen by what happens when it is *not* asked and answered. The power and function of coalitions come rapidly into the conflict process.

7. *Where are the possibilities for change in the power structure?* You are looking for areas of negotiation which previously may not have been recognized. These "change areas" are areas of mutual interdependence. The hope of positive conflict management lies in the answer to this question.

8. *Who exercises the right to label the conflict?* The first one to mark the communication as "conflict" may be using a power tactic. However, a person sensing higher power in the relationship might deny the presence of conflict. He could demand that the other go away and pretend no conflict exists. This person demonstrates greater influence since he has refused to allow the communication relationship to be defined as conflict.

9. *Who demonstrates the least interest?* If one individual appears to show less interest, this might indicate power since this individual demonstrates less dependence on the relationship. She does not seem to have as much invested in the relationship, so therefore a loss would not be felt as keenly. She can risk more which means greater freedom in the conflict process. This freedom translates to an increase in power or influence.

The Sharing of Power or Influence

Usually influence in any conflict situation needs to be shared by the participants. Where an equal sharing of power exists, the chances of a negotiated settlement are much higher. Three principles emerge from the concept of shared power/influence:

1. *Conflict participants have a better opportunity to make a long-range relationship work if some equity of power exists in the relationship.* Married couples have learned the value of give and take. Over time each of these partners exercises influence over the other. Even with the most dominant of personalities, some sharing or influence must come if the marriage is to function at all in the direction God intended. This may be at the core of what Paul wrote to the church in Ephesus: "Submit to one another out of reverence for Christ" (Eph. 5:21). To submit is to allow the power or influence of the other to rule.

2. *The effective use of power/influence includes restraint in its use in order that it can be retained.* The argument Paul used when referring to questionable activities supports this principle. There is a big difference between "I can, but I won't" and "I cannot." Somewhere in those two statements lies the difference between liberty and legalism.

3. *It is not the powerful, but the powerless who become the most violent.* This fact sobers us as we reflect on its veracity. Judas Iscariot may have felt a sense of powerlessness when it became clear that Jesus of Nazareth was not going to use His miraculous power to throw off the Roman oppression. In Judas's powerlessness he took violent action as he sold out to the enemies of Jesus Christ.

Frustration due to lack of perceived power may have turned more than one person to a life of drugs, crime, and violent behavior.

In every conflict situation we seek to influence the adversary toward our positions. We discover power at the core of the choices we make during conflict. Since we function in a relational interdependence, we can and do mediate the goal attainments of each other. Therefore we need a clear understanding of power relations which will open up new options for our conflict behaviors.[7]

Notes

1. Joyce Hocker Frost and William W. Wilmot, *Interpersonal Conflict* (Dubuque, Iowa: William C. Brown Publishers, 1978), 47.

2. See Everett Shostrom's *Man, the Manipulator: The Inner Journey from Manipulation to Actualization* (Nashville: Abingdon Press, 1967) for a fuller discussion of this concept.

3. Jay Haley, "An Interactional Description of Schizophrenia," *Psychiatry* 22 (1959):321-332.

4. Frost and Wilmot, *Interpersonal Conflict*, 51.

5. R. M. Emerson, "Power-Dependence Relations," *American Sociological Review* 27 (1962):31-41.

6. R. P. French and B. Raven, "The Bases of Social Power," *Group Dynamics*, ed. Dorwin Cartwright and Alvin Zander, (New York: Harper and Row, Publishers, 1960), 601-623.

7. Frost and Wilmot, *Interpersonal Conflict*, 62.

18

NEGOTIATION AND BARGAINING IN CONFLICT MANAGEMENT

The terms *negotiation* and *bargaining* differ to some extent in meaning, but in this chapter we will use them interchangeably. The following definition incorporates the primary concept of these words: *"the process whereby two or more parties attempt to settle what each shall give and take, or perform and receive, in a transaction between them."*[1]

Structural Characteristics of Bargaining Relationships

Five structural components must be present for a genuine bargaining experience to occur.

Number of Parties Involved

At least two parties must be involved. The participants may be comprised of more than two people conflicting over one or more issues, but a minimum of two parties is required. Rarely, if ever, will a single issue or item be the total substance for engaging in negotiation. Other issues are also at stake.

Church leaders may be exceedingly zealous for missions and continually negotiate for a high percent of the total budget to be earmarked for that cause. In order to see this accomplished, they soon discover that they need more men and women in leadership areas who think as they do. So what was first a negotiation for more mission money now becomes a crusade to put mission-minded people in leadership positions.

The fact that we all operate out of an historical frame of

Communication and Conflict Management

reference also causes us to negotiate along multiple lines. We
agree to someone else's favorite ministry so that later the
person will agree to the cause we lead. Nothing occurs in a
vacuum. Our past events and relationships usually influence
our present behavior. At times, this can become quite political
and reduce ministry to "who owes whom the most debts."
However, even with the danger, the practice of soliciting people to our side so that our bargaining power increases seems
fairly common on any board or committee.

Conflict of Interest

The parties have a conflict of interest with respect to one or
more different issues. The issues may be primary or secondary,
universal or restricted within the group, related or nonre-
lated, but one or more issues must be present.

The meeting of the pastoral council in Jerusalem (Acts 15)
provides a picture of multiple conflict issues in the early
church. The gospel needed clarification. Was a Gentile person
required to become a Jew in order to have proper standing
with the Lord? Some said yes, others said no. The council met
to decide this question.

They also considered: Could the Gentiles totally ignore the
teaching and standards of the Old Testament? The council's
final statement that these believing Gentiles should, "abstain
from food sacrificed to idols, from blood, from the meat of
strangled animals and from sexual immorality" (Acts 15:29),
supports this second issue. These prohibitions were necessary
so that no offense would come to Jewish brothers in Christ.

Leadership in the first-century church appears as a more
subtle point. Would the church heed the advice of the believing Pharisees? Would Peter have the final voice? Would
Barnabas and Paul win the day with their testimony of the
signs and wonders they had witnessed? The most influential
leader in the Acts record appears to have been James as he
gave his judgment "that we should not make it difficult for the
Gentiles who are turning to God" (v. 19). Some amount of
negotiation seems always bound up in the question: Whom
will we follow in this issue?

Relationship of Parties

Regardless of the existence of prior experience or acquaint-
ance with one another, the parties are at least temporarily

joined together in a special kind of voluntary relationship. For bargaining to exist, the conflicting parties must believe they participate by choice rather than compulsion. We might ask why this seems so important? At the very core of bargaining and negotiation we find the will of the individual. If we violate a person's will, voluntary judgment becomes impossible, and we witness coercion, not negotiation. The spirit associated with the bargaining process assumes a freedom that must be protected. A person entering negotiation must believe that some possible compromise exists. If we have no possibility of haggling, negotiation has been killed.

Each bargainer must choose whether to enter into and remain in this special relationship. Each must also be able to choose when to enter and how long to remain in negotiation association.

While the ethics of Jacob and Laban in Genesis could well be questioned, they developed the negotiation process to an art form. Jacob negotiated for Rachel with Laban and ended up with Leah! He renegotiated the marriage contract and obtained Rachel (Gen. 29:25-29). Within Jacob's own family Leah, the less loved one, negotiated Jacob's love by providing Rachel with the coveted mandrakes and thus bearing Jacob's fifth son, Issachar.

The bargaining between Jacob and Laban continued until nearly all of Laban's flock became Jacob's flock (Gen. 30:27-43). How long should Jacob have bargained with Laban? Finally, Jacob and his wives decided it was time to leave. His wages had been changed ten times, and, although Jacob recognized that God had protected him, he knew he had to obey the voice of God calling him to return to his homeland (Gen. 31:3). Jacob and Laban modeled a temporary joining together of two tricksters who, in their cunning, illustrate the voluntary choice of each to know when to enter and when to exit the bargaining scene.

Desires of Parties

Activity in the relationship concerns (1) the division or exchange of one or more specific resources and/or (2) the resolution of one or more intangible issues among the parties or among those whom they represent. Both parties wish for the same resources, but both cannot have what is desired. The classic story of Solomon's wisdom illustrates the struggle that often accompanies the negotiation process. Two mothers claimed the same living child. Neither mother desired the dead baby. So Solomon demonstrated his wise heart by suggesting the baby be cut in half so that each mother could share equally. The true mother would rather surrender the child than see the baby destroyed. Solomon negotiated the settlement by revealing the true mother (1 Kings 3:27).

Since none of us possess the wisdom of Solomon, not all our negotiations end as well; but we can determine the scarce resource to which both parties lay claim. This at least starts us down the right road in the bargaining process.

Steps in Bargaining Process

The activity usually involves the presentation of demands or proposals by one party, evaluation of these by the other, followed by concessions and counter proposals. The activity is thus *sequential* rather than *simultaneous*. There are at least three sequential steps to any given bargaining process: (1) the demand or proposal by one party; (2) the evaluation of these by the other party; and (3) the concessions and counter proposals by either party.

Perhaps the most classic negotiation in Scripture was the contest between God, represented by Moses, and the false gods of Egypt, represented by Pharaoh and his men (Ex. 7:6—11: 10).

Moses repeatedly demanded, "Let us go,...and sacrifice unto the Lord our God" (Ex. 5:3, KJV; 8:1). Pharaoh countered with, "These people are lazy! They have too much time on their hands. Keep the same quota and take away the straw we have been providing. Make them gather it as well as make the required number of bricks" (author's paraphrase). The contest then began between Yahweh and the gods of Egypt. By the time the second plague (frogs) appeared, Pharaoh seemed to have given in to Moses' demand, but then he had a change of heart (Ex. 8:1-15).

This pattern continued until the plague of flies. At that time Pharaoh offered a counter proposal: go sacrifice to your God in the land. When Moses declined this offer, the king said, "I will let you go to offer sacrifices to the Lord your God in the desert, but you must not go very far" (8:28). Once the flies were removed Pharaoh again hardened his heart. After the plague on livestock, boils, and hail, Pharaoh again admitted his sin and granted permission for God's people to leave.

This, too, was short-lived. His heart was hardened again. With the threat of the locust plague, Pharaoh gave permission, but he wanted to know exactly who would go with Moses (10:8). Moses assured Pharaoh that absolutely everyone would go to make this sacrifice. Pharaoh, still in a bargaining mood, counter proposed that only the men would go (10:11). End of negotiation. The locusts came. Pharaoh said they could go, then changed his mind. After the plague of darkness Pharaoh told Moses, "Go, worship the Lord. Even your women and children may go with you; only leave your flocks and herds behind" (10:24). In the final outcome of this negotiation process the Egyptian firstborn died, followed by the death of Pharaoh's army in the Red Sea.

The first twelve chapters of Exodus provide an excellent case study for the sequential development of the negotiation process. The Scripture records proposal followed by counterproposal followed by counter, counterproposal. We learn a valuable lesson from this historic event: some issues are not negotiable. Even so, the process of bargaining and counterbargaining is fascinating to observe.

In any negotiation situation the presence of an audience must be considered. No one bargains in a vacuum.

The Presence of Audiences

An audience is any group, physically or nonphysically present, which is somehow affected by the bargaining process. They may be dependent or nondependent on the bargaining process. The size, composition, immediacy, and identity of the audience will affect the bargainers. Audiences transmit evaluations by providing feedback in a variety of forms ranging from nonverbal facial expressions and gestures to more highly structured written messages. The feedback may be given at any point in the conflict or bargaining process. The power of audience feedback should not be underestimated.

The audience's influence on Pilate when he judged Christ may be difficult to determine. Pilate tried to appease them by suggesting a beating followed by release. Immediately the people cried out "Away with this man! Release Barabbas to us!" (Luke 23:18). He certainly heard the mass of people incited by the religious leaders, crying "Crucify Him! Crucify Him!" Add to this his awareness of the accusation the Jews kept shouting: "If you let this man go, you are no friend of Caesar. Anyone who claims to be a king opposes Caesar" (John 19:12). The presence of a hostile audience greatly influenced Pilate's involvement in the case of Jesus of Nazareth.

Importance of an Audience in Evaluation

The mere presence of an audience (including psychological presence) motivates bargainers to seek positive, and avoid negative, evaluation—especially when the audience is important to the bargainers. The external audience helps to keep the bargaining process honest. The effect of the negotiator's behavior before a watching world provides a check-and-balance-system so that grave injustices are less likely to occur.

The particular audience we desire to influence plays a large part in what motivates us. If a representative of a motorcycle gang meets with the city council to gain permission to parade through town on a given day, he will not negotiate away those things held valuable by the gang. If the council should place a new-and-clean-clothes-condition on their parade, the motorcyclist might find himself working with something the group deems nonnegotiable. On the other hand, if maximal speed for the day of the parade was set at 40 MPH, the motorcyclist might consider this a possibility. In many ways, negotiators view themselves as representatives of a larger body of people. This real or imagined audience serves as a reference point for what we will use as bargaining chips and how we will engage in this process.

Acceptance from our audience carries more significance for the negotiator than approval from the person we work with in the bargaining process. A wife convinced she obtained a bargain on a newly purchased dress will want to share this news with her husband or nearest friends. She wants this representative audience to be pleased with her judgment. It might be nice if the store clerk also genuinely believed she acquired a bargain, but the clerk's opinion does not really count.

In a church setting the people who make up an official board may also head up given committees. For example, one board member may chair the worship committee. If the official board discusses the use of envelopes for individual records of money contributed, the worship committee chair will probably structure responses to fairly represent the committee. Perhaps the committee had a lengthy discussion about this matter only to decide against using the envelopes. Ethically, that must be revealed in the official board discussion.

This shows us the influence of a smaller audience. The church as a whole serves as a larger audience with far more power, but sometimes with a much lesser-known opinion. Effective negotiators know not only their audience, but the audience of the persons with whom they bargain. This information makes possible a better definition as to what may be negotiated. At the point where the two audiences of the bargainers intersect, we discover a place of bona fide compromise. This territory may be large or small, clearly known or unknown, easy to enter or hard to enter; but it must be found if successful bargaining is to occur on both sides of the table.

Accountability to an Audience

If a bargainer is accountable to an audience for positive evaluation, then accountability is the mechanism by which he or she may be controlled. Obviously, we must know the audience of the one with whom we bargain. We need answers to questions such as: How dependent is this fellow bargainer on that audience? Is the size of that audience important? How does that audience relate to my audience? Are there some areas of shared audience? What influence does that audience have? The more we know about the other's audience and accountability to this group, the wiser we can be in negotiation.

Influence of an Audience

Audiences, especially dependent ones, generate pressures toward loyalty, commitment, and advocacy of their preferred positions. This suggests a tighter rein on bargainers who must cope with a dependent audience. They do not have the freedom to instigate short-range conflict for long-range goals. The surprise element is greatly curtailed.

A dependent audience is usually highly predictable. Therefore, someone closely linked to this type of group loses bargaining power. The progress one makes at a bargaining table will be slower and more methodical. One should not expect quick victories but rather plan on considerable time in the bargaining process. One must report back to the "mother group" in detailed fashion and with great regularity. Keeping the audience happy is paramount and may be as crucial as achievement at the negotiation table.

A particular group worthy of our consideration is the third party to the negotiation process. We want to examine how a third party functions.

The Functions Served By Third Parties

Third parties or mediators have value when they can function in an uninhibited manner.

1. *They reduce irrationality.* In some negotiation proceedings the people involved become so blinded by their own positions that the facts of the situation become blurred. A third party helps to keep a quieter tone and clear view of what is actually transpiring. In some cases a third party provides an opportunity for the individuals to vent their feelings without fear of personal incrimination.

2. *They reduce nonrationality.* When negotiation is going nowhere, a third party can intervene and enable the participants to objectively see potential gains and losses. One may also need to help the parties focus on what has been accomplished. At moments when nonrationality prevails, it is crucial to tag any and all gains (even small ones) and bring them to clear light.

3. *They help the bargainers explore alternative solutions.* At times so much rigidity may be present that a mediator is necessary to restate the actual issue(s) so that the negotiators can begin a creative ideation process. The more areas of mutual satisfaction that can surface, the greater the possible satisfaction in the negotiation outcome. A third party helps to

keep these multiple options alive so participants can determine the most acceptable one.

4. *They provide opportunities for graceful retreat or face-saving.* This face-saving may occur only in the eyes of an adversary or an audience. The third party can reduce the public exposure of the individual negotiators. When retreat from the discussion table becomes necessary, third parties can control the pace of it or assume as much responsibility as they desire for concessions made. In this way they take the heat off the negotiating parties.

5. *They facilitate constructive communication between opposing parties.* Effective third parties serve as a bridge which each side of a negotiation can travel. They help reduce the formality of a complicated negotiation. This does require a certain amount of optimism in persons who function as mediators.

6. *They regulate the costs of conflict.* The amount of public exposure to the process of negotiation rests in the hands of the mediators. If both sides are reluctant to negotiate, they have the weapons of public opinion to bring into the situation. This may include both reward and retribution.

There comes a time when issues must be shared with the leaders of a church and may need to be dispensed church wide. One of the powerful tools of the first-century church was the high esteem all believers had for the corporate fellowship (Acts 2). With nearly twenty centuries completed, the power of corporate fellowship appears to be greatly reduced in most local churches. In the first century though it hurt to be disciplined by a local body of believers, Christians felt incomplete without this corporate bonding.

Today, churches rarely even consider disciplining a believer. The disciplined person can simply unite with another church across town. We have lost the power of the corporate fellowship of believers. Effective third parties have historically been able to use the influence of the whole on the individual parts.

7. *They regulate public intervention or interference.* The better part of wisdom may be to keep the press from some negotiations for a period of time. A productive mediator is a wise gatekeeper. Not every conflict which comes to the negotiation table should be public knowledge in a local assembly. The

effective third party person must be an individual whom both sides can trust to keep negotiation procedures quiet when necessary.

8. *They identify and promote the use of additional resources not initially apparent to the parties.* This suggests that the third parties should be well versed as to the nature of the negotiation. They need to be more knowledgeable than either of the participants if their services will be viewed as valuable. Experience in mediation between conflicting parties with similar problems may increase the value of a third party. In the local church setting he or she should have a reputation for applied wisdom when working with the Word of God and people.

9. *They establish and reinforce norms and rules of procedure.* In heated negotiations some exchanges are legitimate and some are not. Third parties must know what is deemed as acceptable. They should be as well acquainted with the participants in the negotiation as possible. They will know the value of a recess when matters start to move out of hand. Most effective mediators in church settings know, appreciate, and practice a healthy prayer ministry. They serve both as protectors and facilitators.

Negotiation requires a voluntary, on-going relationship where proposals and counter proposals characterize the communication process. These messages sent and received in a conflict setting are greatly influenced by audiences who have vested interest. To some extent these people who observe the conflicting parties exercise control over the bargaining process. Third parties who enter a conflict experience often facilitate progress toward a resolution of the conflict.

Note
1. Jeffrey Z. Rubin and Bert R. Brown, *The Social Psychology of Bargaining and Negotiation* (New York: Academic Press, 1975), 2.

19

COALITIONS IN CONFLICT MANAGEMENT

The official church board convened on Thursday for its monthly meeting. After prayer, each person examined the printed agenda and mentally estimated the length of the meeting. The board swiftly made decisions on some minor matters. But then the nine board members could not agree about the future direction of the music ministry.

Three felt the time had come to employ an additional full-time paid staff member. Four members felt the current lay volunteer director should continue, with more guidance given by the board. Two board members voiced their conviction that a part-time paid staff member was the solution. The difference in these three groups created conflict that will likely stymie the board's progress.

Coalitions often form to assist us with this dilemma. The two members desiring a part-time staff position will probably join one of the other two groups so that the board can achieve a majority opinion. As a rule, the greater the number of parties directly involved in a bargaining situation, the greater the increase of difficulty in coordination. The more a variety of problems are introduced that originate from the conflicting interest and interdependences among the parties, the more complex coalitions become.

For example, the children of Israel when settling in the promised land were told to destroy all of the existing nations. Through a ruse the Gibeonites deceived God's people and acquired a peace treaty (coalition) with Israel (Josh. 9:15). The complexity of the situation surfaced when the five kings of the Amorites decided to attack the Gibeonites (Josh. 10:5). Since the Jews had established a coalition with the Gibeonites, Joshua found himself protecting these people who were not of Israel (vv. 7-10).

Coalitions may form in a planned fashion as a result of a structural design. If three of the deacons work together on an educational subcommittee, the chances are excellent these will form a coalition on other issues when the entire deacon board meets.

Coalitions can come in a more subtle, almost unconscious, fashion. When a difference surfaces during the process of discussion, some deacons may find themselves lining up with other deacons on a regular basis. No outward intention creates this union. It just seems to happen. It may relate to comparable personalities or a similar background which allows these unplanned coalitions to develop.

Coalition Defined

The unification of the power or resources (or both) of two or more parties so that they stand a better chance of obtaining a desired outcome or of controlling others not included in the coalition.[1]

Coalitions appear most frequently when multiparty conflict occurs. The more parties who find direct attachment to the conflict issue the greater the number of coalitions which are likely to form. This becomes evident when several positions exist with reference to the conflict issue. This principle finds illustration when an unexpected money gift must be allocated within a congregationally governed church. The moderator may open the meeting so that all members may voice their opinions. If they collectively attempt to decide how the money gift should be dispersed, the number of ideas may parallel the number in attendance. After much discussion or debate, coalitions will begin to form. The missions advocates will link with each other. Those in favor of building improvements will join forces. Some members may surface who desire to designate the money for the pastoral staff. The educational interest will probably unite. Another group pleads for the money to go for youth work. Each special interest group can detail many reasons why the money should be allocated for their particular cause. At times, the coalitions appear to be endless. In comparing two-party and multiparty bargaining, Jeffrey Rubin and Bert Brown (1975) have noted this difference:

> In multiparty bargaining, pressures toward coalescence are generated when self-perceptions of weakness, disadvantage, or insufficiency of resources needed to obtain an outcome drive at least two bargainers to join forces in order to maintain or increase their individual strength, so that they are neither viewed nor treated as weak by others who are also involved in the exchange.[2]

Coalition Formation

Research abounds in this area. Consider the four major theories about coalition formation:

Minimal Resource Theory

This school of thought views the coalition as forming on the basis of what each prospective coalition member can bring to the group. No one member possesses sufficient power to accomplish the desired outcome. The perceived strength comes when each of these inferior forces unite. Whatever the coalition can accomplish will be distributed in proportion to what each member has invested.

We see an example of this when two or three assistant pastors unite to influence a senior pastor toward their desired position. Their individual power does not begin to compare with the force of their coalition. Each assistant pastor must view his combined resources with other assistants as more influential than the power he has alone for the coalition to be formed.

When resources are combined, some form of compromise usually accompanies the new coalition. The minister of music will not totally endorse everything the minister of youth might desire. But neither will the minister of youth support all items on the music minister's agenda. Each person needs a clear view of priorities when he or she joins with another to receive an adequate hearing. The questions—Where can I be flexible, and in what areas must I remain firm?—constantly structure the new relationship.

Minimal Power Theory

Supporters of this theory equate power with attractiveness. This attractiveness anticipates what power this person(s) would bring as a partner. Each person assesses individual power as insufficient. The thinking runs, *If I join with this person, can our combined strength likely be a winning coalition?* If an affirmative answer comes, then a coalition forms.

A certain amount of chance accompanies this formation theory. The person reasons, *My best guess leads me to believe if Jane and I were together on this issue, the rest of the group would agree as well.* Where this type of thinking dominates, a coalition will usually form.

The apostle Paul's desire to include younger men in ministry might illustrate this coalition theory. Dramatic differences characterized the role of John Mark versus the position of Timothy as members of Paul's early missionary team.

John Mark had apparently accompanied Paul and Barnabas as they began the first missionary journey (Acts 13:4-12). When the team reached Perga in Pamphylia, John Mark left to return to Jerusalem (v. 13). Paul did not approve of this departure. When he and Barnabas determined to revisit the churches, the issue of John Mark's returning with them created sharp disagreement. The conflict was so severe it split this first missionary team (Acts 15:36-41).

The next chapter in Acts opens with the record of Timothy joining the missionary team (Acts 16:1-3). Paul desired his presence as the Lord used them to spread the gospel and establish churches on their journeys. Timothy's contribution was deemed a positive influence on the team's ministry.

Anticompetitive Theory

When we belong to a smaller, less influential group we seek to unite with others so that we can stand against a common target. This greater strength helps maximize our joint outcomes while still maintaining the solidarity of the group. This rests on two foundational ideas: (1) We normally negatively value and avoid anything that will disrupt group solidarity. Our desire for group cohesiveness motivates us more than the urge to fulfill our personal agendas. (2) Superordinate goals provide us a basis for unification, regardless of differences in initial power or resource contribution. We will lay aside our differences for the greater good of the group. This formation theory implies that, "what the entire group produces becomes more valuable than continued insistence for my position."

This formation concept views time as basic to coalition formation. When a group wrestles with a decision over a prolonged period of time, eventually the person committed to the higher good of the group will form a new coalition. This demands surrender of what one may consider "best" for what one values as "good" or "better."

For example, suppose the conflict issue was whether the church should continue to organize and produce a daily vacation Bible school. One half of the board stands strongly positioned to continue this traditional summer ministry. The other half argues for a more contemporary day-camp ministry approach. It appears to be so deadlocked that neither ministry will be implemented.

At this point some of the members supporting the day-camp idea switch over to the VBS group. Why does this occur? One reason might be because these members have determined that *some* summer ministry for the children beats *no* summer ministry for the youth. If these board members who changed became convinced that the conflict was destroying both opportunities, they could likely vote for what they considered a higher good.

Confusion Theory

The complexity of the situation dictates that coalitions be formed. These usually come into being in a nonsystematic manner. Random factors create the coalitions which combine. The desire to make sense of what occurs forces two or more individuals to join forces. Some minimal relationship must exist for coalition attraction to be stimulated. Some cite times of crisis as an indication of how this theory works.

If an earthquake suddenly devastated a public building, people who would not otherwise likely form a coalition would work together in a heroic rescue effort. In a less traumatic picture, two college students who failed a mid-term examination might join together so that the conflict created by failure could be better managed. Wisdom might dictate that this new coalition also add a student who scored a *B* or better to their new group.

Each of the previous four coalition theories contributes to our understanding of coalition formation. These theories provide us with different perspectives as we attempt to answer the same question: Why do coalitions form? While some might argue that they are contradictory, a better position views them as complementary. A coalition will usually have multiple reasons leading to its formation. One of the four theories may dominate, but other reasons may also be present to a lesser degree.

Each situation must be examined in its own context. When we have discovered what makes a coalition form in a given set of circumstances it helps us trace the relationships which exist. The detection of coalitions also assists us in tracking the role that power occupies within a group.

T. A. Caplow's chart outlines the relationship of power to the prediction of coalition formation. This chart presents the probability element in a functional manner.

The dynamic of each situation changes as the relative value differs.

#1 A = 1; B = 1; C = 1. Since each person has an equal power index, one cannot predict how the coalition will form. A and B could combine against C; B and C could unite against A; or A and C could join to defeat B. Where true equality of power exists, other dimensions may determine how the coalition forms. Factors outside the group may influence which coalition of individuals will occur. This coalition formation may require more time since no one person can dominate alone. The competition element usually stands out as strong when the group experiences this personal triple equality. Frequently, in a group where no leader has been designated these relationships can develop.

#2 A = 3; B = 2; C = 2. Since A has more power than B or C individually possess, the coalition will occur between the weaker parties, B and C. A has no reason to join with B or with C. In head to head confrontation A could defeat either B or C. This reveals the nature of coalitions as a forced alliance. The weaker parties might not otherwise choose each other, but since they must deal with A, they will unite.

Caplovian Coalition Predictions (Adapted)[3]

Index of relative power for each member			Type of Power relationship	Predicted coalition	Character of alliance
	A	B	C			
# 1	1	1	1	All equal A = B = C	Any pair	Two parties pair to outweigh third
# 2	3	2	2	One stronger A GT B; B = C; A LT B + C	BC	Two weaker parties pair to outweigh the stronger
# 3	1	2	2	One weaker A LT B; B = C	AB or AC	Each stronger party seeks the weaker to outweigh other stronger party
# 4	3	1	1	One all powerful A GT B + C B = C	None	Coalition useless; parties cannot outweigh stronger
# 5	4	3	2	All different A GT B GT C; A LT B + C	AB or AC	Any coalition of the two outweighs the third
# 6	4	2	1	All Different A GT B GT C; A GT B + C	None	Coalition useless; weaker parties cannot outweigh stronger

#3 $A = 1; B = 2; C = 2$. Neither B nor C requires the help of the other to defeat A. But since their power is equal they cannot overcome each other. Therefore, both B and C will find A attractive to offset the problem of their equality. Each desires to tip the scales in his favor. A provides the solution to this equality problem.

#4 A = 3; B = 1; C = 1. In this instance equal power shows up in B and C. But the total power of the two falls short of the power variable A possesses. Coalition becomes wasted effort since it can effect nothing. Therefore, it will not occur in this power distribution.

#5 A = 4; B = 3; C = 2. This configuration resembles 2 (A = 3; B = 2; C = 2). But the major difference concerns the equality possessed by B and C in the second example. In the present picture each of the people have different relative power indications. The reason A will unite with B or C is because A has more to lose than B or C. Therefore, A will take the initiative so as not to be overpowered.

#6 A = 4; B = 2; C = 1. This picture approximates the scene in   4 (A = 3; B = 1; C = 1). Some distinction exists since the distribution of power does differ between B and C. But this coalition of B and C becomes futile when measured against the strength of A. The hopelessness of the situation will probably be registered by C before B comprehends the impossibility of the situation.

Conditions Likely to Form Coalitions

If distribution of power or other resources necessary for obtaining an outcome exists, coalitions are likely to form. Conversely, when power or other resources reside exclusively in one person or place, coalitions do not form. A dictatorial rule will not permit coalition development. People oppose autocratic rule by speaking with the voice of rebellion or more passive resignation, but not coalition.

We find the ideal context for coalitions in highly competitive, multiparty bargaining relationships. When juxtaposed with types of church government, the congregational form will produce more coalitions at the grass roots level. A representative type of church government will use coalitions with a two-tiered approach. Those seeking to influence the ruling body will join forces to ensure that their representative knows of the importance of their cause. Also among the representatives, coalitions will form to influence the actual decisions enacted.

Chances for coalitions are enhanced when one of the parties

views himself as disadvantaged with respect to obtaining some outcome and does not consider it fruitless to join forces with another in pursuit of the outcome sought. Perceived weakness or disadvantage fuels coalition formation.

If the children's ministry in a church has the reputation of lesser importance than teaching an adult class, individual Sunday School teachers in the primary department may find themselves joining voices to achieve recognition for one or all of the teachers. Coalitions reveal where perceived weaknesses exist.

Desirability of a Coalition Partner

Principle 1

When coalitions are not seen as useless, weaker parties are likely to seek each other out and exclude decidedly stronger parties from their alliances. This argues for a small group of new believers meeting together on a regular basis. If an older, stronger believer joins the group, its growth effectiveness may diminish. A certain homogeneity proves beneficial to those who picture themselves progressing at the same rate. This does not rule out a respected shepherd or leader to guide the group, but it does argue for similar group consistency.

Principle 2

The attractiveness of a coalition mate varies with each situation; alliances will tend to form among individuals who see themselves as sharing a common disadvantage at the hands of another. We sometimes witness the birth of a new church because people have been mutually hurt by the leadership of a previous church. "Misery loves company" may not be the best of motives for forming these alliances, but it does occur.

Some individuals within the same church find solace with each other after each has fought against a local "tribal chief" and lost the battle. The expression of their mutual thought seems to be, *If we unify on the next issue of conflict, maybe we can win!* Coalitions form against a definite, stronger adversary.

Principle 3

A high-power party who also has an announced strong probability of victory may be viewed as an attractive coalition partner. We are creatures who continually examine the odds. If triumph appears imminent we want to jump on the winner's wagon. When board members of a church see the most influential member of the board making a decision which will be well received by the constituency, they find it easy to add their support.

Division of Outcomes in Coalitions

First, equality of initial power or resources among coalition members will likely result in an equal division of outcomes. However, differential power or resources likely results in an unequal distribution, with members possessing greater power or resources generally demanding a larger share of the outcomes. Distributive justice prevails when coalitions are successful. What one invested parallels what one shares when the coalition achieves its goal. This may be defined as time, money, or energy. The more one contributed to the coalition, the more one can expect to receive from the coalition victory.

Second, difference in status ranking may also affect the distribution of outcomes in a coalition, with the greater percentage going to high-status members. Believers do not usually care to consider status consideration. We are all equal in sin, equal in Christ, and of equal importance to God. Even so, status implies greater responsibility or ability in some fashion. Coalition distribution of rewards does not ignore ranking. If advancement becomes possible for a coalition member, the individual with the higher status will receive the promotion. This often removes him or her from the coalition which provided the strength for victory. We continue to honor status even among the weaker who had to unite to accomplish their goal.

Conclusion

Coalitions help to counterbalance the imbalance created by inappropriate strength and weakness within any organization. They center on power as it functions within any group. They help us see where weaknesses surface and how strength can be adjusted by weaker parties unifying. In conflict, coalitions become part of an equalizing force so that a stronger adversary cannot bully a weaker opponent.

Notes

1. Jeffrey Z. Rubin and Bert R. Brown, *The Social Psychology of Bargaining and Negotiation* (New York: Academic Press, 1975) 64.

2. Ibid., 65.

3. This adaptation of Caplow's chart appears in *The Social Psychology of Bargaining and Negotiation* by Jeffrey Z. Rubin and Bert R. Brown (New York: Academic Press, 1975), 66. For the original see T. A. Caplow, "A Theory of Coalitions in Triads," *American Journal of Sociology* 21 (1956):489-493.

20

CONFLICT AND MANAGEMENT STYLES

When we face a fight we usually respond on the basis of how we have faced similar encounters. The response pattern may be influenced by the issue or the individual. For example, if one finds controlling the conversation during an argument works best with one's spouse, one will usually opt for this style when engaged in conflict.

A conflict management style may be intentionally or nonintentionally selected. It may vary depending on the particular set of circumstances which surround the conflict experience. However, usually each of us exhibits a preference for a particular conflict management style. Norman Shawchuck (1983) defined style in his book on *How to Manage Conflict*: "Each style consists of a basic set of assumptions along with specific behaviors, gestures, expressions, and words that, when taken together, serve to comprise that particular style."[1]

Three Major Styles

Putnam and Wilson (1982) grouped the primary styles of conflict management in the following manner:
• Nonconfrontation: indirect strategies for handling a conflict; choices to avoid or withdraw from a disagreement; such communicative behaviors as silence, glossing over the differences, and concealing ill feelings.
• Solution-orientation: direct communication about the conflict; behaviors that aim to find a solution, to integrate the needs of both parties, and to give in or compromise on issues.
• Control: direct communication about the disagreement; arguing persistently for one's position, taking control of the interaction, and advocating one's position.[2]

Nonconfrontation

The *nonconfrontation* style tries to sidestep disagreements when they arise. This individual shies away from topics which are the source of disputes. She usually tries to ease conflict, claiming differences are trivial. Frequently this person will keep quiet about her views so conflict can be avoided.

On occasion this style serves as the most appropriate behavior. If the conflicting issue does not merit the energy being expended, then nonconfrontation becomes the wiser choice. The color of carpet in a new church should not become the major reason for leaving a church. As Vance Havner once put it, "A bulldog could beat a skunk in a fight any day, but it just ain't worth it."[3] Wisdom will dictate when we should engage in conflict or practice restraint.

Frequently in the Book of Proverbs we receive wise counsel to avoid conflict. "It is to a man's honor to avoid strife,/ but every fool is quick to quarrel" (Prov. 20:3).[4] When a fight appears imminent, we should consider the following questions: (1) Is this issue worth the conflict involvement? (2) Does this conflict make any difference in light of eternity? (3) Am I anticipating a fight because I have a personal agenda? These types of questions may influence an individual to live with the tension rather than engage in full-scale war.

At times conflict avoidance may indicate weakness or sin. If church purity needs to be defended and we practice nonconfrontation, we fail to respond in a biblical manner. The church at Corinth illustrated the negative side of nonconfrontation in conflict management (1 Cor. 5:1-13). Immorality had entered the assembly with no one taking a stand against it. They were proud of their toleration of the situation when God said they should have been filled with grief. Action was the appropriate response. The immoral man claiming to be a believer should have been removed from the fellowship. However, they arrogantly practiced nonconfrontation. God condemned their boasting and toleration of impurity among them.

We must have discernment from God to know when to confront and when not to confront in conflict issues. When purity in living or doctrine surfaces as the issue, nonconfrontation does not become an option. We must exercise care that we are accurately interpreting "purity" and "doctrine" in the factual arena. *Confrontation becomes proper only when we live in the accurate world of facts and not the inferential world of opinions.* Unfortunately, conflict too often centers on our ideas, wishes, and opinions—not on factual validity.

Solution

The *solution* style seeks to meet the opposition at the midpoint of differences. Everybody's ideas are considered as we attempt to settle disagreements. This person will combine a variety of viewpoints to find a workable answer. He or she frequently will give a little if the other party reciprocates by giving a little.

The first Jerusalem council pictured men working together seeking a solution to a difficult problem (Acts 15). The critical question was: How Jewish must a person become in order to be a Christian? The dispute was debated sharply. Some Judean men made circumcision a condition for salvation. Paul and Barnabas had repeatedly witnessed Gentiles coming to Jesus Christ without any connection to Judaism. The Pharisees insisted that obedience to the law of Moses was required for genuine conversion.

After hearing Peter's testimony and the report of Paul and Barnabas, James cited Old Testament teaching (Amos 9:11-12) including Gentiles in God's overall plan. Some restrictions were suggested (Acts 15:20), but the Gentiles were to be received on the basis of grace, not the keeping of Old Testament law. Multiple ideas were voiced to create this workable solution at the Jerusalem council. While persons did not need to become Jews to be saved, they should not be insensitive to some of the elements of the Mosaic code.

Solution seems to be the ideal style for managing conflict. Yet every Christian leader will find occasions when solution will not be available. Not all parties should contribute to a solution if the issue involves orthodox versus unorthodox doctrine. We dare not slight the deity of Jesus Christ to reduce conflict with the followers of Jehovah's Witness teaching. Usually we are attracted to solution as the most viable conflict management style. But at times nonconfrontation or control may provide the more valid stance for conflict management.

Control

The *control* style dominates arguments until the other person understands his or her position. Such people often insist upon their own points of view. They assert opinions forcefully and stand firm in personal views during the disagreement. Emotional attachment often accompanies the desire to make sure a personal stance wins a fair hearing. When sin overtakes a brother or sister, God expects us to take action. We are taught to restore individuals who have been caught in sin (Gal. 6:1-5). This ministry should be done by the mature or spiritual believer because it requires great care. This "restoring" action depicts the setting of a bone by a doctor or the mending of a net by a fisherman. Both instances require precise knowledge and control of the process. Quick, careless words or behavior create disastrous consequences. The more the control-conflict management style becomes necessary, the more we must make certain we are walking in obedience to God.

A Fivefold Division of Conflict Style

Communicologists have further defined conflict styles into five categories. Blake and Moulton (1964) suggested a fivefold division of conflict management.[5]

Forcing

This results from production-oriented management styles and signifies the use of competitive behaviors to win one's position, even if it means ignoring the needs of the opponent. Forcing reveals the use of power, particularly expert or legitimate power in winning an argument.

The pastor or senior board member might be tempted to run roughshod over a younger, more inexperienced church leader by forcing personal views on the novice. The inappropriate use of Greek and Hebrew can help the possessor to force a certain position on the less trained. This style uses power to bully the opposition into submission. The person on the receiving end usually feels highly victimized when suffering this treatment.

Confrontation

Sometimes we label this problem solving: "collaborating and integrating." It consists in facing a conflict directly, evaluating causes, and examining possible solutions. To reach creative solutions, participants must exchange information and integrate alternative points of view.

Paul legitimately confronted Peter at Antioch because Peter was wrong (Gal. 2:11-14). Peter's relationship with the Gentiles changed when those of the circumcision arrived. Paul challenged Peter face-to-face about his behavior. This hypocrisy demanded an answer since it was leading others astray. Most people do not enjoy confronting others, but it becomes necessary when an important issue such as the gospel is at stake.

Not all issues require confrontation. When Paul wrote to the church at Philippi, he mentioned that some were preaching the gospel out of envy and rivalry attempting to add greater frustration to his imprisonment (Phil. 1:12-18). His response was not confrontational: "But what does it matter? The important thing is that in every way, whether from false motives or true, Christ is preached. And because of this I rejoice. Yes, and I will continue to rejoice" (Phil. 1:18). The difference between these Philippian evangelists and Peter was seen in who suffered in the conflict. In Galatians the gospel was suffering, and this demanded confrontation. In Philippians Paul was suffering, and this did not require confrontation. How frequently we confuse these two areas. We want to confront the personal attack, but we allow attacks on the gospel to go unchallenged!

Smoothing

We designate this style as accommodation, referring to behaviors that are glossed over or concealed. Differences are played down by emphasizing common interests. Our relationship with our fellow combatants concerns us far more than any particular conflict issue or outcome. The desire to get along with each other far exceeds any will to win the battle.

Early in Genesis (13:5-9), Abram demonstrated a smoothing style of conflict management when trouble arose with his nephew Lot. The land proved to be a limited resource. It could

not support the flocks and herds of both Abram and Lot. The
quarreling between Abram's herdsmen and Lot's herdsmen
occurred with greater frequency. Something must be done to
alleviate the problem. In this situation Abram said:

> Let's not have any quarreling between you and me, or be-
> tween your herdsmen and mine, for we are brothers. Is not
> the whole land before you? Let's part company. If you go to
> the left, I'll go to the right; if you go to the right, I'll go to the
> left (vv. 8-9).

The relationship between the two families was viewed as
stronger than the conflicting problem. They considered it
worth protecting.

When the identity of the conflicting parties proves stronger
than the conflicting issues, the style of smoothing will more
likely occur. In Genesis the family relationship was the glue
that kept Abram and Lot from warfare. Today the spiritual
relationship between two leaders may be strong enough to
weather conflicts when they come. When conflict wins the day,
it almost always reveals weak relationships.

Avoiding

We see this best illustrated by physical withdrawal or refusal to discuss the conflict. To sidestep the issue becomes the
artful display of this style. The withdrawal may be psychological or physical. This individual views no fight as worth the
cost of the conflict. Denial of the presence of conflict marks
this style. This can and does become a refusal to cope with
reality. We can pretend only so far. As a target, a person may
refuse to admit that such a thing as a gun exists, but the
bullet holes in the target's chest argue otherwise.

Immediate avoidance may indicate wisdom if the emotional
level runs so high that destructive conflict becomes ensured. A
parent should delay punishment of a child if his or her emotional index has soared beyond reasonable response. Also,
delayed penalties have a certain therapeutic value for both
the parent and the child.

Compromise

This style works energetically toward "splitting the difference." The person employing this strategy seeks the goal of

the middle ground. We view neither party as totally right. This basic assumption believes that somewhere between the two conflicting positions lies a common ground which all parties can and will accept. Mediators use this management style more than combatants. It presupposes an objectivity to all the issues and people involved in the conflict process. Rewards or penalties are shared equally.

When I was a child, my father would often practice this style of conflict management. On one occasion my older sister and I were having a severe conflict. The years have blurred the conflict issue, but I shall never forget my father's management style. He questioned both of us as to the problem. We were equally convincing concerning our innocence and the other party's culpability. Since my father was not present to determine who started what, his solution was a compromise. He decided to spank both of us. My older sister had seniority, so he used the yardstick on her first. He broke the yardstick. At this point I laughed and assured him he could not whip me since the yardstick was broken. What faulty logic! With hand-measured equality he administered corrective procedures I have never forgotten. Compromises can serve as a viable way to manage conflict.

Shawchuck's Descriptions of Conflict Management Style[6]

Each of Shawchuck's five styles possess certain distinct characteristics. The following descriptions may prove helpful as you consider your style and the style of your adversary. In each of Shawchuck's descriptions he used an animal to depict the behavior of the style.

Avoiding (the Turtle)

The driving force for these persons seeks to dodge or to stay out of the conflict, to avoid being identified with either side. Noninvolvement has uppermost value to these individuals.

They make every effort to create a situation which causes other people to assume responsibility for conflict management.

Passiveness becomes the *modus operandi*. This may be visible by the individuals physically withdrawing from the conflict situation.

The nonassertive nature of this style frustrates others because the persons neither seek their own interests nor the interests of anyone else.

This style uses silence. A direct question does not merit a reply if it means more involvement in the situation.

The individual may see the situation as hopeless or trivial but plans absolutely no involvement in the conflict arena.

This individual seems to be saying: "I don't care enough about the issue to invest time and energy into solving it," or, "Even though I care, it is not appropriate for me to become involved; it is someone else's problem."

The long-term effect of this style produces frustration, compliance with little commitment, and ultimately, deep-seated hostility.

Accommodating (the Teddy Bear)

The driving force of this style seeks to preserve the relationship at all cost. People are far more significant than any particular problem which may develop. Whatever will hurt or damage the relationship the least becomes the chosen behavior. The teddy bear who cuddles with everyone best illustrates this position.

Quick steps are taken to "resolve" conflict. Since peace reigns supreme we must have it at all costs.

This person often says, "Let's forgive and forget." This thinking prevails even when the issues have had little or no discussion. Communication serves only one purpose— to help us build better relationships.

This individual rapidly assumes whatever blame must be allocated. This person reasons, "If someone else assumed the blame they might feel badly, so I will assume it to keep him or her from feeling badly."

Hard work characterizes this style since the other person must be pleased to safeguard the relationship. Some individuals prove difficult to please, but this style will put forth every effort to satisfy the other person.

The constant message—"Our getting along with each other means far more than the conflict issue"—drives the behavior of this person.

The long-term outcome of this individual style suggests

outward cooperation, strong people lover, and a huge desire to maintain relationships.

Collaborating (the Owl)

The person using this style seeks the participation of all parties in defining the conflict and in agreeing with the procedure that all will view as proper conflict management. This person looks for mutually agreeable steps that please the most people. The wisdom of the owl provides the picture for this style of management.

This person believes that all parties have something to say, and each one should be heard.

Everyone's goal shares importance and should be honored. This proves problematic when it becomes obvious one party's goals cannot be achieved.

The conflict episode will ultimately strengthen the relationships within the organization. Inherently, a strong belief that conflict can be managed marks this concept. Optimism and hope distinguish this style more than any other.

The collaborator assumes all the conflicting parties can voice differences without destroying the existing relationship. He or she also believes that opponents will follow the rules of legitimate combat. This can create difficulties in the actual management of conflict.

This management style demands cooperation from the conflicting parties. In conflict, cooperation can easily fade into the background becoming almost invisible.

The long-term effect should be stronger trust and relationships. Implementation of solution should be easier.

Compromising (the Fox)

This style seeks to furnish each side of the conflict with a little bit of winning so that each will allow a little bit of losing. The risk of manipulation can mark this style. The fox portrays this position.

The common good becomes the basic assumption. No one can be fully satisfied with the outcome, but since all desire to continue the relationship, the parties will give and take.

This person protects the progress toward striking a middle position. When extreme positions have been taken in the conflict, the task of guarding the middle position becomes more difficult. To vary in either direction gives the appearance of favoring one adversary over the other.

A strong amount of persuasion, negotiation, and bargaining are all a dynamic part of this style. Patience and persistency must be employed for this style to be effective.

Compromisers embrace the driving directive, "We must all submit our personal desires to serve the common good."

This style seems most popular when the price of an extreme position (aggression or avoidance) becomes too costly for all parties involved.

When opponents are of mutual strength, and rigidly committed to different outcomes, compromise surfaces as a popular style. They find themselves convinced that they cannot win the others to their position. Therefore they give some to gain some.

The long-term effect produced by this style usually shows up as halfhearted relationship allegiance and disguising old issues as new ones.

Competing (the Shark)

The primary objective focuses on winning. The philosophy of this style says, "In any conflict you can only win or lose." This person intends to win while making sure the other loses. Aggressiveness and domineering often are the tactics used. The shark represents the power and drive of this management style.

Personal goals reign supreme. "What is best for me is best for the organization" dominates such thinking.

Others often see these individuals as aggressive, domineering, and uncooperative. They obtain reputations for walking all over other people to achieve personal goals and ambitions.

Competitors value control. If control diminishes, failure becomes likely. Conversely, if personal control increases, the conflict finds more productive management.

Task-oriented activity characterizes a high amount of behavior. Relationship building becomes wasted activity. Executing an agenda in the time allotted thrills this conflict style.

Either overtly or covertly, the message sent by this person

reads, "I know what is best for all parties involved, and my thinking is best for the organization."

This style may not always be cruel. A fatherly, dictatorial leader may choose this style, exercising it in a benevolent manner.

The long-term effect reveals conformity or resignation to the fact that nothing significant can be changed. Persons using this style do not want change if change is different from their thinking. Hostility goes underground, and negative feedback becomes extinct.

Notes

1. Norman Shawchuck, *How to Manage Conflict in the Church,* vol. 1 (Irvine, Calif.: Spiritual Growth Resources, 1983), 22.

2. Linda L. Putnam and Charmaine E. Wilson, "Communication Strategies in Organizational Conflicts: Reliability and Validity of a Measurement Scale" in *Communication Yearbook,* vol. 6, ed. Michael Burgoon (Beverly Hills: Sage Publications, 1982), 647.

3. Vance Havner speaking at Moody Bible Institute Founder's Week in the 1980s.

4. See also Proverbs 16:6; 19:11; 21:19; 22:24-25.

5. R. R. H. Shephard Blake and J. S. Moulton, *Managing Intergroup Conflict in Industry* (Houston: Gulf Press, 1964).

6. Shawchuck, *How to Manage Conflict,* 23-27.

21

————— →》》》 《《《← —————

STRATEGIES AND TACTICS
USED IN MANAGING CONFLICT

A strategy reveals our plan of action when anticipating conflict. It may be carefully constructed or more loosely arranged. A conflict strategy should be planned in accordance with our conflict goals. The actions taken to reach the conflict goals appear as conflict tactics. No one can completely predict all the choices which could transpire when individuals engage in conflict. Even so, wise managers will consider possible conflict tactics which they may employ or that may be employed against them. We will place these tactics into four categories: (1) avoidance tactics, (2) escalation tactics, (3) maintenance tactics, (4) and reduction tactics.

Avoidance Tactics

Avoidance has neither positive nor negative connotations. We typically practice it when we are in the early stages of forming a relationship. When we overuse avoidance, we produce a static quality in the relationship, and little growth occurs. However, since avoidance can be appropriate and beneficial, employment of these tactics should be noted.

Postponement

Some conflicts will not work well with this tactic. Most fights would benefit from a "cooling period" which this suggests. George Bach and Peter Wyden, in *The Intimate Enemy* (1968), popularized the phrase: "fighting by appointment."[1] Setting a future time for conflict often helps since an immediate emotional attachment can cloud valid judgments. It does presuppose a willingness from both conflicting parties to wait.

This usually means the postponed appointment will occur soon and possess more realism. We must acknowledge any present emotional stress for any future meeting to be effective.

Controlling the Process

This delay tactic seeks to control *how* the conflict process will proceed. The person who designs the rules begins with a higher power base when actual conflict negotiation commences. When conflicting parties write a mutually defined conflict agenda, this avoidance tactic becomes highly productive. Some issues can be eliminated, parties can assess power, and coalitions can be predicted when we clearly establish the "how" of the conflict.

Resorting to Formal Rules

This usually takes the form of a vote. The problem arises since it can be a premature vote that will simply delay the actual conflict. This happens when we do not give consideration to the consequences of the group which loses when we vote. Cheap resolution results. Alan C. Filley (1975) has observed that the power issue in the conflict is not solved since we bring in the power from elsewhere instead of working it out among the participants in the conflict.[2] Arbitrary breaks by a chairman to avoid conflict illustrate another form of avoidance.

Changing the Physical Environment

This tactic seeks to either influence a greater intimacy by moving closer to the individual (and therefore seeking to reduce the conflict) or moving away from the opponent and enhancing the conflict. The extreme use of this tactic occurs when one physically removes oneself from the anticipated conflict location. If one perceives bodily injury and feels totally outnumbered or tricked into a conflict situation one does not want to participate in, then leaving the scene may be the wisest choice.

After one of His confrontations with the religious leaders, they picked up stones to kill Jesus when He made Himself equal to Abram. The apostle John told us He hid Himself, slipping away from the temple guards (8:59). Changing the physical environment may be the best tactic in some situations.

Tacit Coordination

We often experience this when we feel that much of what the conflict dealt with has been decided ahead of time. We may observe known opponents cooperating much more than expected. Joyce Frost and William Wilmot (1978) summarized this; "Full communication about the actual conflict is impossible or undesirable, yet there is a certain amount of unspoken understanding present."[3]

This tactic appears while we are engaged in conflict. We can seldom predict it. We recognize someone's prior activity has influenced present behavior. The element of surprise occurs to the person who receives the action of this tactic. Sometimes this takes the form of "splitting the difference." When a scarce resource such as money becomes the area of conflict, tacit coordination may be employed to avoid the energy needed for that conflict.

Precuing

When we give information about ourselves before the conflict, we can help define the extent we will go in a specific conflict. The more congruent our verbal and nonverbal behavior appears, the more believable the data we precued will be received. This also results in more consistent predictions made of our future behavior.

Gunnysacking and Dump Trucking

An individual using this tactic will hide gripes, keep count of grievances, hold grudges, and suppress smaller conflicts until he or she empties all these items at once on his or her opponent. These avoidance tactics are highly destructive and usually misunderstood by the antagonist. Sometimes this practice occurs when the goal is not to manage the conflict but to do damage to the opponent. The ugliness of this tactic surfaces in resignations, shouting matches, divorces, and bitter misunderstandings. Gunnysacking runs contrary to the principle of managing conflict in the early stages. Usually the earlier we confront a tension, the easier we can manage it.

Coercive Tactics

We use the word *bully* to describe this tactic. Physical, psychological, social, or even spiritual "pulling rank" serve as examples of how this coercive tactic functions. When the organizational hierarchy becomes more complex, we have greater probability this tactic will be employed. "Emotional blackmail" can develop when one party agrees not to insist on a certain issue if the other party will reciprocate by avoiding a different sensitive issue.

Linguistic Manipulation

This tactic uses "labeling" as a conflict avoidance. "We are not really in conflict; we just have minor differences." Or the opposite could be claimed: "You never agree with me on anything!" The overstatement of the situation often serves as a linguistic control to avoid conflict. With this tactic we state the greater so that the lesser issue becomes lost in the overstatement. We are so skilled with this avoidance tactic we may use it without consciously being aware of its presence or power.

Refusal to Recognize the Conflict

When one party faces definite conflict and the other party refuses to admit reality, the result can be a painful, disconfirming encounter. Refusal to recognize conflict demonstrates shortsightedness and usually creates a more severe conflict. It may occur when the stakes in the conflict are higher than one party wants to admit. But to pretend the conflict does not exist or will go away without recognition fools no one, and makes the overall management of conflict far more difficult. We simply delay meaningful management to a later time.

Fogging

This takes the form of agreeing with part of a complaint but ignoring the other part. For example:

JIM: You can't ever make up your mind about what you want to do. You take forever!

JEAN: I *do* take a long time.

For one reason or another Jean does not want conflict at this moment, so she *fogs* by agreeing with part but not all of what Jim has said. Whenever anyone considers oneself in a lower power position, this tactic becomes popular. It also may be productively used when one is not so sure one wants to be drawn into a specific conflict. Partial agreement disarms the opponent while the other delays the actual conflict experience.

Escalation Tactics

These tactics are promoted when we want to place more pressure on the other person(s) to change. In escalation tactics, involvement increases, conflict issues increase and are sharply defined, and parties polarize. We count on interdependence as we seek a workable response from our opponents. At times we vigorously solicit this response.

Labeling

Two types of labeling are worth noting. (1) Naming the other person (or party) and (2) labeling the conflict or relationship. Consider:

Tom: You're nothing but a closet charismatic!

Bill: You're only a disguised Stoic philosopher!

Jan: You're always trying to mother me!

Jill: Well, you seem so childish in your decisions!

We engage in labeling because it serves as a quick way to depict our views of other persons' motives and provides more fuel to escalate the conflict. The Tom and Bill example reveals simple name calling as a labeling device. The Jan and Jill illustration focuses more on the relationship. To some extent Jan and Jill agree about the relationship, but they each express quite different perspectives on this shared relationship. We exercise the labeling tactic more frequently when the conflict becomes more heated.

Issue Expansion

This occurs when we extend the conflict beyond the immediate issue. The content of the conflict simply shows us the tip of the conflict issue(s). A complaint about the tardiness of the board's chairman leads to the fact that he monopolizes the discussion which leads to the fact he plays favorites. The deeper problem may be the feelings of inferiority the complaining person has toward the chairman. When we expand the issue, we escalate the conflict.

Coalition Formation

Coalitions relate to power or influence. They become a part of escalation tactics because (1) they highlight the disparity of power between the conflict participants, and (2) they demonstrate an attempt to shift the power balance. If a coalition would not alter the overall power balance, it would seldom form. Since coalitions form naturally and escalate conflicts, wise leaders make sure meetings include everyone in the decision-making process, so the need for coalitions decreases.

Threats

We define a threat as one party willing to inflict punishment or harm on the other in order to achieve a personal goal. Threats, real or implied, are the most basic tactics used to escalate conflict. A threat used as a warning device can have a positive effect in a conflict situation.

Consider the final stage of church discipline as outlined by Jesus Christ (Matt. 18:15-17). Once the offended party has visited the person causing the offense, the next recourse is to take two other believers so the matter can be established by the presence of two witnesses. If this fails to bring about reconciliation, we are to tell it to the church. The Lord instructs the church then to treat this individual as a pagan or tax collector. Threat becomes meaningful when we link it to promise.

If a threat falls somewhere between an argument and the use of brute force, productive use in conflict becomes possible. Threats, to be useful, must be credible. This means the party using the threat must be able and willing to carry out the consequences. It also presupposes the other party wants to avoid the consequences which the threat will ensure.

Constricting the Other

The more we box in our opponents, the more they will fight for freedom. We often impose time limitations that may unwittingly escalate conflict since these restrictions may allow insufficient time for adequate consideration of the alternatives. Victims of constriction will usually fight more vigorously since they feel cornered. When constriction escalates conflict faster than the conflict parties deem appropriate, revolution or rebellion may occur.

Breaking the Relational Rules

We commonly designate this as "hitting below the belt." It can take the form of a personal attack that violates the conflictual rules which may be implicit or explicit. When these "rules" are broken, escalation of conflict follows. Betrayal is an emotional, dramatic, and frightening experience.

In Genesis the brothers of Joseph clearly illustrate the breaking of relational rules when they put him in a well, then sold him as a slave to the Midianites (37:12-36).

Maintenance Tactics

The moves used when we engage in maintenance tactics will neither avoid nor escalate the conflict for any of the conflict participants. The level of tension remains somewhat constant for all. Power becomes equalized among the adversaries. The tactics suggested below may be appropriate or inappropriate depending on the situation.

Quid Pro Quo

"Getting something for something" describes this tactic. The gains and losses of each party are outlined so that wins and losses are accepted equally. The trading idea rests on the assumption that the conflicting parties will treat each other as equals. This tactic rests on the assumption that innate justice will satisfy the adversaries, at least temporarily.

Jacob's experiences with Laban in Genesis picture this tactic. Jacob felt it was reasonable to expect just behavior from his uncle Laban. Instead Jacob found his wages changed ten times (31:38-41).

Agreement on Relational Rules

Ground rules are established so that a productive focus on the real conflict can occur. We permit no character assassination but honest personal feelings are welcomed. The more formal the conflict, the more time will be invested in working out the agreement of these relational rules. Usually this time invested on rules will speed up the management of conflict later in the process.

Reduction Tactics

Fractionation

This process breaks down one big conflict into several smaller, more manageable units. It allows for smaller progress to occur in visible ways and therefore encourages better positive management of the greater conflict. Patience and plodding sometimes characterize this tactic. It works best when emotional involvement has stabilized, and all parties are content to let the conflict process move at a lower pace. This sizing technique also works best when the conflict demonstrates complexity and longevity.

Negative Inquiry

We have brought this concept from the assertiveness training background. When criticized, the individual receiving criticism responds by asking for more information, not less, about what the other person finds objectionable. Psychologically it disarms our opponents when we do not engage in self-defense; instead, we make ourselves more vulnerable to continued attack.

In strong substantive conflict it may not prove to be as effective. It seems to work best when conflict can be managed rapidly. When the conflict process requires weeks and months, negative inquiry proves less effective.

Metacommunication

People using this tactic talk about the communication as it occurs. "I could have,... but I didn't" demonstrates metacommunication. The idea expressed is, "I'm working to manage this conflict by not using more drastic measures." Another form of metacommunication tosses the issue to the adversary by asking, "What do you think I ought to do?" In short-term conflict, metacommunication disarms the adversary and enables more productive communication to occur.

Response to All Levels of the Conflict

In this concept, we request our opponents to give us both the content and the relationship levels of the conflict. We want the "facts" and the "feelings" to be given. Be ready to receive both if you ask for them. When we use this tactic well, deep-level conflicts can be addressed. The relationship between the combatants must be strong for this tactic to be used effectively. Where the relationship lacks strength, more harm may be experienced than if it were not employed.

The Position Paper

This concept accepts the premise that the flat statement (position) will frequently be followed by qualifiers or softening statements. More intimate relationships reveal, for example, that a person will make a strong statement against compromise and then turn around and compromise. It becomes a reduction tactic since it has a certain cathartic effect.

Compromise

Often used in conflict as a reduction device. When each party can win some things and lose other things, it finds a use similar to fractionation. The danger with this tactic is that no one goes away satisfied. At best it becomes a bitter-sweet experience.

Establishment of Outside Criteria

When we set a time frame, we are employing an outside criterion on the conflicting parties. If prior agreement as to how a decision will be made can be established, the parties are submitting to outside criteria.

Outside mediation also helps to serve as a reduction tactic. When both conflicting parties agree to abide by the mediation, conflict often has a more objective solution. This agreement must be genuine. More than one pastor has been called to be an outside mediator in husband-wife conflict only to find one or both of the conflicting parties did not plan to abide by the mediation.

Conclusion

Conflict management allows us to employ a variety of tactical tools. These tools allow us to avoid, escalate, maintain, or reduce a given conflict. The effective use of these tactics depends upon the situation and conflict issues we face. Your personal strategy and desire to effectively manage conflict should help govern a wise use of these tactics.

Notes
1. George R. Bach and Peter Wyden, *The Intimate Enemy* (New York: Avon Books, 1968).
2. Alan C. Filley, *Interpersonal Conflict Resolution* (Glenview, Ill.: Scott, Foresman & Co., 1975).
3. Joyce Frost and William W. Wilmot, *Interpersonal Conflict* (Dubuque, Iowa: William C. Brown Company Publishers, 1978), 118.

22

MANAGING CONFLICT
DESTRUCTIVELY
OR CONSTRUCTIVELY

Mr. Smith was upset. He completely expected a different response from his pastor. About six months ago Smith's grandfather died and left $10,000 to the church. Mr. Smith was proud of the fact he had such a godly heritage. After all, most of the elderly just left their money to their children, but not Mr. Smith's grandfather. He had considered the needs of the Lord and His church.

Now the pastor and the leaders were planning to spend the money the wrong way. They had this silly notion that some of the missionaries needed a cost-of-living increase. But Mr. Smith was sure his grandfather intended to give the money toward paving the parking lot. His grandfather was not opposed to missions, but everyone knows a strong base is needed at home so the church can send those missionaries overseas. Missionaries need to sacrifice anyway, so they can be more Christlike.

At first Mr. Smith thought he would just let the church leaders decide what to do with the money. But the more he thought about it, the more he became convinced his grandfather's wishes should be honored, It was true his grandfather did not stipulate what to do with the $10,000, but who would know his wishes better than a grandson! Mr. Smith felt certain if he and his grandfather had discussed this gift of money, Grandpa would have earmarked it for paving the parking lot.

It was just terrible that the church leaders wouldn't listen to reason! At this point Mr. Smith would have even settled for $5,000 for the missionaries and $5,000 toward paving the lot. But the church leaders insisted on the money going to those people who only come around with their slides once every four years!

Now Mr. Smith plans to leave this church with its insensitive leaders and find a church that cares!

Does this sound familiar? The names and issues may change but conflict often destroys the harmony within the local church. How can conflict be managed constructively instead of destructively?

> *It is not the presence of conflict that causes chaos and disaster, but the harmful and ineffective way it is managed.* It is the lack of skills in managing conflict that leads to problems. When conflicts are skillfully managed, they are of value.[1]

If these words are accurate, we need to know how to make positive use of conflict. What skills should we be developing? How can we tell when we manage conflict wrongly in our interpersonal relationships? In this chapter we will trace the difference between destructive and constructive use of the inevitable conflict which arises in all of our lives.

Destructive Use of Conflict

Conflict becomes destructive when internal strife robs us of effective association and ministry with those around us. Our relationships with others never remain stagnant. We continually grow closer or farther apart in our human experiences.

Does an unusual amount of internal strife exist in your life? Three signals may help you determine the destructive conflict in your life.

• *Time.* As God's children we know we are to exercise our God-given spiritual abilities for God's glory. However, if the internal struggle requires most (and sometimes nearly all) of our time, then we can be severely limited in our service for the Lord.

Our heated involvement in fighting leaves us little time to minister as God intended. The Lord has given us a mandate to make disciples of all nations (Matt. 28:19-20). He expects us to penetrate the world around us with the gospel of Jesus

Christ. When we crowd our schedules with conflict-related appointments, we have little time left to share the good news of Jesus Christ. When criticism or conflict strikes, how much time do we consume with the problem? Does your thinking constantly run to the difficulty? If you find your schedule crowded with helping God's people work out their difficulties, the conflict may be more destructive than you first realized.

• *Energy.* When we use most of our body's physical strength to war with other persons, conflict moves in a nonproductive direction. As we repeatedly mismanage conflict, a pattern emerges that saps vitality and weakens our efforts to minister effectively for Christ. Creative energy for Christ becomes dissipated. Internal fighting can so fatigue us we have little strength left for positive ministry. We may become dispirited in the work of the Lord when we minister only in the negative arena of conflict. When this happens, we become exhausted in civil war efforts with other believers and make ourselves most unattractive to a world who needs the life God offers.

• *Vision.* Destructive use of conflict causes us to sacrifice the future on the altar of the present. Our primary objective focuses on survival. We can become so absorbed with internal power plays and bickering that we forget what ought to occur in our immediate lives as well as the far-reaching future. Future plans, goals, and objectives become sidetracked in our lives because we are consumed with our struggle for stability. Collectively, the positive force a body of believers ought to have can be so changed that negative and ugly behavior prevails. Where vision falters, discouragement soon develops. The leadership tires of constant fighting as the people slip into a drab "maintenance only" mode of spiritual existence. Your awareness of vision should help you measure how much destructive conflict exists in your life. Does your life focus on the past more than the future? Are present troubles clouding specific, worthwhile plans for the future? Destructive management of conflict may be part of the problem.

Conflict becomes destructive when nonshared or conflicting goals or values are clearly evident. If one leader believes worship should characterize a church's ministry while another leader views evangelism as the congregation's primary function, potential destructive conflict surfaces from their leadership values. More than one conflict experience will likely occur when values differ dramatically. If the differences exist only at an activity level, the conflict will probably not be as severe. More intense conflict comes when primary goals conflict.

This may be subtle at first, since everyone agrees we need both evangelism and worship. When scarce resources such as people, money, or time are introduced, then the true values begin to emerge. When we pit one important area against another important area, the priority system becomes obvious. At this level, nonshared or conflicting goals can create strong destructive conflict. This type of destructive power frequently causes the relationship to be broken if mutual goals or values cannot be defined and accepted.

Conflict becomes destructive when incompatible, irreconcilable role definitions exist. For example, if a pastor views his ministry as overseeing the flock as a leader, but the people view him as only a preacher, destructive conflict will probably develop. He will want to introduce new ideas as to how the church can reach the lost, educate in the Sunday School, and develop a women or men's program. Some of the lay leaders will likely inform the pastor that they really appreciate his preaching, and, since he does this well, he ought to minister from his strengths and leave administration to them. The board and the pastor do not share the same concept of the pastoral office. The conflict occurs in the definition of the role of the pastor. The lay leaders do not view themselves as opposing the pastor. They like the pastor. They love their pastor! But they expect him to function only in the pulpit. We are not examining a personality problem. It would not matter who was pastor. The role of pastor to these people does not include administration. This type of situation must have redefinition of the role which can be mutually accepted, or a change in the relationship will probably occur.

Conflict becomes destructive when threat of a broken relationship dominates the decision-making process. When a number of alternatives exist, conflict can usually be properly managed. When we reduce the alternatives, conflict accelerates to the point where it breaks the relationship. If the leadership of a church becomes unhappy with the work of a pastor, they may approach him in several ways:

• You are fired! Usually when this happens, poor communication as well as inadequate interpersonal skills have dominated their relationship.

• If the lay leaders say to the pastor, "We see some problems and would like to work with you on them," they may offer to send the pastor to some specific conference which they believe will strengthen the needy area.

• They may respond more indirectly: "What do you think about pastoral visitation?" if felt need arises in this area. This approach seeks to work with the pastor instead of against him. Hidden in this question they are asking, "Is this pastor interested in improving his ministry in the areas we see as important?"

• The lay leaders in question may resign and refuse to confront the pastor about the issue. This response usually carries emotional baggage with it. These individuals become warped in their view of service and often refuse to engage in any lay leadership again. They stay in the church as pew-warmers refusing to exercise their God-given abilities.

• The lay leaders in question may resign and leave the assembly to join another church across town where the "pastor really pastors."

Conflict becomes destructive when desire or motivation to continue the relationship no longer exists. *An interdependent relationship can survive only as long as both parties will it to survive.* If one of the parties no longer commits to the overall relationship, it will die. When a marriage experiences conflict, a mutual desire must be present to stop a total breakdown in the relationship.

The destructive nature of conflict appears when lines of communication voluntarily or involuntarily close. Sometimes we experience more severe conflict when parties communicate. Nevertheless, it is improbable that less communication will produce less conflict. When we close the communication lines or choose to ignore an adversary, we strike a deadly blow at a deep relationship level.

Destructive conflict can be detected when we notice a lack of accuracy in communication. Exactness between the message we send and the message received becomes hopelessly distorted. Tragedy comes when no one seeks to clarify the communication messages. To reduce the destructive force of conflict we need to ask questions, rephrase, summarize, and engage in any efforts possible to protect the meaning of the words we use.

The destructive ability conflict possesses cannot be minimized. But we can control conflict and manage it in a productive manner.

Constructive Use of Conflict

The following eight principles are vital if we want to manage conflict constructively:

1. *Learn to respond to conflict in its earliest stages.* Tension needs to be discussed. Conflict moves in a cyclical fashion. Tension develops in the first stage and then leads to a role disparity. We either question our part in this relationship, our opponent's part, or both roles in the situation. This questioning then deepens to the point we start case building. In time, we plan to prove our adversary wrong. Therefore evidence must be gathered to bring an accusation that can lead to a trial and conviction of this other individual.

Once we have built a sufficient case, we will confront an enemy. The confrontation leads to some type of adjustment. This may run the gamut from totally breaking the relationship to one of the parties completely agreeing with the other. Once again, tension starts to develop that brings us full cycle in the conflict process.

When we sense tension moving in a negative direction, we must muster the courage to address it. Waiting and hoping it will go away usually becomes futile activity based on wishful desires. The earlier we face the problem, the easier we can appropriately manage the conflict. The longer we delay approaching a conflict, the more likely it will turn into destructive conflict which usually carries heavy emotional baggage.

2. *Keep everyone centered on the conflict issue(s).* We are constantly tempted to turn from the issue of conflict and make personal attacks on our adversary. We make a close tie be-

tween the individuals and the issue. "If they feel this way, then they must be..." characterizes our mind-sets when we are immersed in conflict.

The longer we experience a specific conflict, the more likely true conflict issues will become clouded by drifting away from the main issue or introducing unwarranted emotional or personal attacks. We must work together on the conflict issue while in disagreement if positive management of conflict is to occur. We must stress our cooperation in the big picture even though we oppose each other in this specific snapshot.

3. *Monitor the conflict process keeping four essential rules enforced:*
   • Make sure all parties are allowed to disagree without feeling guilty.
   • Each individual must be allowed to state his or her position with energy and exactness.
   • Protection from being hurt and hurting others must be sustained.
   • Remind conflicting parties when they achieve even small amounts of progress.

Some people automatically associate guilt with disagreement. We must learn to separate the two. Disagreement does not have to lead to conflict. The fact that parties differ adds creativity and innovation to the group process. Often how we express these disagreements produces guilt or strengthens the overall relationship.

The value of guaranteeing energy and exactness protects us from early jumping to conclusions. If we allow our opponents this privilege, facts have a fair opportunity to influence both parties. Sometimes clearness cannot be attained because energy was denied one of the adversaries. If one party needs to state feelings or facts in forceful fashion, those present must allow this.

The balance to stating things with energy comes when we protect all parties from hurt. This includes self-inflicted wounds which can be a ploy for longer-range advantage. The familiar "put-downs" have been outlawed from the procedure. If the facts of the situation create hurt, this cannot and should not be softened or denied. Yet we must be certain we are working with factual data, not hearsay or inference.

The difference becomes so magnified we need to remind all conflicting parties of the small gains. When either opponent becomes convinced zero progress has been made or will be made, a stalemate in the conflict-management process occurs. Each adversary will easily comprehend the differences he or she has with the other person. When the differences are so obvious, our vision becomes blurred as to the progress achieved. Productive conflict management tags any progress and spotlights it to both parties regularly.

4. *Help the parties to see creative options available to them.* The process of conflict has a restricting element in it. It seems increasingly more difficult for adversaries to find creative alternatives as conflict continues. The squeezing effect tightens its hold on the conflicting parties unless someone works hard to surface viable alternatives which each side could and should consider.

5. *Put your energy into helping the conflicting parties to view every conflict as a problem to be solved.* Hope must be present and usually needs to be encouraged if conflict is to be managed. The more involved all parties concerned are, the better likelihood of positive conflict management. A danger comes when either party senses an unwarranted coalition has formed to oppose the other. Input and involvement by all parties must be seen as essential if ownership is expected. Norman Shawchuck (1983) supported this concept in *How to Manage Conflict*: "Always remember: People tend to support what they have helped to create."[2]

6. *Produce authentic and worthwhile information about conflict issue(s).* Can we measure the level of trust? What context will be present where the conflict will be processed? Will this be a face-to-face situation or will a mediator be used? What history do we have of this present conflict episode? Questions of this type must be asked and answered if we are to productively manage conflict. We usually have to sift through faulty facts in most conflicts. Be careful about assuming anything. Verify everything. The human ability to jump to conclusions based on nonfactual data can be astounding!

More information about a specific conflict is better than less information. The data gathered should be shared with all parties involved in the conflict. Protect equality for all parties as much as possible.

7. *Provide a context for independent and knowledgeable choices.* Each of the conflicting people must be free to make personal, informed choices based on the facts at hand. Guard against any hint of manipulation. Personal responsibility must be honored at all times. When we violate personal responsibility, we create more difficult and dangerous conflict for a future day. Search for those areas where enough agreement exists to form a basis for later appropriate conflict management.

We must also understand what areas are totally in disagreement. The question of how the parties will live and function directly relates to how each views the areas of agreement and disagreement.

8. *Encourage personal commitment to the plan of action which wins mutual agreement.* It may be wise to use written statements reflecting each party's promise to fulfill the mutual agreement. We must seek to motivate the adversaries to live up to what they have verbally acknowledged. Personal responsibility should not be taken for granted. Agreement does not guarantee commitment to a course of action. We have not properly managed conflict until we forecast how the parties can better manage their future relationship. Productive management of conflict focuses on preventive measures as well as corrective elements. Each party must possess an understanding of the days ahead if the conflict hopes to experience any degree of closure.

Conclusion

In each conflict event we possess the potential for constructive or destructive management of conflict. When conflict occupies most of our time, energy, or vision, we will experience more destructive conflict. We manage conflict more productively when we address it early with all parties focusing on the problem to be solved, working hard to surface as many creative alternatives as possible. Constructive management of conflict works to build relationships with others while not sacrificing clear, biblical convictions.

Notes
1. David W. Johnson, *Human Relations and Your Career: A Guide to Interpersonal Skills* (Englewood Cliffs: Prentice-Hall, 1978), 247.
2. Norman Shawchuck, *How to Manage Conflict in the Church*, vol. 1 (Irvine, Calif.: Spiritual Growth Resources, 1983), 46.

23

STRESS: CAUSES AND THE CURE

Cardiologist Dr. Meyer Friedman has done a good bit of research on stress and what he called "Type A behavior." Interestingly, he linked it specifically with inadequate self-esteem or insecurity and said, "Seventy percent to 80% of those in our program at the Institute said 'no' when asked if they had adequate and unconditional affection and admiration from both parents."[1]

Friedman went on to suggest that "Type A behavior" affects 75 percent of the male population in any American city and that these "patients" do not necessarily want to get rid of their disorder. Essentially they are people addicted to wanting too many things in too little time or wanting things to be exactly arranged to suit them. Friedman seems quite convinced that behavior which gives rise to stress is a psychophysical phenomenon:

> Type A behavior is very simple. It is a sense of time-urgency, or impatience, and free-floating hostility—easily aroused anger at the most trivial events of daily living—nothing more and nothing less. It has nothing to do with long hours, it has nothing to do with creative energy, or enthusiasm. It is a health disorder.[2]

Frank Minirth and Paul Meier cited the work of Hans Selye whom they called "the most widely recognized authority on stress." Selye defined stress as a body's response to any demand made upon it. He identified two types: "(1) *distress*—excessive levels of continued, damaging stress, and (2) *eustress*—a good, positive kind of stress one feels at times of happiness, fulfillment, or satisfaction."[3]

Minirth and colleagues distinguished between "stress" and "burnout" by referring to them as the cause and the results: "Too much stress over too long a time can result in burnout. Too much burnout, without learning and applying certain coping techniques, can lead to clinical depression."

The Right to Fail

The above heading is the title of an article published in the sixties by Albert J. Sullivan of Boston University.[4] Sullivan argued that leadership places people in constant tension in which they must strive to maintain equilibrium between the pull toward change and the pull against it.

Creativity and Conservatism

These polar points could also be referred to as *creativity* and *conservatism*. According to Sullivan, "Leadership is pulled between these two poles; in parallel, it maintains the equilibrium. If the creative pole attracts too strongly, productive energy can be dissipated down beautiful, but blind, alleys; if the conservative pole wins the tug-of-war, the end is sterility and drabness."[5]

One of the problems we face in the church and other Christian organizations is allowing conservatism in decision making and leadership to control our efforts to such an extent that we deny ourselves and everyone around us "the right to fail." Because the prevention of failure is the essence of conservatism, a denial of the right to fail stifles creativity in the organization.

Three Problems in Developing Creativity

Several problems rise immediately as we consider this issue in relationship to stress. First of all, creative people do not commonly enjoy the financial dimensions of planning and decision making. Nevertheless, the creation of new ideas usually carries with it the responsibility for some budget construction. It is quite easy to throw creative people into stress by forcing them to attach price tags to every good idea they come up with.

Secondly, an organization can live in such daily threat of

budgetary restrictions that it stifles creativity. People who would normally be creative force themselves to think conservatively and face the stress of behaving in ways other than those which characterize their familiar behavior.

The third issue at stake here is the negative lens through which we view failure. Rather than another pit stop on the raceway to new ideas, failure carries a personal price tag in current society which few seem willing to pay, primarily because those of us who lead are not willing to let them fail.

Trial and Error

Let me clarify my remarks. The stress factor comes not in the experience of failing, nor even in the risk entailed. Both of those can contribute to stress, but the real stress rests in the hassle and harassment that comes because we deny people the right to fail. Let us go back to James Kouzes and Barry Posner whose wisdom we have tapped on numerous occasions throughout these chapters:

> The point of this discussion is not to promote failure for failure's sake. We do not advocate for a moment that failure ought to be the objective of any business. Instead, we advocate learning. Leaders do not look for someone to blame when mistakes are made in the name of innovation. Instead they ask: "What can be learned from the experience?" The two very finest teachers of business are named *trial* and *error*.[6]

These authors also speak about a "hearty attitude" in which leaders held solidly to certain commitments, both personal and professional, exercised control over their own lives, and welcomed the challenges of leadership:

> People with a hearty attitude, then, take the stress of life in stride. When they encounter a stressful event—whether positive or negative—(1) they consider it interesting, (2) they feel that they can influence the outcome, and (3) they see it as an opportunity for development. This optimistic appraisal of events increases their capacity to take decisive steps to alter the situation. Instead of avoiding the problem, they choose action to confront—and control—it. Heartiness con-

tributes to a person's ability to cope with stress by transforming stressful events into manageable or desirable situations,
rather than regressing and avoiding the issue.[7]

Stress in Ministry[8]

Recent Research

Studies show that pastoral stress has become a major factor
in disqualifying or driving people from the ministry. Research
by John Gleason identifies 43 potential stressors with the top
five being proliferation of activities, perfectionism, no time for
study, role conflicts, and unwelcome surprises. In a different
survey, Paul Robbins sees the top five as problems with parishioners, overwork, local church problems, feeling of futility,
and conflicts within the congregation. There seems to be a fine
line there between items, but the central focus is clearly
congregational life.

A comprehensive survey directed by Craig Ellison in con-
junction with the *Journal of Psychology and Theology* divided
respondents into three groups: senior pastor with staff, senior
pastor without staff, and associate pastor. For all three groups
stress was the number one item, and the top five in each group
are listed as follows:[9]

Senior Pastor/Staff	Senior Pastor/No staff	Associate Pastor
stress	stress	stress
disappointment	frustration	frustration
spiritual dryness	inadequacy	anxiety
inadequacy	disappointment	spiritual dryness
anxiety	fear of failure	fear of failure

Common Categories

Certain groupings can be selected to identify ministerial
stressors and how they affect the work we do:

1. *Personality stressors* include such things as low self-
esteem, the issue of perfectionism (noted above), status orientation marked by aggression, ambition and competitiveness,
and the lack of personal identity. Note how this last item
relates to our earlier discussions about a realistic self-concept.

2. *Social stressors* pick up things like unrealistic expectations, time and family demands, financial difficulties and

interpersonal demands. The U.S. Department of Labor, identifying occupations by salary ranked from highest to lowest, listed clergymen at level 317 in a list of 432 occupations. The interpersonal demands focus on such things as the development of significant others and the loneliness of leadership.

3. *Spiritual stressors* include such things as general dryness, guilt, or the presence of sin either recognized or unrecognized in one's life.

4. *Career stressors* include many of the above but highlight particularly those factors which relate to the work of the ministry.

Lay Leader Stress

What does the Christian leader do about stress in lay leaders? Like many diseases, the analysis or diagnosis seems a bit easier than the prognosis. However, we can employ some simple and biblical patterns to retain the good people we have and allow them to become reproducing leaders. Remember the following axioms about stressful situations:

1. *Stress is a mind/body response to imbalance and frustration.* When one of the people we supervise seems to struggle in some type of stressful situation, we should assume imbalance or disequilibrium somewhere in that person's life.

2. *Stress is no stranger to Christians.* A worthless and simplistic homily suggests that because people belong to Jesus Christ they have become immune to stress factors in modern society. However, Christians need to learn that reading Psalm 23 will not cure problems of bitterness and friction between them.

3. *Stress is a result of how we perceive problems and pressures.* Sometimes we perceive correctly, indicating genuine stress. Sometimes, however, we guess wrong, and the stress we imagine is not really there. At those points wiser, more experienced leaders can help us get around the stress problem.

4. *Stress lies within ourselves—not in inanimate objects or situations.* Flip Wilson's "The devil made me do it" line may very well be true about the behavior of some people, but a lawn mower cannot "make" one angry. Failure of one's car to start cannot "create" frustration. Frustration and anger lie

within us, and conflict with those obstinate motorized monsters merely offers an occasion to erupt.

5. *Stress excess may be a matter of choice.* Some people serve on too many committees, working for the Lord in too many different ways. It may be better to burn out for God than to rust out, but better options are available. We can carefully, wisely, wear out, using spiritual and physical resources at a reasonable rather than foolish rate.

Remember our key learning idea here: experience. Stress will always come, and if those stressful experiences teach us how to handle them, how to change and adjust our perceptions, and how to trust the God who can mold every situation and solve every problem, we have come a long way toward developing our own leadership.

Don Huddle, whether or not he was intentionally writing from a Christian perspective, vividly described a mature Christian leader counseling a subordinate under stress when he wrote:

> The person in a stress situation needs support, and the best types are *understanding* (that the pain of emotional distress is real and not "all in your head"); *listening* (remembering that the superior can offer only emergency help and cannot hold himself responsible for other people's troubles); and *referring* (guiding the person with the behavioral problems to professional sources—not necessarily a psychiatrist).[10]

Fear of Success

One common and oft-occurring source of stress has been identified in industrial research as "competition anxiety." The competitive spirit thrives in Western culture, and this issue has been surfacing with regularity for the past two or three decades. In addition to the research done in business and industry, education has recently taken a long hard look at the negative effects of classroom competition at all levels.

Reflected in Competition Anxiety

As early as Zaleznik's *Human Dilemmas of Leadership*,[11] management studies took note of the fact that developing executives experiencing difficulty living in competitive environments struggled to be effective in leadership roles. Interestingly, Zaleznik pointed up the fear of *failure* as one polar cause of competition anxiety and fear of *success* as the other. Both destroy initiative and creativity, driving promising leaders to take refuge in the flurry of group activity.

Exemplified in Jonah

Fear of success evokes memories of an ancient Jonah syndrome. If we understand Jonah's dialogue with God correctly, his paranoia at being called to Nineveh stemmed not from a fear of failure (what the pagan Ninevites would do to a Hebrew prophet), but rather from a genuine fear that God in His loving grace would pardon a nation as fearsome and vicious as Nineveh. In short, Jonah was afraid he might win.

Often the fear of success becomes something of a morbid cycle characterized by hostile and aggressive acts followed by guilt and retribution. People in such a situation may seem outgoing and extroverted, but that drive and initiative tends to dim when battered by the feelings of guilt acquired while moving up the hierarchy.

Experienced in Guilt

For one thing, success tends to move one into positions already occupied by others, perhaps a friend. Consequently, advancement may bring with it the subsequent desire to reverse or make amends for some seemingly wrong behavior that caused the displacement of the other person.

Behaviorally, people who fear success tend to work hard in a competitive environment moving satisfactorily toward goal achievements. But just when they seem about to achieve the goal, to attain success, they put on the brakes and stop short of the reward that could bring with it the issues described above.

Truly a major antidote to both problems and to competition anxiety in general is a healthy recognition of the grace of God. Christian leaders must see all that they have and all they can be as a product of God's sovereign grace working in their lives and ministries. Titles, honors, abilities, and offices attained—

these and many more badges of success must be laid at the feet of the Lord who made them possible.

In the same manner, a recognition of God's sovereign control over our lives can remedy fear of failure. To be sure, we may very well be responsible for our own failures because of sloth, sin, or just plain carelessness. Yet many times when we have worked as hard as we can, we still seem to fall short of goals that seem so important. In those moments we must remember that God can close doors as well as open them.

The Contribution of Small Groups to Stress Reduction

Much of the research on small groups has stemmed from sociological foundations relating to the development of significant others in our lives. There is a catch-22 here, however, since conflicts often arise in group activity (board meetings, for example), and those conflicts give rise to stress.

Process of Reduction

A good bit of stress reduction can take place within a properly functioning small group. Group members can help each other develop a system for managing stress through self-analysis, structuring a plan for reduction, checking that plan for the evaluation of progress, and sharing victories along the way. Mutual prayer and support among significant others looms large in stress management.

In the effective group a relaxed atmosphere works toward the reduction of tension. People are involved, interested, and virtually everyone participates in the discussion. Stress can also be reduced in a group when the members understand their goals and have some clear idea of how to attain them. Group members need a willingness to listen to each other, providing every idea a fair hearing.

Handling Disagreements

Of course disagreement occurs from time to time. Good groups are comfortable with this and do not avoid confrontation; they simply control it. Suppressing disagreements simply pushes the stress factor further down into the lives of the individuals involved. The group must surface these matters, not suppress them. Good groups reach most decisions by a kind of consensus in which people are either eager (or at lest willing) to go along with the group's plan. Keep in mind we do not need an *apparent* consensus but a real willingness to work together toward common goals. Criticism is frequent, frank, and expected but offered in love. Do not welcome personal attacks either covert or overt. Keep hidden agendas at a minimum, though only the rare group can dispense with them entirely.

Leaders of such groups do not dominate, nor do the groups defer to them unduly. Indeed, the genuine leadership role shifts among members from time to time, depending on the topic and the circumstances. All members serve as resources and thereby mitigate any struggle for power.

Mutual Assistance

We are not referring here to a group designed for stress reduction or conflict management. We are referring to the normal groups that make up the life of congregations and Christian organizations: committees, boards, and task forces. Care for mutual physical, emotional, and spiritual health leads members to be alert to the potential of the group for stress reduction, even though that may not be its primary objective for existence.

Members in such a group help each other say no to unreasonable demands. They assist one another in learning to settle for limited objectives. They discuss important priorities, allowing group members to think through the real issues they should "die for" and those they should dismiss as insignificant or trivial.

One more thought: good groups tend to be self-conscious about their own operations. Frequently they stop to examine how well they are doing and what roadblocks may be interfering with effectiveness.

Many times the road into stress has been a long and tortuous one. One might conclude, therefore, that the road out might also be somewhat arduous, and that conclusion would be correct. Of course, God can miraculously and immediately deliver one from any physical, emotional, or spiritual trauma.

More commonly, He brings us back slowly through rest, obedience, trust, and waiting.

Many paths on the road back seem to be dead ends, and we struggle to work through the maze of deliverance. The promises of Scripture center on the healing power of the gracious Father and the following paragraph represents just one among many passages dealing with that hope:

> Do you not know?
>   Have you not heard?
> The Lord is the everlasting God,
>   the Creator of the ends of the earth.
> He will not grow tired or weary,
>   and his understanding no one can fathom.
> He gives strength to the weary
>   and increases the power of the weak.
> Even youths grow tired and weary,
>   and young men stumble and fall;
> but those who hope in the Lord
>   will renew their strength.
> They will soar on wings like eagles;
>   they will run and not grow weary,
>   they will walk and not be faint.
>   (Isa. 40:28-31)

Notes

1. Meyer Friedman, "Type A Behavior and Your Heart," *Commonwealth,* August 3, 1987, 330.

2. Ibid.

3. Frank B. Minirth and Paul D. Meier, et al, *How to Beat Burnout* (Chicago: Moody Press, 1986), 15-16.

4. Albert J. Sullivan, "The Right to Fail," *Journal of Higher Education* 34 (April 1963).

5. Ibid., 191.

6. James M. Kouzes and Barry Z. Posner, *The Leadership Challenge* (San Francisco: Jossey-Bass Publishers, 1987), 64.

7. Ibid., 67.

8. Much of this section is borrowed from Kenneth O. Gangel, *Feeding and Leading* (Wheaton: Victor Books, 1989), 314-17.

9. Craig W. Ellison and William S. Mattila, "The Need of Evangelical Leaders in the United States," *Journal of Psychology and Theology* 11, no. 1 (1983):31-32.

10. Don Huddle, "How to Live with Stress on the Job," *Personnel Magazine,* March-April 1967, 7.

11. Abraham Zaleznik, *Human Dilemmas of Leadership* (New York: Harper and Row, 1966).

24

THE WORKAHOLIC
SYNDROME

Workaholics arise out of a success-oriented culture. That syndrome of behaviors we now call "workaholism" consists of problems related to success addiction and performance dependency.

Television commercials of the eighties focused this most clearly in the stock broker who arises at some ridiculously early hour to check the European markets and cannot sit through a meal without being interrupted by business phone calls. Interestingly, the commercial presents the broker as the kind of person we should want in our corner. "Hire us," the company seems to be saying. "We will give you a broker who is hooked on workaholic success addiction and performance dependency," and handling your account can make him even sicker.

It would be nice if we could keep all the words of our study sorted out. But workaholism, tension, stress, and burnout form an almost seamless garment of the problem we discuss in these last two chapters. The order in the above sentence more or less describes the flow of the problem.

In the chapter on workaholism which appears in the book *How to Beat Burnout,* Frank Minirth and Paul Meier offer the following introductory paragraph:

> When most people hear the word *burnout,* they think of the hard-driving business person who never stops for coffee breaks or relaxing lunches, and who insists on taking work home at night, or even on vacations. There are, of course, occasional situations where such a workstyle is necessary. If that work-style has been practiced long term, however, its necessity is as much in the mind of the workaholic as in the reality of the situation.[1]

In this chapter we want to weave these various elements together, talking about conflict, stress, and how they relate to the workaholic syndrome.

Causes of Executive Stress

In the first frame of a cartoon, Charlie Brown and Linus stare at a rock wall as Linus laments, "I can't believe Lucy cemented my blanket into this rock wall." But Charlie Brown comforts him: "You don't need your blanket anymore—you said so yourself—this rock wall is your therapy. Every time you have a little stress in your life, you can come out here and add a few rocks to your wall." In the final frame, Linus throws up his arms in desperation and shouts at Charlie Brown, "There aren't that many rocks in the world!"

Stress from Competition

In the secular business world, the anxious, overstressed executive who pours down pills to placate his angry ulcer entered the business folklore in the 1930s. The problem has become much more complex since then, and we now know that causes of stress among executives vary widely and include inability to cope with change, failure to accept thwarted ambitions, and promotions to jobs beyond their capacity (the "Peter Principle"). Closely akin to all this is the conflict that comes from personality clashes and the competition between home life and work coupled with fears about the security of retirement.

Several interesting studies suggest that the worst stress in some of the highest levels of workaholism is experienced by middle managers who seem to be constantly fighting both the top and the bottom of the organization chart. They have no control over changes their companies require them to put into effect, yet they become the targets of subordinates' unhappiness and criticism. Like a field captain in an infantry unit, they find themselves saying to the followers, "I have to obey orders just like you."

Soon stressed-out workaholics begin to show the common symptoms—frequent lost time, lack of job control, new nervous habits, missed appointments, and a gradual but noticeable slipping quality in their work.

Stress from Change

Part of the problem is the rapidity of change in the workplace as well as in varied places of ministry. A study by Edgar Mills and John Koval, published in 1971, identified four types of stress which continuing education can help:[2]

1. Job related, local church problems including conflicts with parishioners, within the congregation, or among the church staff.
2. Family-marital problems such as struggles in child raising, death of a spouse, etc.
3. Career unemployment including the inability to continue formal education, uncertainty about one's calling, and similar issues.
4. Personal financial problems, health problems, housing problems, and other problems related to domestic economic issues.

Continuing education programs are as common today as stress, and the linkup for help should be obvious. In professional ministry, the most logical choice would be a doctor of ministry program. Keep in mind, however, that the addition of another responsibility (such as a degree program) could add to the stress rather than alleviate it unless care is taken to protect against that problem.

In addition to continuing formal education, some simple life-style changes can alleviate tension in the life of a leader. As with most things of this kind, they are much easier to list than to practice:

1. Keep a calendar and plan ahead.
2. Set definite office hours.
3. Set both family and recreational time on a regular basis.
4. Learn to say no.
5. Learn to relax.
6. Keep contact with "safe people."

Conflict and Stress

Several years ago The National Institute on Workers Compensation and the American Institute of Stress compiled some valuable lists, which were published in *Newsweek,* for people wanting to escape patterns of stress and workaholism. For example, they identified the "10 Tough Jobs" as follows:[3]

Inner-city high school teacher,
Police officer,
Miner,
Air traffic controller,
Medical intern,
Stock broker,
Journalist,
Customer service/complaint department worker,
Waitress, and
Secretary.

Warning Signs

The same *Newsweek* article identified several "warning signs" usually found in people who carry responsibility without control:

Intestinal distress,
Rapid pulse,
Frequent illness,
Insomnia,
Persistent fatigue,
Irritability,
Nail biting,
Lack of concentration,
Increased use of alcohol and drugs, and
Hunger for sweets.

In a sense then, conflict leads to stress. We learned as early as 1975 that conflict was number one on ministers' lists of the sources of job stress. Sixty-two percent of respondents identified it in first place.

Part of the problem seems to be an almost idealistic view of the Christian organization which suggests that conflict dare never enter. Nevertheless, conflict is less likely to lead to stress when leaders understand that it is inevitable, and where people are interested and involved. Conflict also accelerates as change accelerates, so we should anticipate increasing problems toward the end of the twentieth century as the "future shock" society takes hold.

Conflict Resolution

Throughout this book we have tried to show that conflict is not inherently destructive or constructive; our reaction to it often determines what it will become in our own lives and in the larger group. Rather than facing disintegration of resources, dysfunction of objections, and disassociation of relationships, we need to learn how to handle conflict through diplomacy and negotiation. Conflict resolution can be taught, and the stress it brings can therefore be reduced.

A newsletter produced by the Deitrich Associates typifies the good literature on the subject when it emphasizes the problem-solving approach to integrating issues that have caused and continue to fuel the conflict:

> This person [the problem solver] is actively concerned with satisfying his goals as well as the goals of others. His philosophy and approach are a win/win throughout. He feels that no one's goals must be sacrificed to reach a good solution. He accepts all views as legitimate expressions of personal opinion. He demonstrates trust in others and tries to act in such a way that others will trust him. He is concerned with pushing through to a solution satisfactory to all parties. He is willing to persevere past pain, frustration, and weariness to get the best solution possible.[4]

Marks of the Workaholic

By this time we have developed a fairly thorough profile of the workaholic person. Frank Minirth and Paul Meier talk about obsessive-compulsive personality traits and list no fewer than 42 such traits to describe the workaholic; each of them is a multiple list in itself! Perhaps we can boil all that down into a simple list of ten items representing a fairly common view of workaholism which does not differ significantly from Christian or secular points of view. Here are the ten characteristics:

Inability to accept failure,
Incessant work patterns,
Guilt over low productivity,
Anxiety and depression,

Subject of standards of success,
Leisuretime guilt,
Time consciousness,
Self-denial,
Future orientation, and
Impatience.

In short, the workaholic does not have the faith to face failure.

Biblical Examples

The word *burnout* does not appear in Scripture, but the idea abounds. As early as the Book of Job, we find the lament:

> For sighing comes to me instead of food;
>   my groans pour out like water.
> What I feared has come upon me;
>   what I dreaded has happened to me.
> I have no peace, no quietness;
>   I have no rest, but only turmoil.
>   (3:24-26)

Moses, no less a leader, complained to God, "If this is how you are going to treat me, put me to death right now—if I have found favor in your eyes—and do not let me face my own ruin" (Num. 11:15).

Finally, we are all familiar with Elijah's prayer of frustration, offered in a period of intense burnout: "He came to a broom tree, sat down under it and prayed that he might die. 'I have had enough, Lord,' he said. 'Take my life; I am no better than my ancestors.' Then he lay down under the tree and fell asleep" (1 Kings 19:4-5).

Practical Suggestions for Defeating Workaholism

Such suggestions seem as multiple as the characteristics of workaholism itself. Leaders set the standard in stress reduction within the congregation or Christian organization because defeat of workaholism flows downward not upward. If we want to reduce competition and mediate conflict quickly, communication must flow openly and often; and if we want to calm the environment, then the leaders must set a pace others can follow, and they will watch for stress symptoms in themselves and all their subordinates.

Ten Suggestions

Apart from what leaders might do for you or what you might do for others as a leader, here are some suggestions for defeating a spirit of workaholism in your own life:

1. *See people and respond to them as people.* Take time to talk in the halls or in the coffee-break areas.

2. *Give of yourself instead of things.* Be willing to invest that time to build strong positive friendships.

3. *Enhance your sensory awareness,* the old "stop-and-smell-the-roses" approach to life. Left-brain leadership types tend to focus exclusively on task accomplishment and goal achievement. Smelling, touching, and hearing are not commonly used senses.

4. *Develop a capacity for spontaneity.* Workaholics tend to be too fixed in their schedules—same food for meals at the same time, same chair at meetings, and same routes to and from the office, etc. Leadership success rests so much in long-range planning that the capacity for spontaneity tends to get lost, sacrificed on the altar of other good things.

5. *Make yourself slow down.* Learning techniques of relaxation is important for leaders, especially those in stressful situations or those given to workaholic tendencies. Progressive relaxation tapes are inexpensive and easily obtained at book stores or from various types of medical offices.

6. *Find a pleasant avocation or hobby,* preferably something enjoyable that increases creativity, spontaneity, and sensory awareness. Do not feel guilty when giving yourself to that hobby. Remember the wise words of Reuel Howe who described mature persons as ones who can work without playing and play without feeling they should be working.

7. *Avoid stressful situations if possible.* Of course, it is not always possible. I have to drive to and from my office on a busy interstate and several inner-city streets. I could wish the seminary were located out in the country thirty or forty miles east of the city, but it is not. I can, however, refuse speaking engagements that require seven or eight flight segments on a

weekend, and I can even choose my travel times with enough discretion to avoid major traffic gridlocks on the interstate.

8. *Forgive yourself.* Frank Minirth and Paul Meier reminded us that a common sign of burnout is guilt over trying to be overly responsible or overly committed:

> That unnecessary guilt or false guilt, felt whenever workaholics slow down, may be related to an anxiety regarding their fear of facing what had *not* been accomplished during their times of frenetic workaholic activity, things such as spending time with God, with family, and improving one's own mental and physical health.[5]

9. *Work toward a realistic self-concept.* We covered this in detail in an earlier chapter, but it fits here as a defense against stress and workaholism.

10. *Keep a sharp eye on common stress causes such as struggles in the family, rapidity of change, and problems with finances.* Obviously health factors are an issue here as well.

The Gospel of Luke records a helpful account regarding the pressure in Jesus' ministry:

> While Jesus was in one of the towns, a man came along who was covered with leprosy. When he saw Jesus, he fell with his face to the ground and begged him, "Lord, if you are willing, you can make me clean."
>
> Jesus reached out his hand and touched the man. "I am willing," he said. "Be clean!" And immediately the leprosy left him.
>
> Then Jesus ordered him, "Don't tell anyone, but go, show yourself to the priest and offer the sacrifices that Moses commanded for your cleansing, as a testimony to them."
>
> Yet the news about him spread all the more, so that crowds of people came to hear him and to be healed of their sicknesses. But Jesus often withdrew to lonely places and prayed (5:12-16).

The early verses of our passage describe a harried minister rushing from place to place, besieged by people, carrying out popular procedures. Then we see the Lord decide to "take a break." He did not leave the ministry; He did not quit; He did

not stamp off in anger; He did not vow never to serve on
another committee; He did not leave the church and start
another one; He simply took a break for meditation. He went
away from the people who besieged Him and spent some quiet
time with the Father. Any leader who wants to reproduce
leaders capable of reproducing other leaders must learn that
balance.

> Dear Lord and Father of mankind,
> Forgive our foolish ways;
> Reclothe us in our rightful mind;
> In purer lives thy service find,
> In deeper rev'rence, praise.
>
> Drop Thy still dews of quietness,
> Till all our strivings cease;
> Take from our souls the strain and stress,
> And let our ordered lives confess
> The beauty of thy peace.
>
> ....
>
> In simple trust like theirs who heard,
> Beside the Syrian Sea,
> The gracious calling of the Lord,
> Let us, like them, without a word,
> Rise up and follow Thee.[6]

Notes

1. Frank B. Minirth and Paul D. Meier, *How to Beat Burnout* (Chicgo:
Moody Press, 1986), 59.

2. Edgar W. Mills and John P. Koval, *Stress in the Ministry* (Washington,
D.C.: Ministry Studies Board, 1971), 7.

3. Annetta Miller, "Stress on the Job," *Newsweek,* 25 April 1988, 43.

4. Deitrich Associates, "Conflict: Causes and Cures," *The Value of People
Review* 2 (November 1982):2.

5. Minirth and Meier, *Burnout,* 60.

6. John G. Whittier, "Dear Lord and Father of Mankind," *Baptist Hymnal*
(Nashville: Convention Press, 1975), 270.